Easy Piano

JUMBO
EASY PIANO STANDARDS

ISBN 978-1-4234-9485-0

HAL•LEONARD®
CORPORATION
7777 W. BLUEMOUND RD. P.O. BOX 13819 MILWAUKEE, WI 53213

Visit Hal Leonard Online at
www.halleonard.com

4	Ac-cent-tchu-ate the Positive	138	Do Nothin' Till You Hear from Me
10	Ain't Misbehavin'	135	Do-Re-Mi
14	All Shook Up	142	Do You Know the Way to San Jose
18	All the Things You Are	146	Easter Parade
7	All the Way	152	Easy Living
22	Always on My Mind	156	Easy to Love (You'd Be So Easy to Love)
25	And I Love Her	149	Everybody's Talkin' (Echoes)
28	April in Paris	158	Feelings (¿Dime?)
34	As Long as He Needs Me	164	A Fine Romance
31	As Long as I Live	168	For All We Know
36	Autumn in New York	161	Gentle on My Mind
42	Autumn Leaves	172	Getting to Know You
39	Baby Elephant Walk	175	Girl Talk
44	Bandstand Boogie	178	Glad to Be Unhappy
47	Basin Street Blues	181	The Glory of Love
50	Baubles, Bangles and Beads	184	Goin' Out of My Head
53	Bella's Lullaby	188	Good Night
56	Bésame Mucho (Kiss Me Much)	192	Happy Trails
60	The Best Things in Life Are Free	194	Harlem Nocturne
66	Beyond the Sea	200	Heart and Soul
70	Big Spender	197	Hello, Dolly!
63	The Blue Room	204	Hey, Look Me Over
74	Blue Velvet	207	Hill Street Blues Theme
77	Born Free	210	Honeysuckle Rose
80	Button Up Your Overcoat	213	I Believe in You
83	By the Time I Get to Phoenix	216	I Could Have Danced All Night
86	Bye Bye Blackbird	220	I Could Write a Book
94	Can't Help Lovin' Dat Man	222	I Don't Want to Walk Without You
98	Can't Smile Without You	225	I Enjoy Being a Girl
102	Candle on the Water	230	I Get Along Without You Very Well (Except Sometimes)
89	The Candy Man		
106	Cherokee (Indian Love Song)	238	I Love Paris
110	Chim Chim Cher-ee	240	I Say a Little Prayer
113	(They Long to Be) Close to You	244	I Walk the Line
116	Come Rain or Come Shine	233	I Whistle a Happy Tune
119	Crazy	248	I Wish I Were in Love Again
122	Cry Me a River	254	I Write the Songs
128	Daddy's Little Girl	251	If
125	Darn That Dream	258	If Ever I Would Leave You
132	Dearly Beloved	262	If I Loved You

265	If I Were a Bell	402	Penthouse Serenade
268	If I Were a Rich Man	405	Put On a Happy Face
276	The Impossible Dream (The Quest)	408	Puttin' On the Ritz
280	In the Mood	411	Que Sera, Sera (Whatever Will Be, Will Be)
273	It Could Happen to You	414	The Rainbow Connection
284	It Never Entered My Mind	418	Rockin' Chair
288	It's a Big Wide Wonderful World	421	A Sleepin' Bee
294	It's Impossible (Somos novios)	424	Small Fry
298	It's So Nice to Have a Man Around the House	427	Small World
291	June in January	430	Softly as in a Morning Sunrise
300	Just One More Chance	436	Somebody Loves You
306	Lazy River	433	Someone Nice Like You
303	Lazybones	438	Something Good
308	Little Girl Blue	441	Sophisticated Lady
311	Long Ago (And Far Away)	444	Spanish Eyes
314	Love Is Just Around the Corner	448	Steppin' Out with My Baby
320	Lover	454	Sunrise, Sunset
317	Lullaby of Birdland	451	Tangerine
324	Make Believe	458	There Will Never Be Another You
330	Manhattan	464	There's a Small Hotel
327	Mister Sandman	461	This Can't Be Love
334	Moon River	468	To Love Again
337	Moonlight Becomes You	471	The Very Thought of You
340	More Than You Know	474	What a Diff'rence a Day Made
343	My Foolish Heart	480	What Now My Love
346	My Heart Will Go On (Love Theme from 'Titanic')	477	Who Can I Turn To (When Nobody Needs Me)
352	My Old Flame	484	Willow Weep for Me
356	My One and Only Love	488	Won't You Be My Neighbor? (It's a Beautiful Day in the Neighborhood)
360	My Ship	490	Yesterdays
364	My Silent Love	492	You Are Beautiful
367	Nadia's Theme	495	You Light Up My Life
370	Never Never Land	498	You'd Be So Nice to Come Home To
374	Never on Sunday	501	You'll Never Walk Alone
380	A Nightingale Sang in Berkeley Square	504	You're Nobody 'til Somebody Loves You
384	On the Street Where You Live	507	Younger Than Springtime
377	Once in Love with Amy	510	Zip-A-Dee-Doo-Dah
388	Once Upon a Time		
392	One Note Samba (Samba de uma nota so)		
396	Only Trust Your Heart		
399	Out of Nowhere		

AC-CENT-TCHU-ATE THE POSITIVE

from the Motion Picture HERE COME THE WAVES

Lyric by JOHNNY MERCER
Music by HAROLD ARLEN

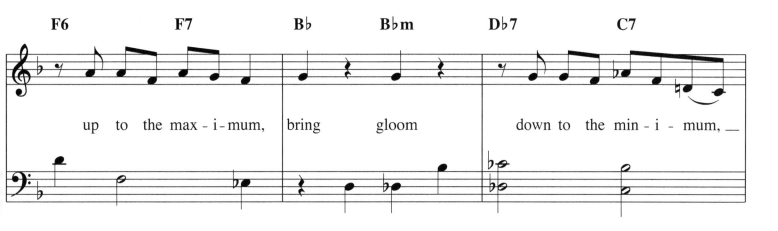

up to the max - i - mum, bring gloom down to the min - i - mum, __

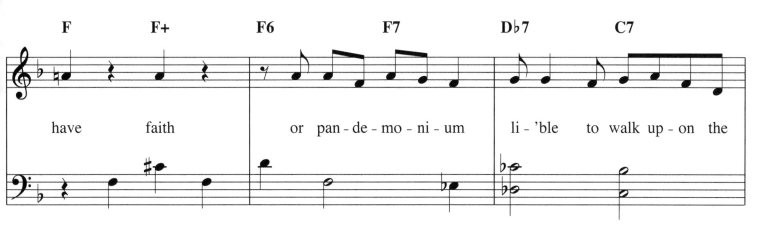

have faith or pan - de - mo - ni - um li - 'ble to walk up - on the

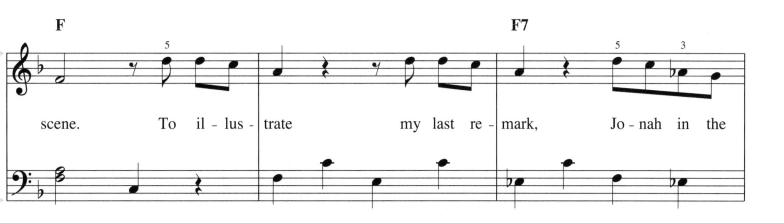

scene. To il - lus - trate my last re - mark, Jo - nah in the

whale, No - ah in the ark. What did they do just when

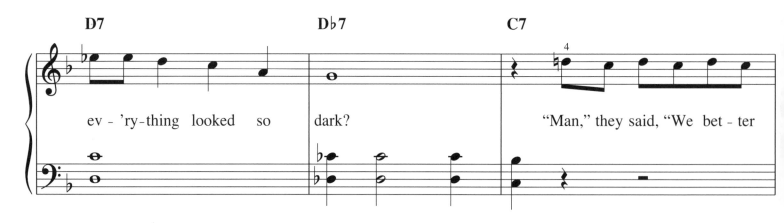

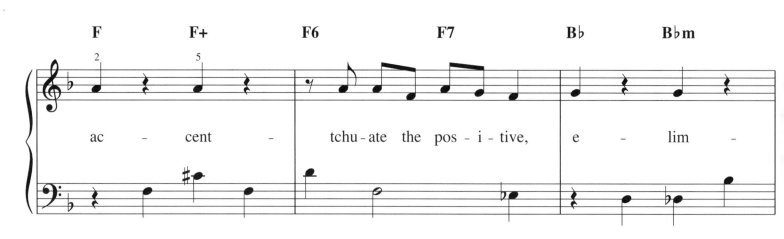

ALL THE WAY
from THE JOKER IS WILD

Words by SAMMY CAHN
Music by JAMES VAN HEUSEN

When some-bod-y loves you, it's no good un-less he loves you
When some-bod-y needs you, it's no good un-less she needs you

all the way.
all the way.

Hap-py to be near you, when you need some-one to cheer you
Through the good or lean years and for all the in-be-tween years,

all the way.
come what may.

Tall - er_____ than the
Who knows_____ where the

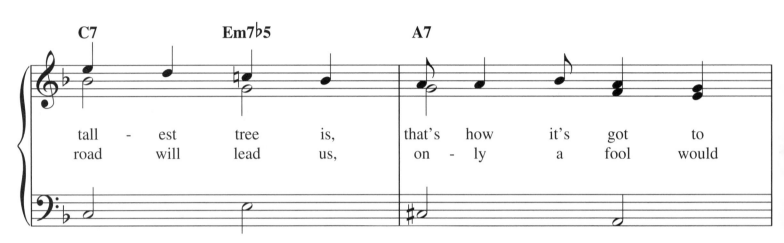

tall - est tree is,
road will lead us,

that's how it's got to
on - ly a fool would

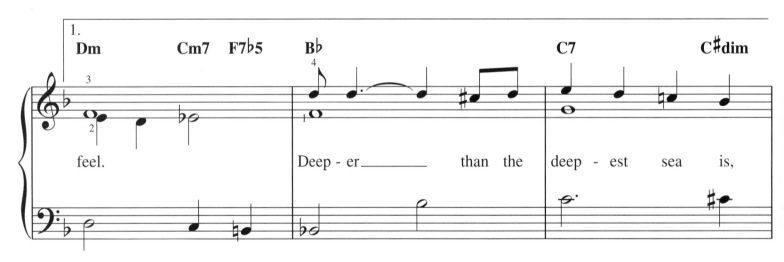

feel.

Deep - er_____ than the deep - est sea is,

that's how deep it goes,___ if it's real.

AIN'T MISBEHAVIN'
from AIN'T MISBEHAVIN'

Words by ANDY RAZAF
Music by THOMAS "FATS" WALLER and HARRY BROOKS

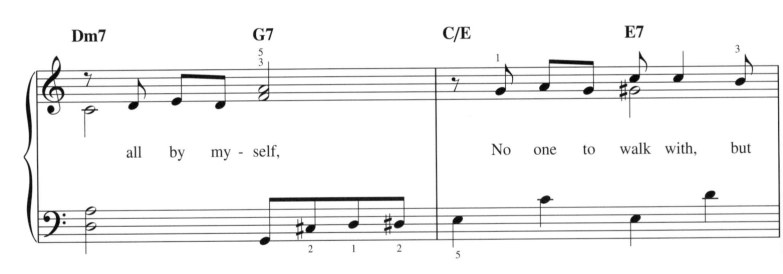

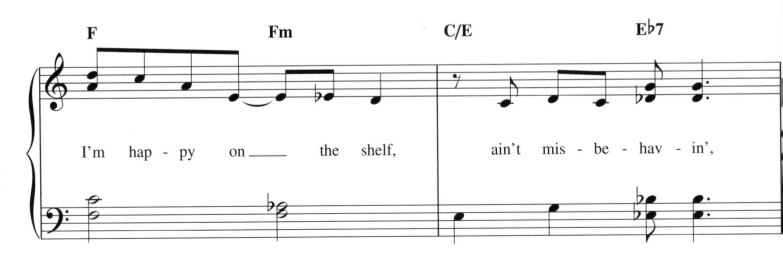

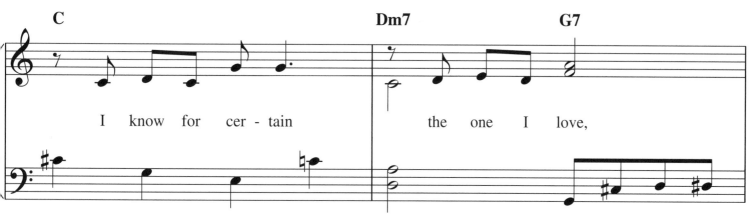

you.   Like Jack Hor - ner

in the cor - ner,   don't go no - where,   what do I care.

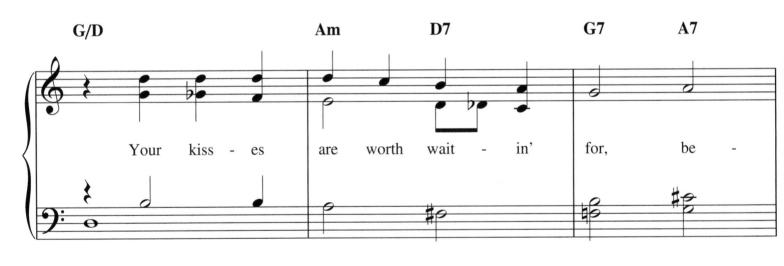

Your kiss - es   are worth wait - in' for,   be -

lieve   me.   I don't stay out late,

13

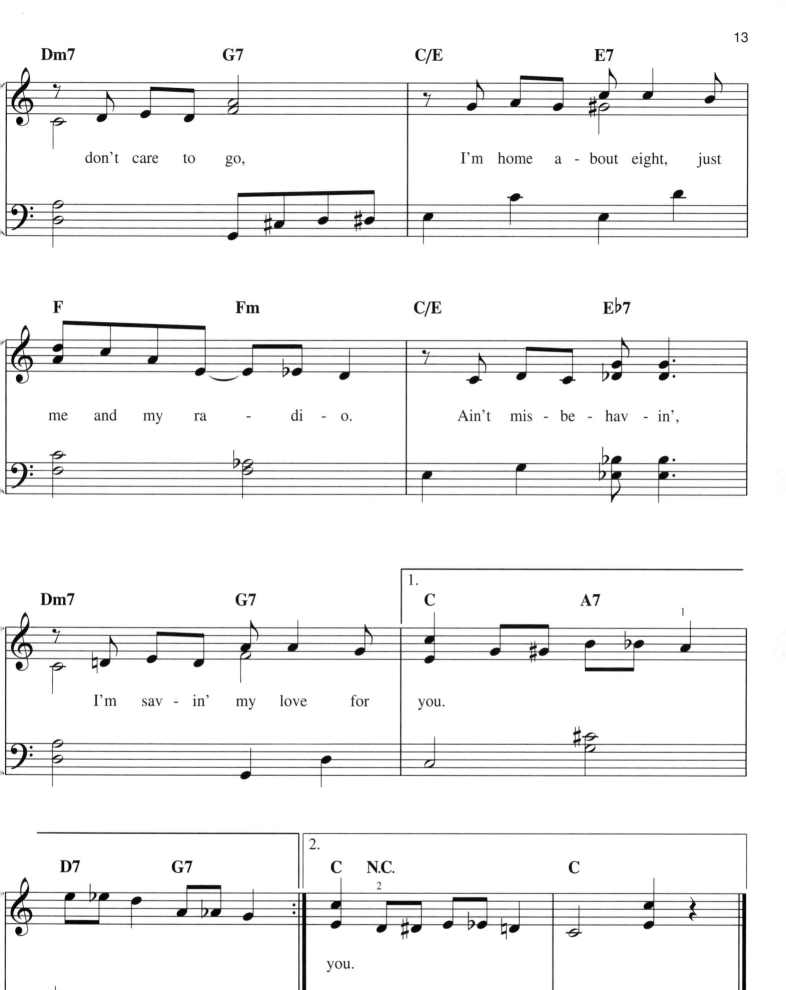

ALL SHOOK UP

Words and Music by OTIS BLACKWELL
and ELVIS PRESLEY

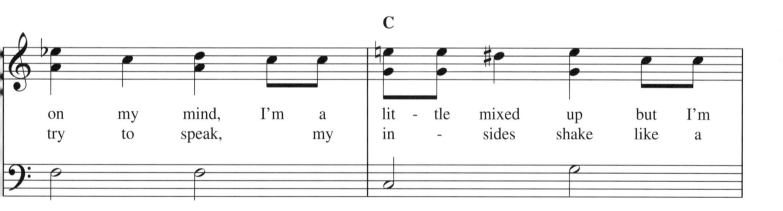

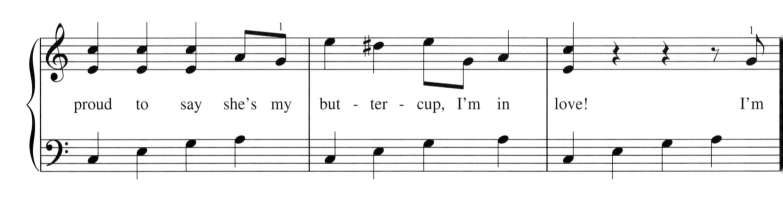

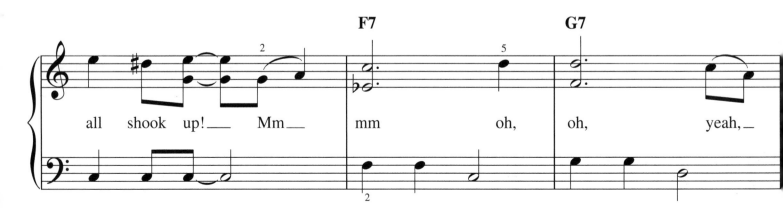

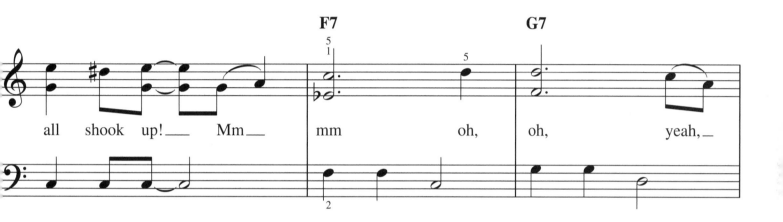

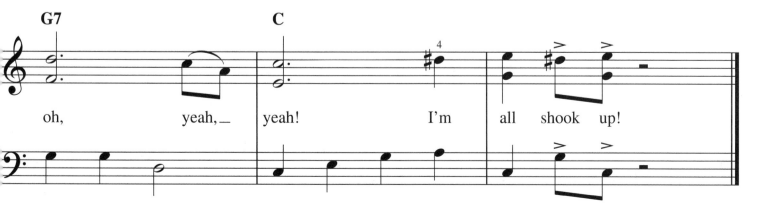

ALL THE THINGS YOU ARE

from VERY WARM FOR MAY

Lyrics by OSCAR HAMMERSTEIN II
Music by JEROME KERN

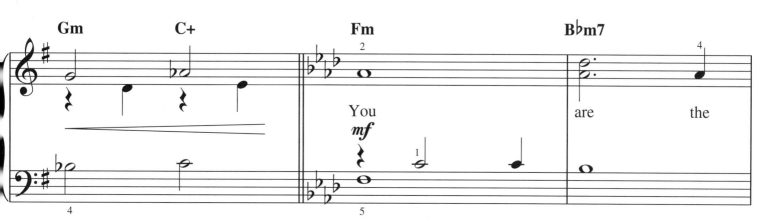

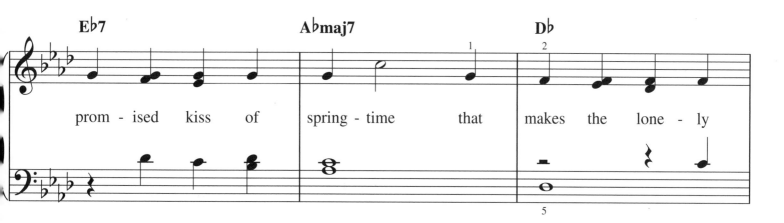

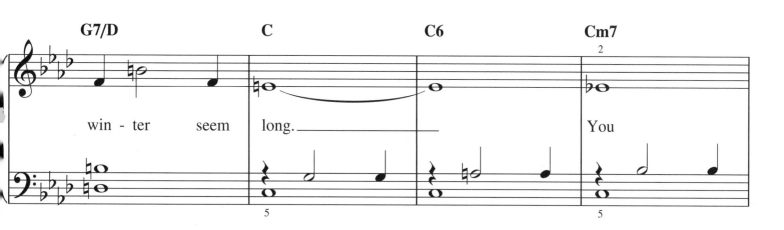

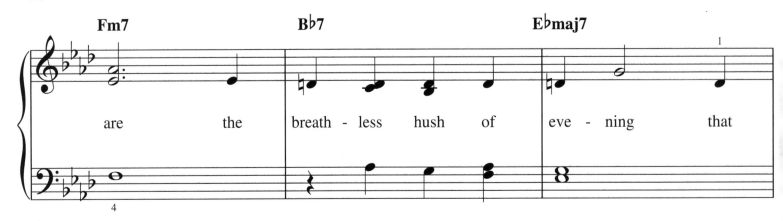

are the breath-less hush of eve-ning that

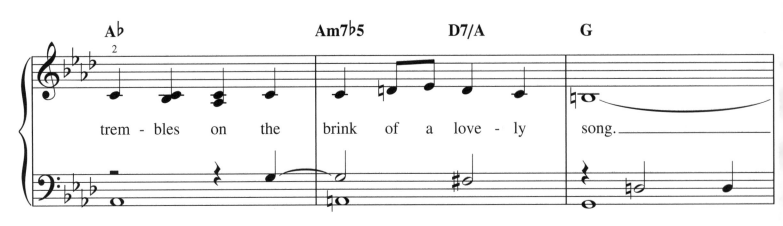

trem-bles on the brink of a love-ly song.

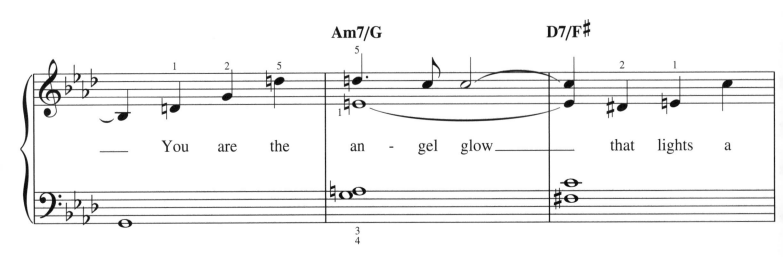

___ You are the an-gel glow___ that lights a

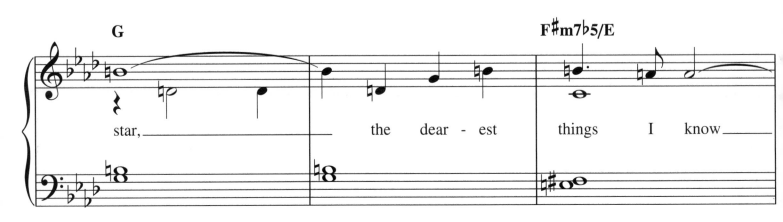

star,___ the dear-est things I know___

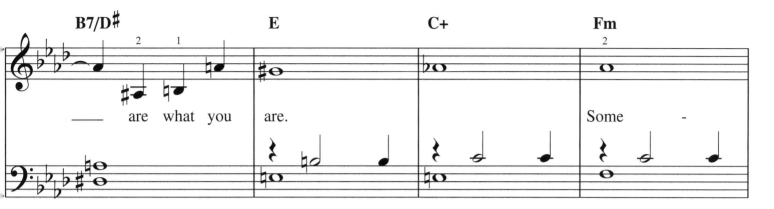

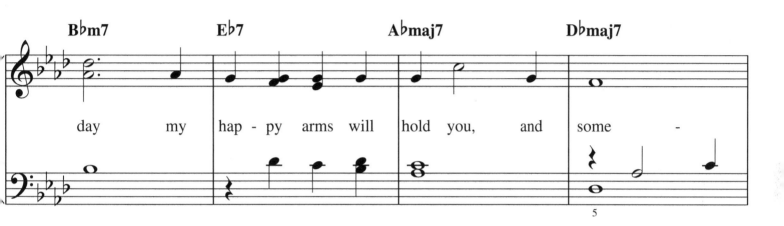

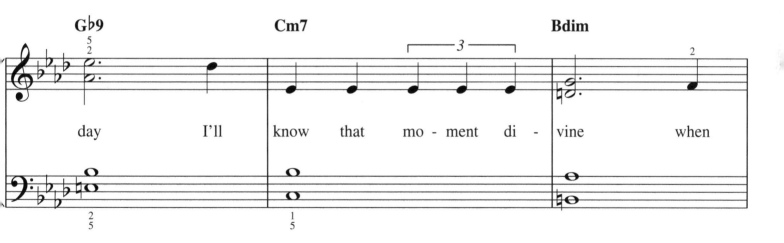

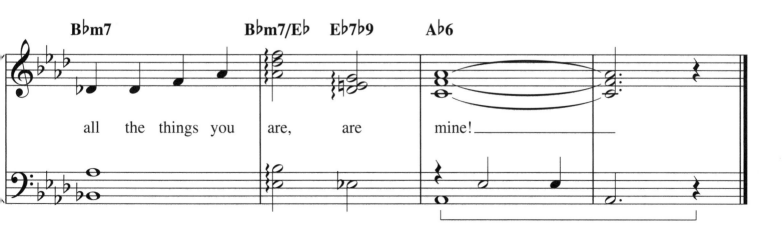

ALWAYS ON MY MIND

Words and Music by WAYNE THOMPSON,
MARK JAMES and JOHNNY CHRISTOPHER

Moderately slow

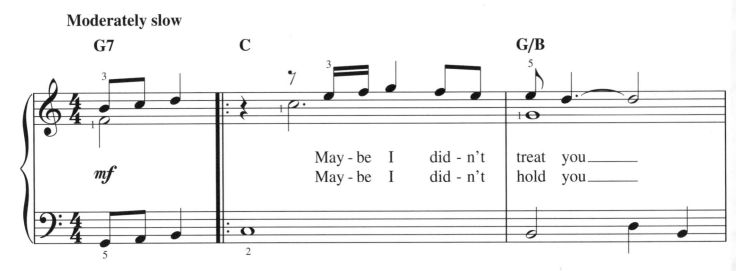

May-be I did-n't treat you_____
May-be I did-n't hold you_____

quite as good_ as I should have.
all those lone-ly, lone-ly times,_

May-be I did-n't
and I guess I nev-er

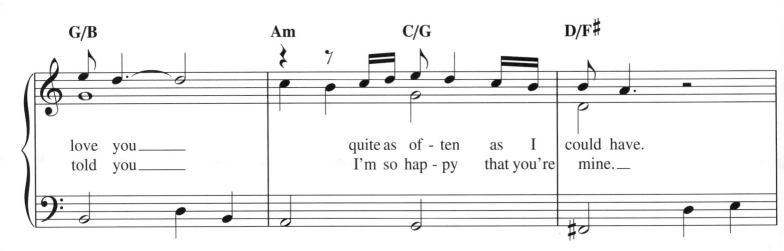

love you_____
told you_____

quite as of-ten as I could have.
I'm so hap-py that you're mine._

tell me that your sweet love_ has-n't died._____ Give_____

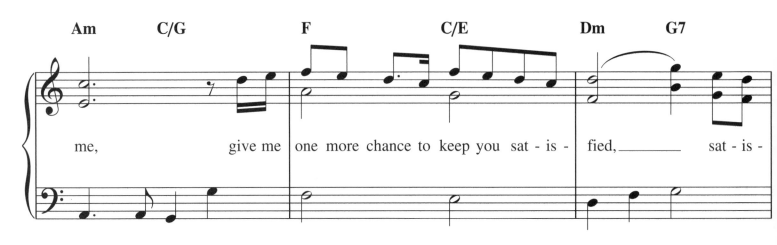

me, give me one more chance to keep you sat - is - fied,_____ sat - is -

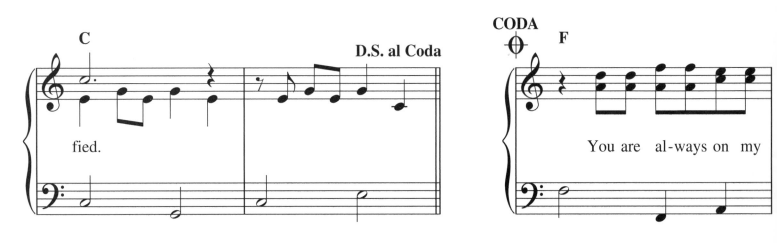

fied. You are al-ways on my

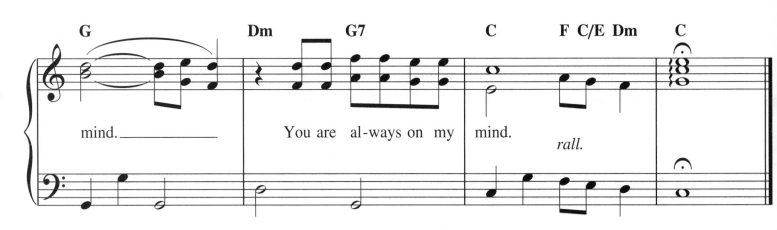

mind._____ You are al-ways on my mind.

AND I LOVE HER

Words and Music by JOHN LENNON
and PAUL McCARTNEY

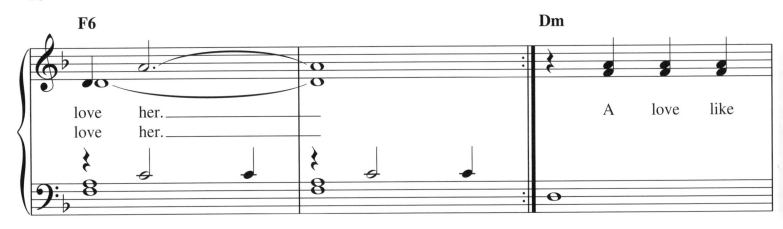

love her.
love her.

A love like

ours

could nev - er die

as long as

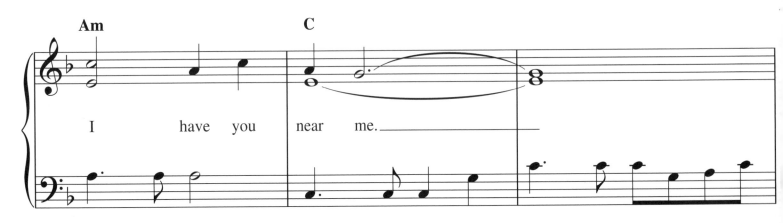

I have you near me.

Bright are the stars that shine, dark is the sky.

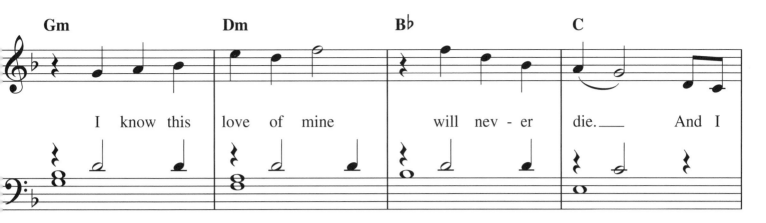

I know this love of mine will nev - er die.___ And I

love her.___

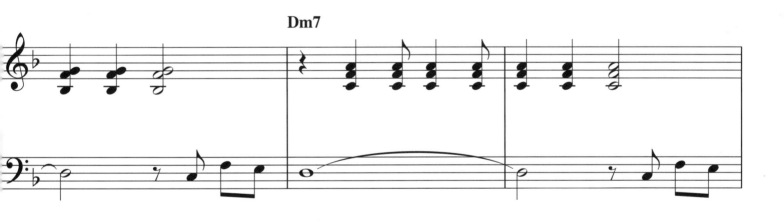

APRIL IN PARIS

Words by E.Y. "YIP" HARBURG
Music by VERNON DUKE

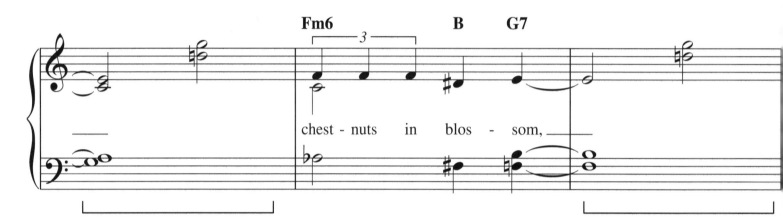

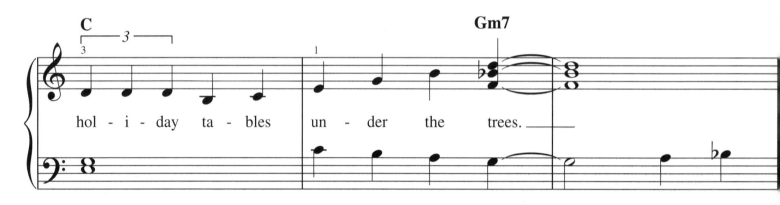

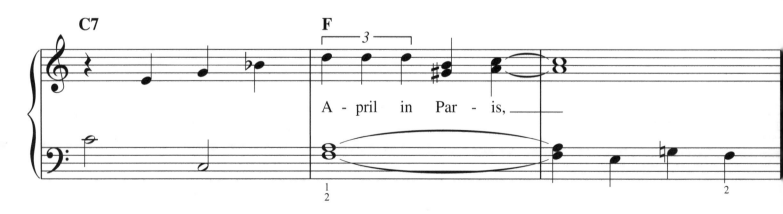

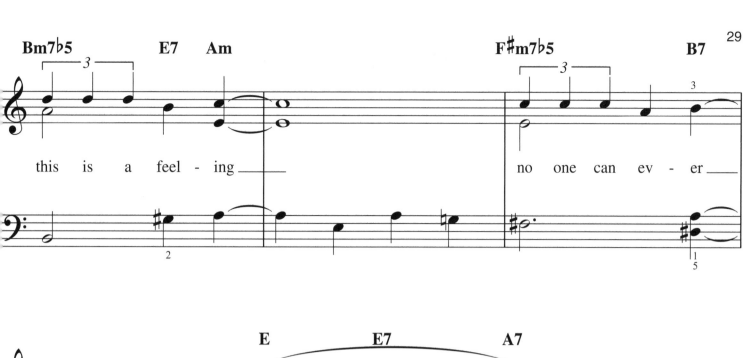

this is a feel - ing ____ no one can ev - er ____

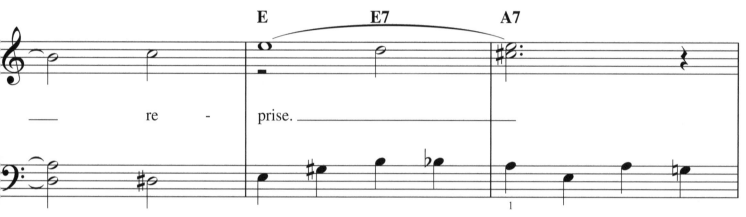

____ re - prise. ____

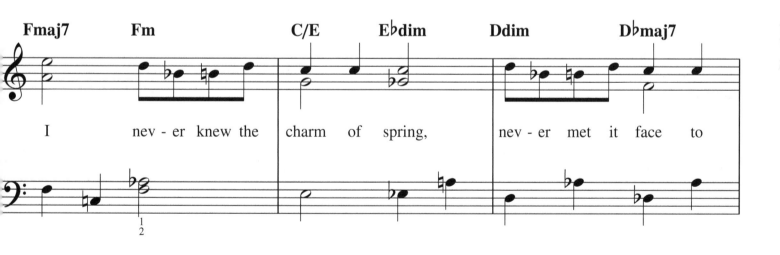

I nev - er knew the charm of spring, nev - er met it face to

face. I nev - er knew my heart could sing,

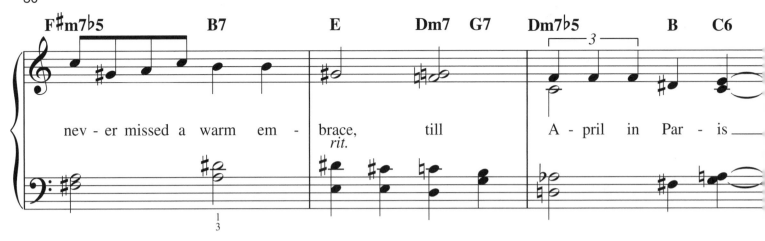

nev - er missed a warm em - brace,   till   A - pril in Par - is ___

rit.

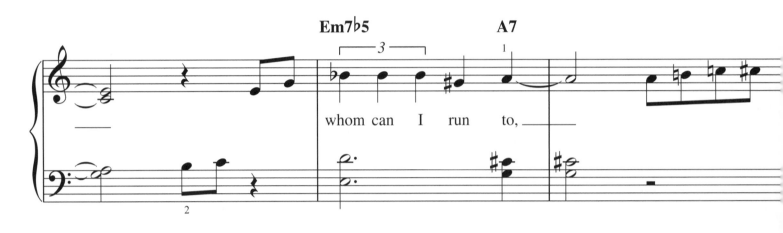

___   whom can   I   run   to, ___

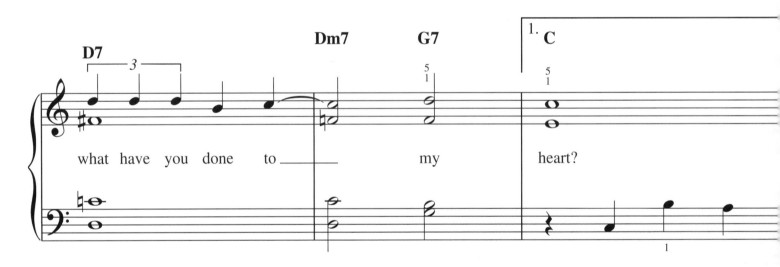

what have you done   to ___   my   heart?

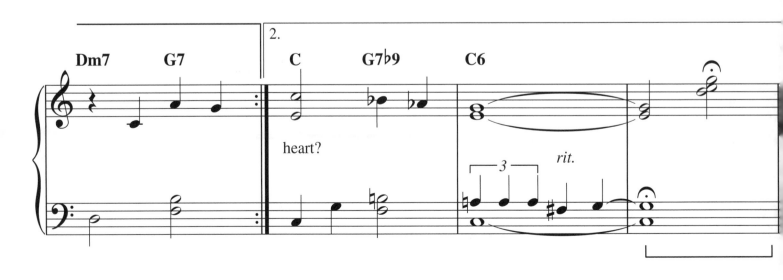

heart?

AS LONG AS I LIVE

Lyric by TED KOEHLER
Music by HAROLD ARLEN

2.

Gm **C7** **F** **F#dim**

I nev - er cared, but

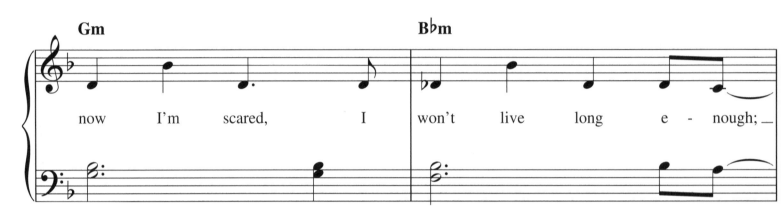

Gm **Bbm**

now I'm scared, I won't live long e - nough; —

F **Dm**

— That's why I wear my rub - bers

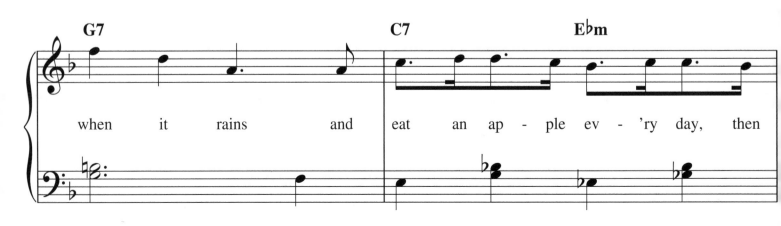

G7 **C7** **Ebm**

when it rains and eat an ap - ple ev - 'ry day, then

see the doc - tor an - y - way. What if I can't __ live to love __

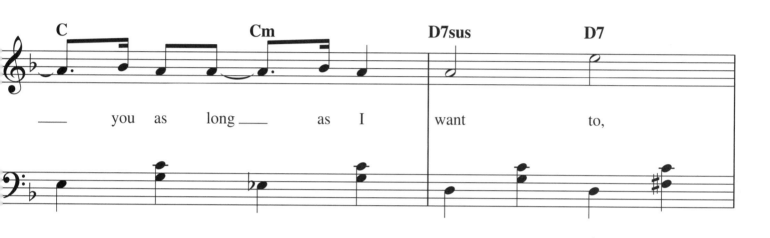

__ you as long __ as I want to,

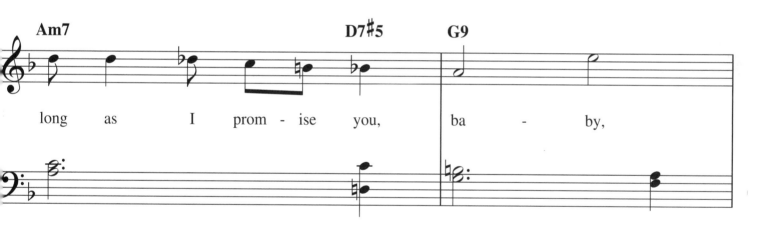

long as I prom - ise you, ba - by,

I'm gon - na love you as long as I live.

AS LONG AS HE NEEDS ME

from the Broadway Musical OLIVER!

Words and Music by
LIONEL BART

AUTUMN IN NEW YORK

Words and Music by
VERNON DUKE

BABY ELEPHANT WALK
from the Paramount Picture HATARI!

By HENRY MANCINI

AUTUMN LEAVES

English lyric by JOHNNY MERCER
French lyric by JACQUES PREVERT
Music by JOSEPH KOSMA

Freely

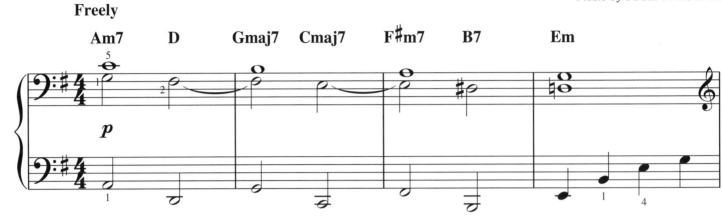

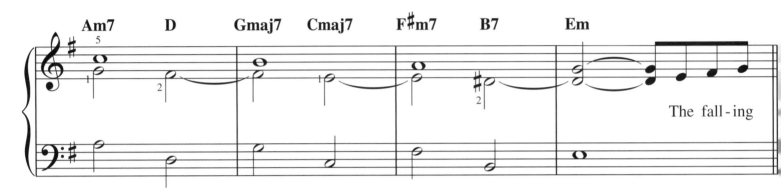

The fall-ing

Slowly

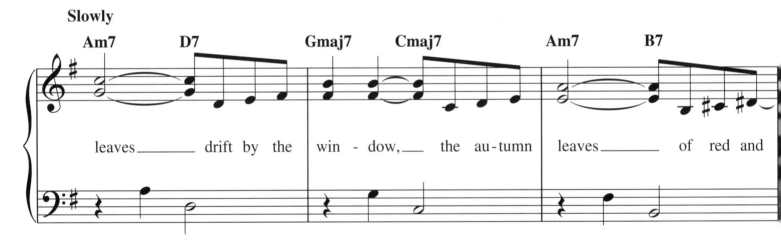

leaves_____ drift by the win - dow,_____ the au-tumn leaves_____ of red and

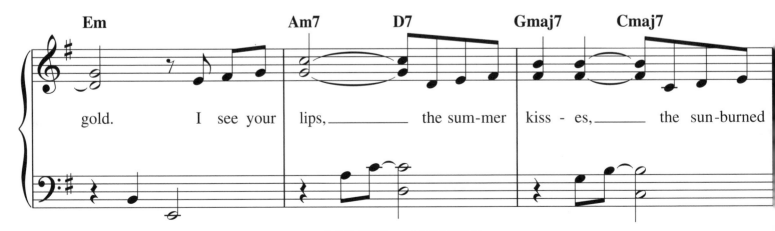

gold. I see your lips,_____ the sum-mer kiss - es,_____ the sun-burned

43

BANDSTAND BOOGIE
from the Television Series AMERICAN BANDSTAND

Special Lyric by BARRY MANILOW and BRUCE SUSSMAN
Music by CHARLES ALBERTINE

drop in (drop!) on all the mu-sic they play on the Band - stand. _
ring - in' (ring!) my mom and dad are so proud, I'm on Band - stand. _

(Band - stand.) _ We're go - in'
(Band - stand.) _ And I'll jump and, hey, I
Now for all you Joes here

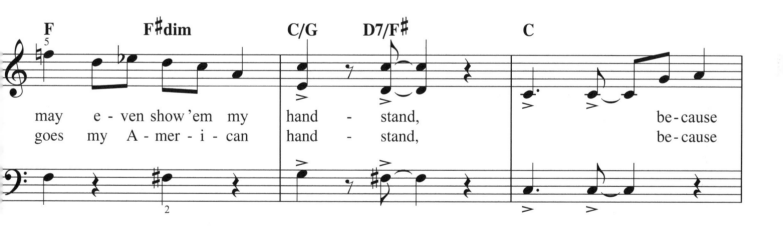

may e - ven show 'em my hand - stand, be - cause
goes my A - mer - i - can hand - stand, be - cause

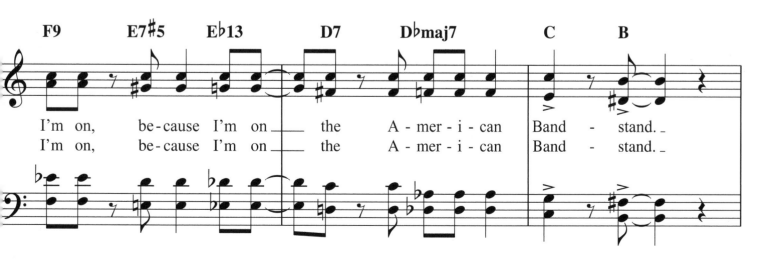

I'm on, be - cause I'm on ___ the A - mer - i - can Band - stand. _
I'm on, be - cause I'm on ___ the A - mer - i - can Band - stand. _

When we / As we dance real slow I'll / I'm show all / show-in' the guys in the

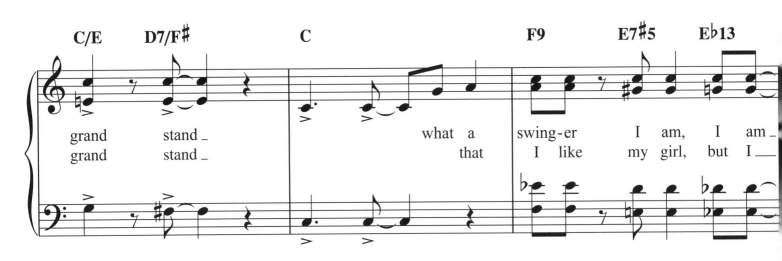

grand stand _ / grand stand _

what a / that swing-er / I like I am, I am _ / my girl, but I _

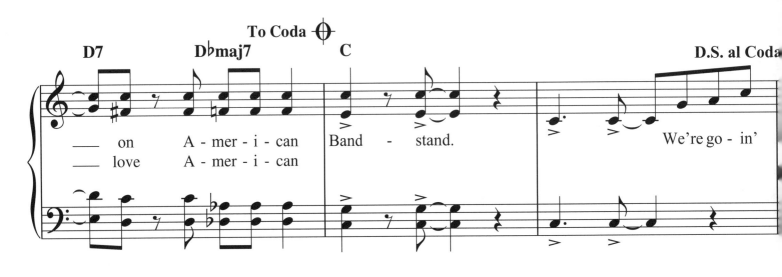

_ on / _ love A-mer-i-can A-mer-i-can Band - stand. We're go-in'

To Coda 🎵

D.S. al Coda

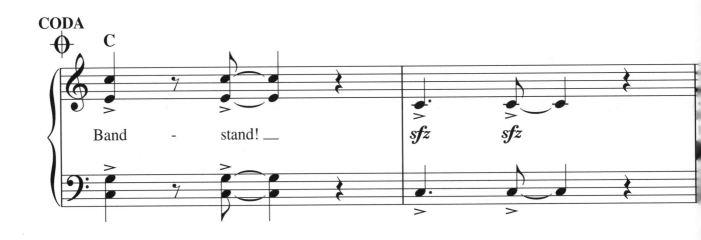

CODA

Band - stand! _

BASIN STREET BLUES

Words and Music by
SPENCER WILLIAMS

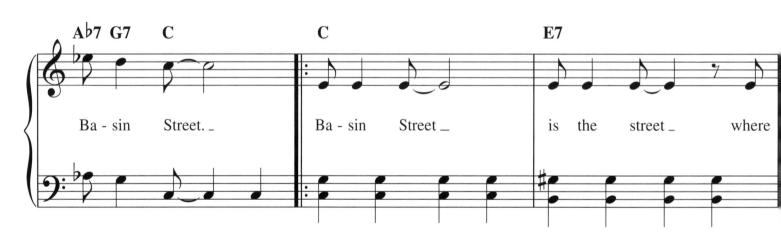

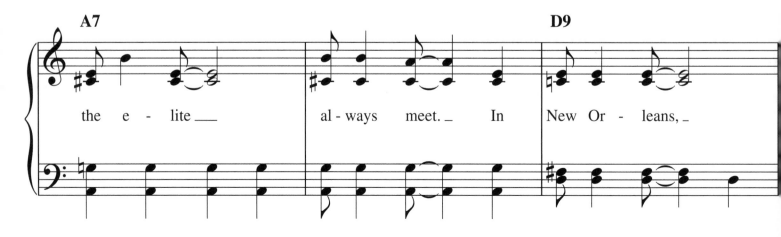

BAUBLES, BANGLES AND BEADS

from KISMET

Words and Music by ROBERT WRIGHT
and GEORGE FORREST
(Music Based on Themes of A. BORODIN)

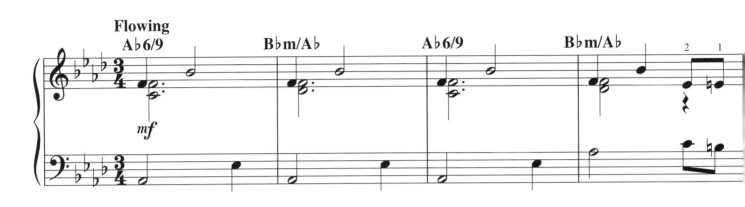

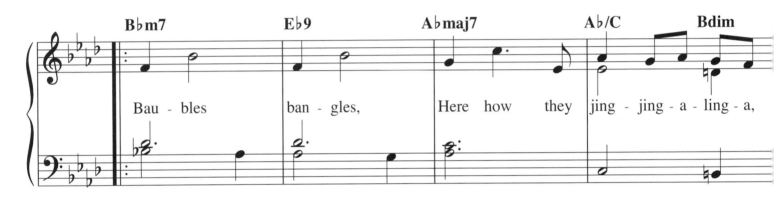

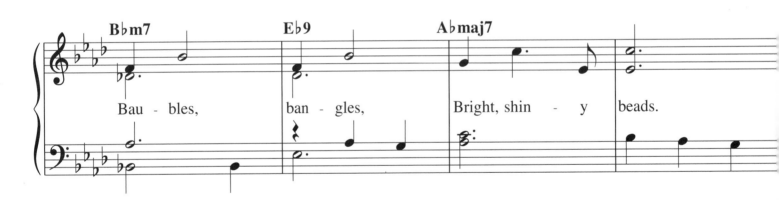

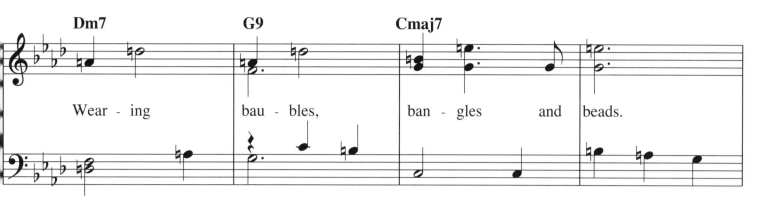

Wear - ing   bau - bles,   ban - gles   and   beads.

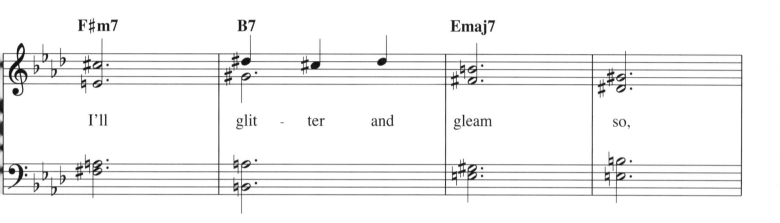

I'll   glit - ter   and   gleam   so,

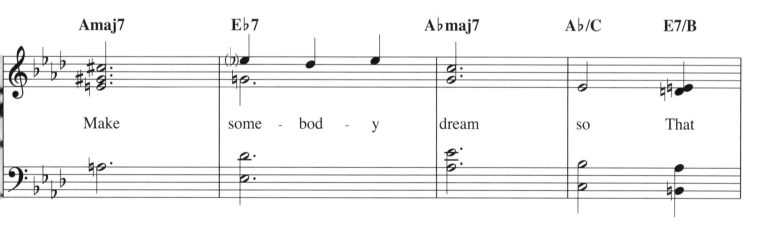

Make   some - bod - y   dream   so   That

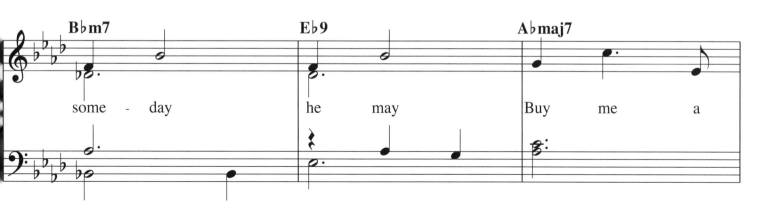

some - day   he   may   Buy   me   a

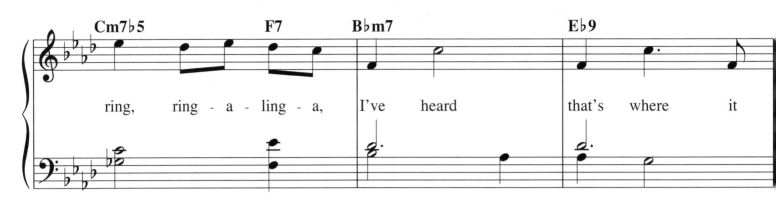

ring, ring - a - ling - a, I've heard that's where it

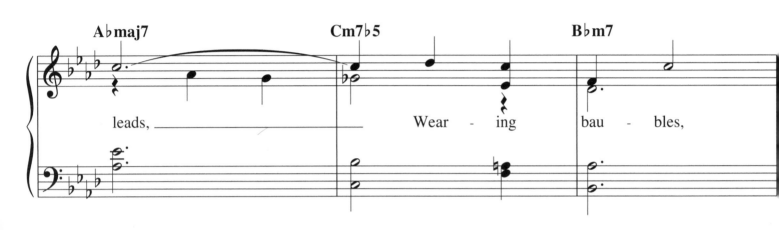

leads, _____ Wear - ing bau - bles,

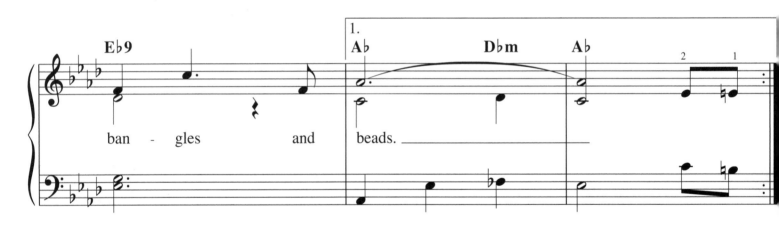

ban - gles and beads. _____

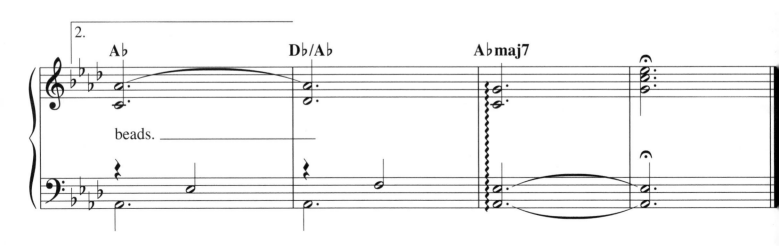

beads. _____

BELLA'S LULLABY

from the Summit Entertainment film TWILIGHT

Composed by
CARTER BURWELL

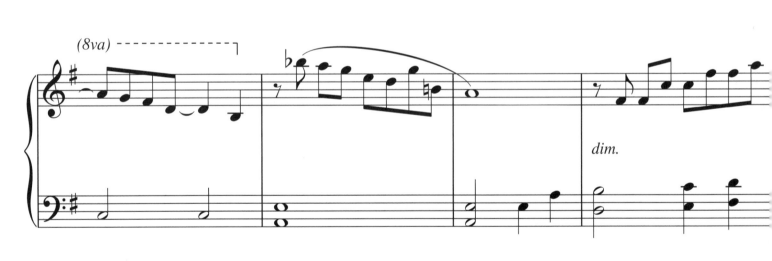

BÉSAME MUCHO
(Kiss Me Much)

Music and Spanish Words by CONSUELO VELAZQUEZ
English Words by SUNNY SKYLAR

Bé - sa - me _____ bé - sa - me mu - cho, _____
Bé - sa - me _____ bé - sa - me mu - cho. _____

co - mo si fue - ra es - tá no - che la úl - ti - ma
Each time I cling to your kiss I hear mu - sic di -

vez; Bé -
vine. *Bé -*

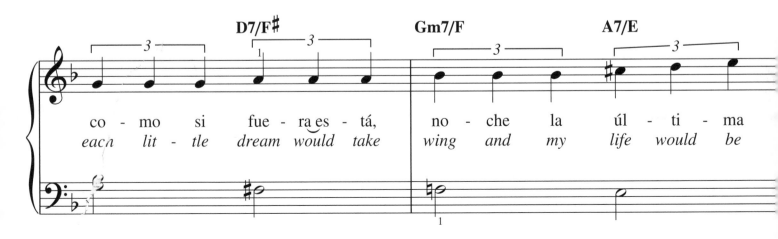

THE BEST THINGS IN LIFE ARE FREE

from GOOD NEWS!

Music and Lyrics by B.G. DeSYLVA
LEW BROWN and RAY HENDERSON

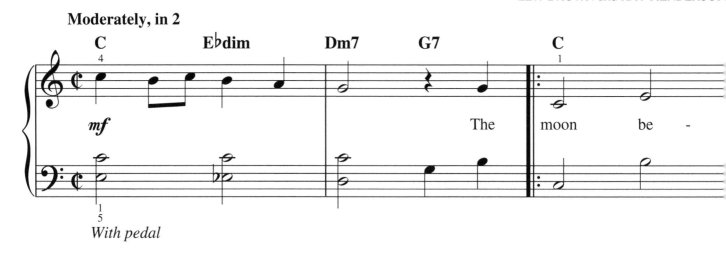

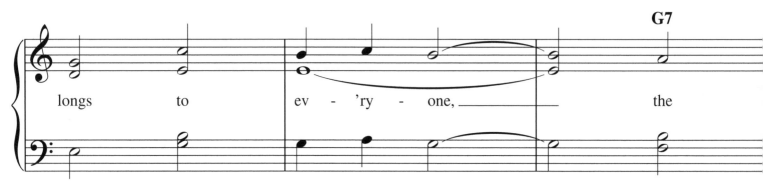

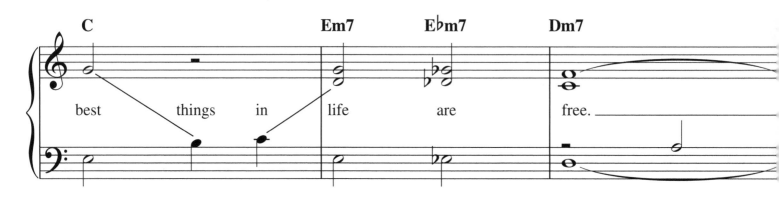

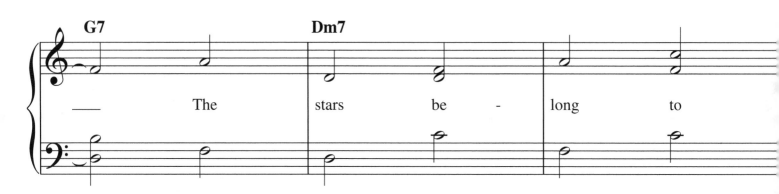

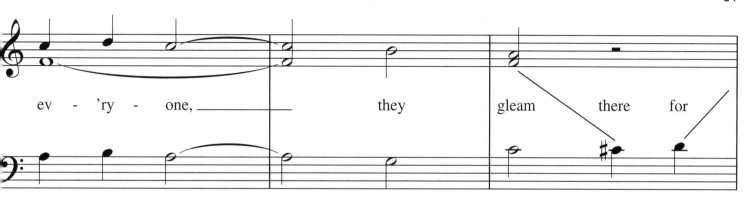

ev - 'ry - one, ____ they gleam there for

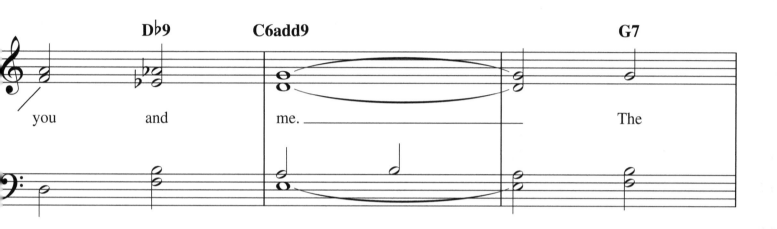

you and me. ____ The

flow - ers in spring, ____ the rob - ins that sing, ____

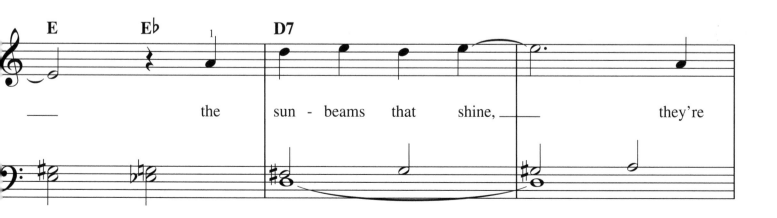

the sun - beams that shine, ____ they're

yours, they're mine! And love can

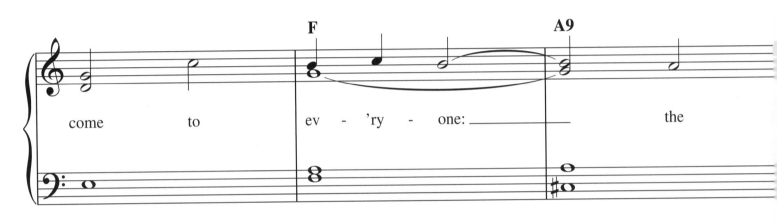

come to ev - 'ry - one: the

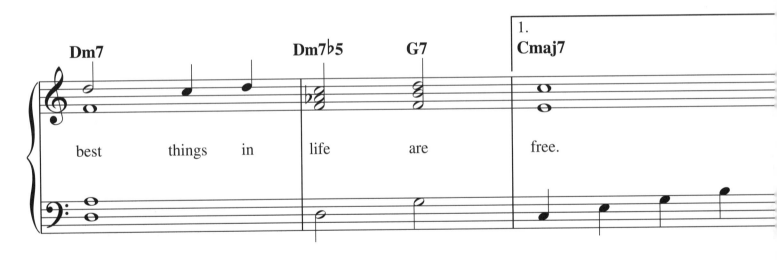

best things in life are free.

The free. *rit.*

THE BLUE ROOM
from THE GIRL FRIEND

Words by LORENZ HART
Music by RICHARD RODGERS

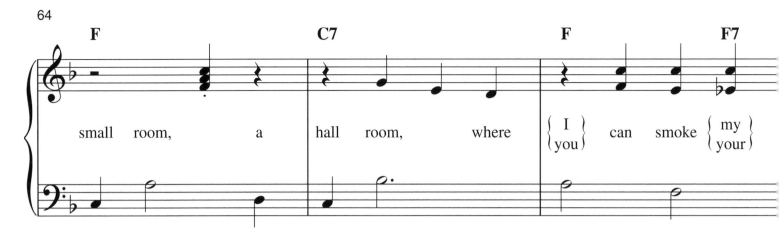

small room, a hall room, where { I / you } can smoke { my / your }

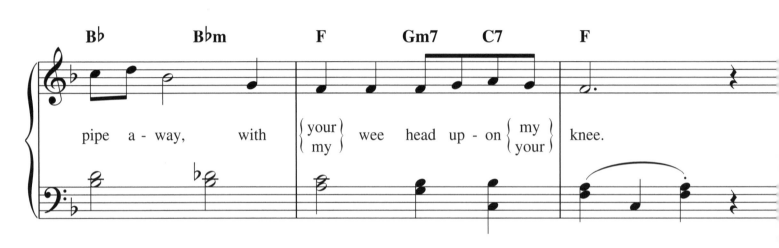

pipe a - way, with { your / my } wee head up - on { my / your } knee.

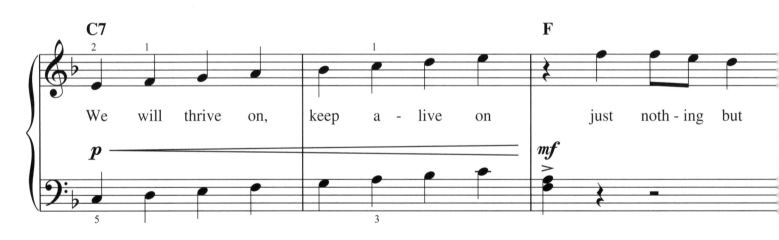

We will thrive on, keep a - live on just noth - ing but

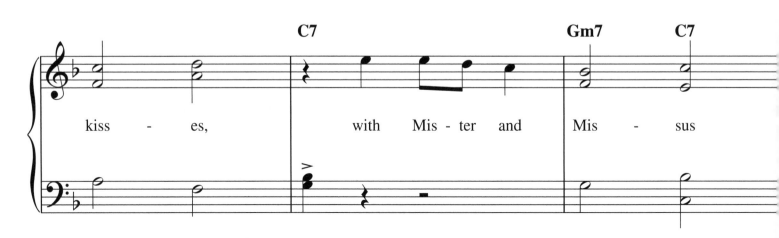

kiss - es, with Mis - ter and Mis - sus

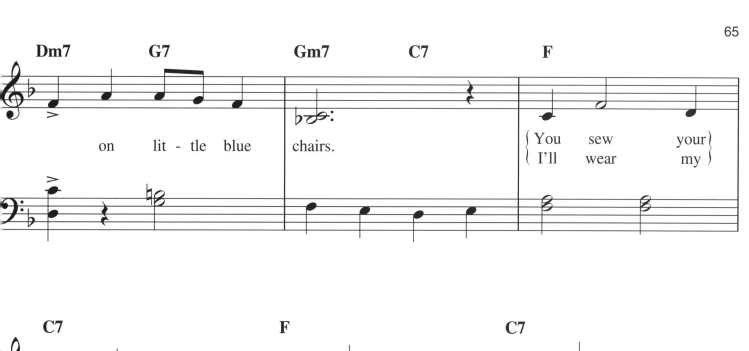

Dm7 **G7** **Gm7** **C7** **F**

on lit - tle blue chairs.

{You sew your}
{I'll wear my}

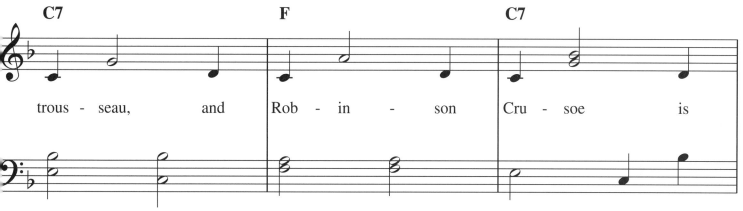

C7 **F** **C7**

trous - seau, and Rob - in - son Cru - soe is

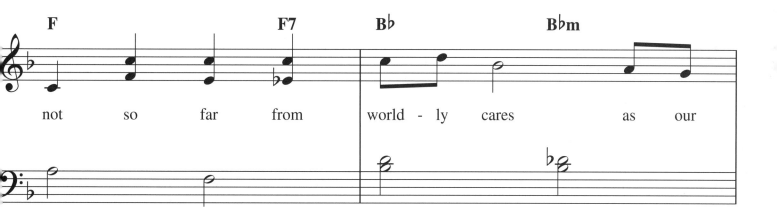

F **F7** **Bb** **Bbm**

not so far from world - ly cares as our

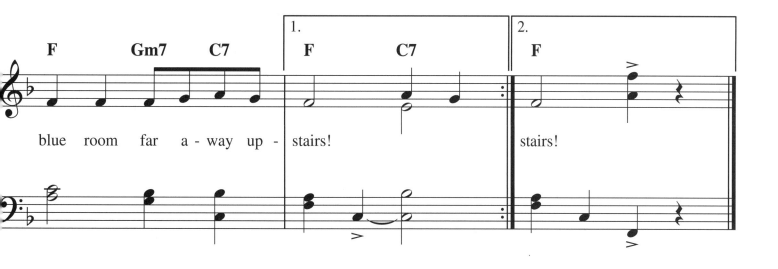

F **Gm7** **C7** 1. **F** **C7** 2. **F**

blue room far a - way up - stairs! stairs!

BEYOND THE SEA

Lyrics by JACK LAWRENCE
Music by CHARLES TRENET and ALBERT LASRY
Original French Lyric to "La Mer" by CHARLES TRENET

Some- where _____ be-yond the sea some - where wait - ing for me, _____ my lov - er stands on gold - en sands _____ and watch - es the

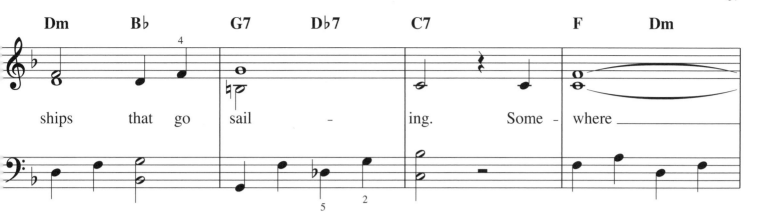

ships that go sail - ing. Some - where

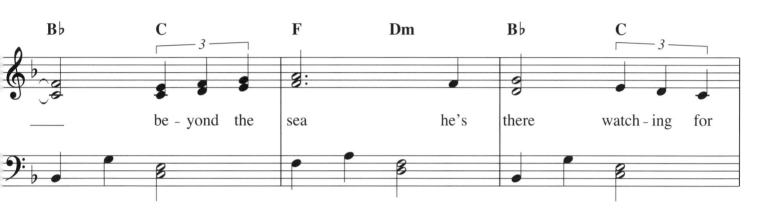

be - yond the sea he's there watch - ing for

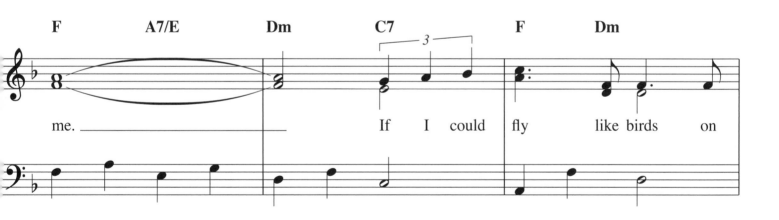

me. If I could fly like birds on

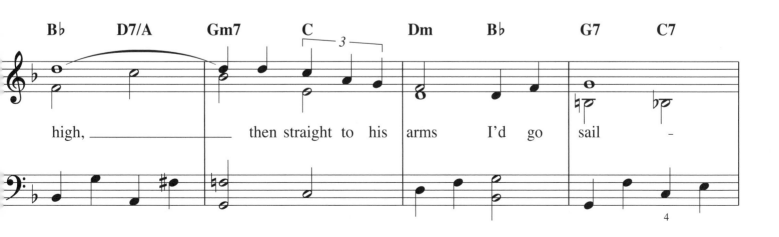

high, then straight to his arms I'd go sail -

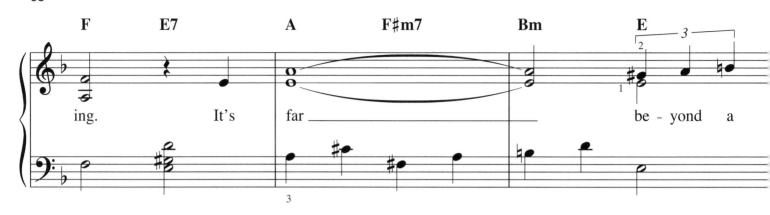

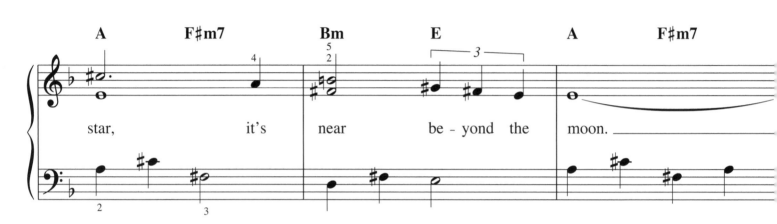

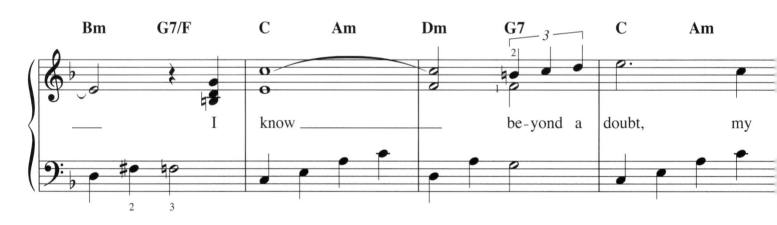

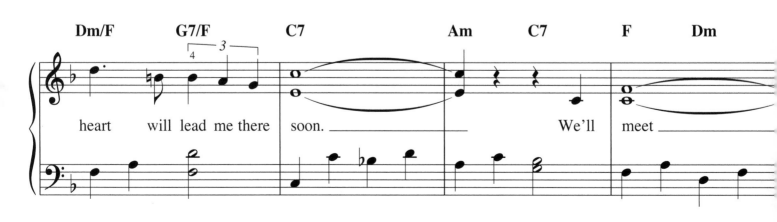

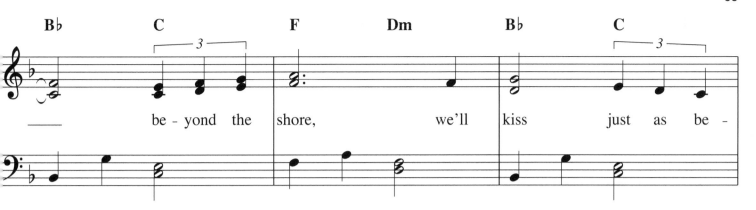

be - yond the shore, we'll kiss just as be -

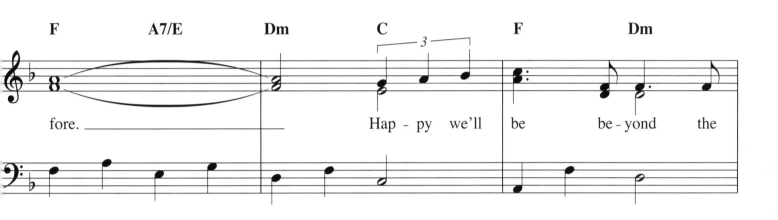

fore. _____ Hap - py we'll be be - yond the

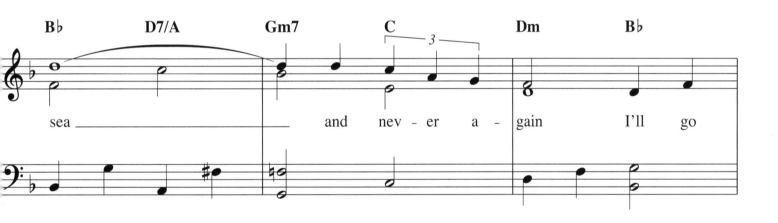

sea _____ and nev - er a - gain I'll go

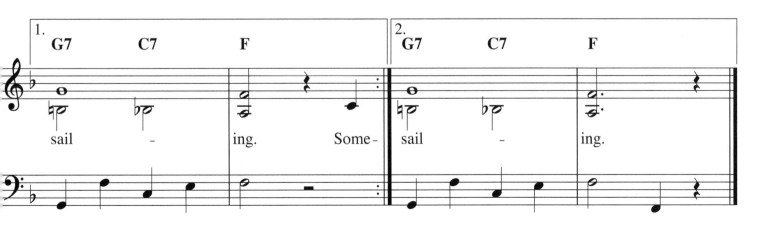

1. sail - ing. Some-

2. sail - ing.

BIG SPENDER

from SWEET CHARITY

Music by CY COLEMAN
Lyrics by DOROTHY FIELDS

Moderately, with a beat

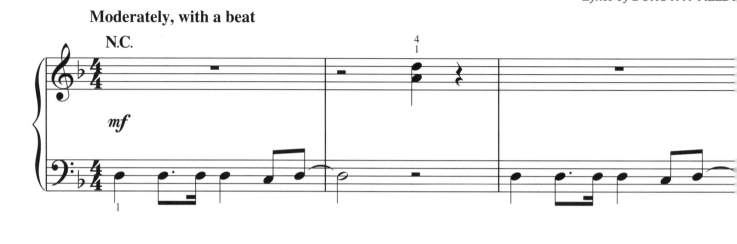

The min-ute you walked in the joint I could see you were a

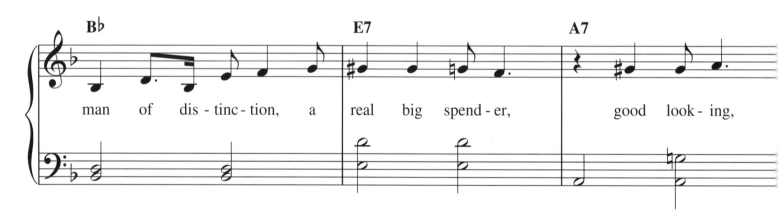

man of dis - tinc - tion, a real big spend - er, good look - ing,

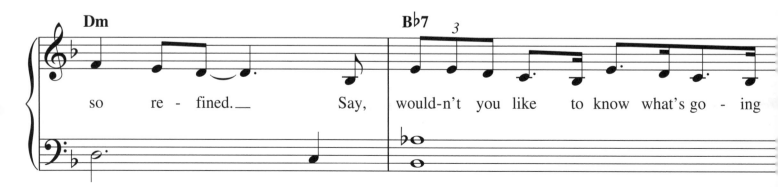

so re - fined.__ Say, would-n't you like to know what's go - ing

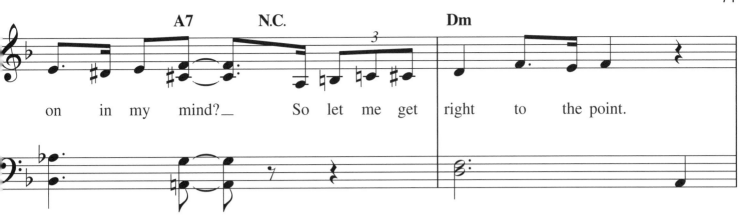

on in my mind?_ So let me get right to the point.

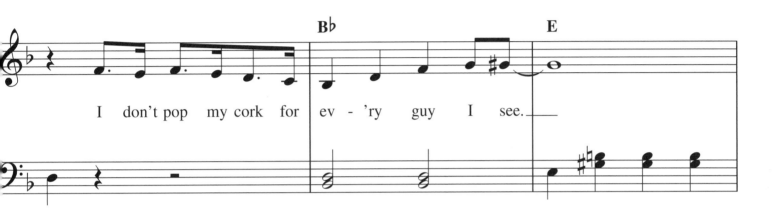

I don't pop my cork for ev - 'ry guy I see._

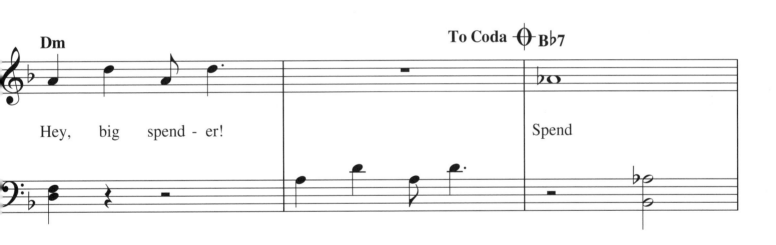

Hey, big spend - er! Spend

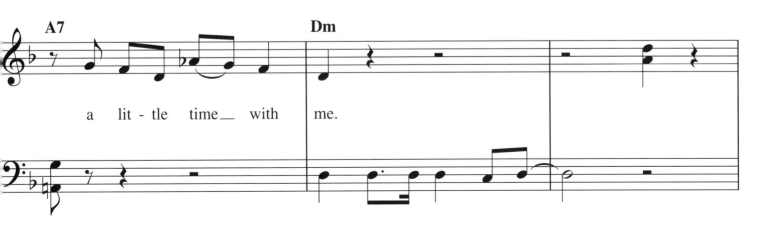

a lit - tle time_ with me.

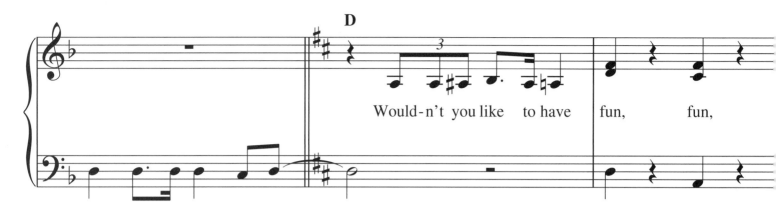

D

Would-n't you like to have fun, fun,

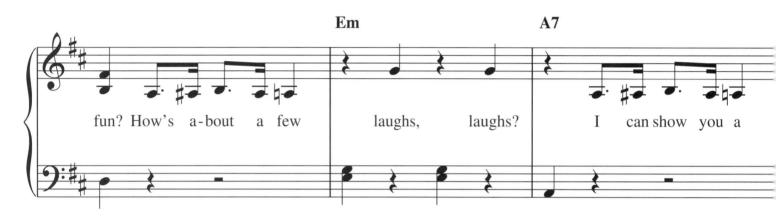

Em   **A7**

fun? How's a-bout a few   laughs, laughs?   I can show you a

B♭7   **A7**   **B♭7**

good time,____   let me show you a   good time.____

A7   **D.S. al Coda**

____   The min-ute you

CODA
E♭m

Hey, big spend-er!

Hey, big spend - er!

Spend a lit - tle time __ with me. Spend __

__ a lit - tle time __ with me. Spend __

__ a lit - tle time __ with me. __

BLUE VELVET

Words and Music by BERNIE WAYNE
and LEE MORRIS

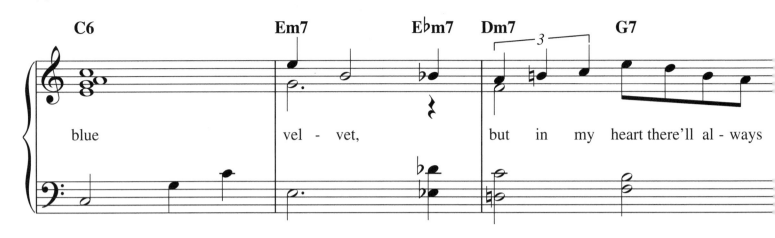

blue   vel - vet,   but in my heart there'll al - ways

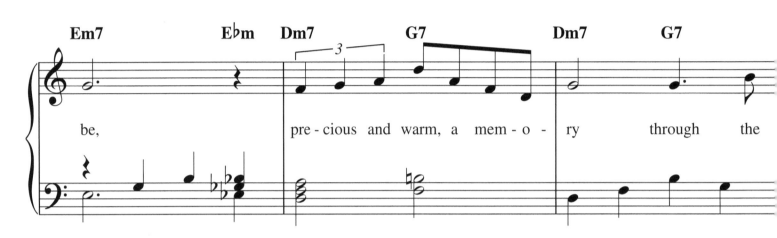

be,   pre - cious and warm, a mem - o - ry   through the

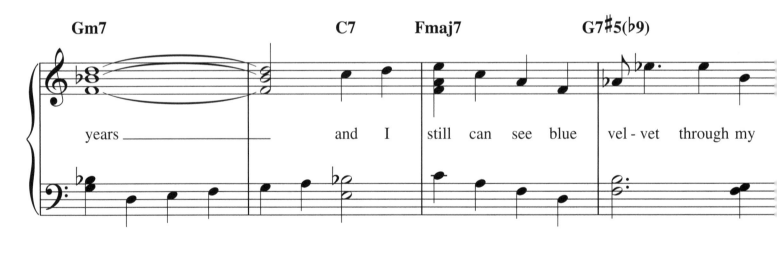

years _____   and I   still can see blue   vel - vet through my

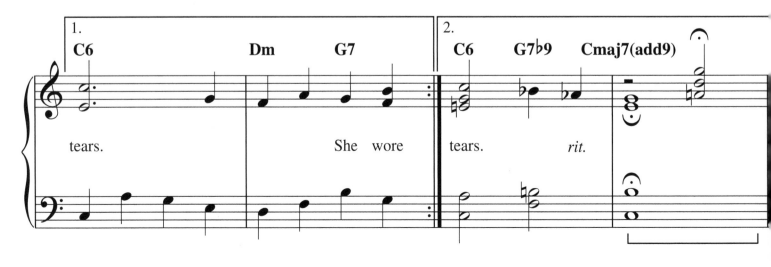

tears.   She wore   tears.   *rit.*

BORN FREE

from the Columbia Pictures' Release BORN FREE

Words by DON BLACK
Music by JOHN BARRY

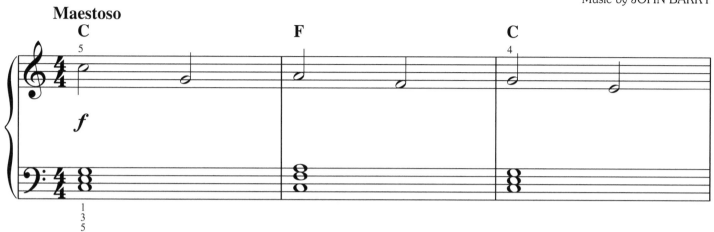

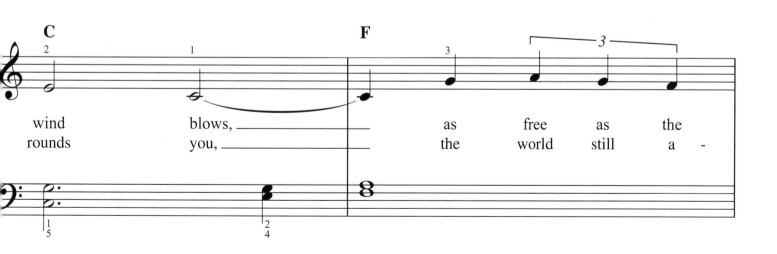

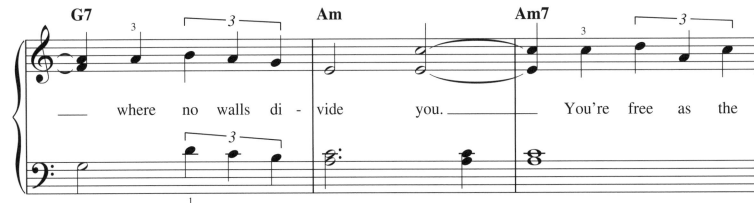

roar - ing tide, so there's no need to hide.
cresc.

f

Born free, _____ and life is worth

liv - ing, _____ but on - ly worth liv - ing 'cause

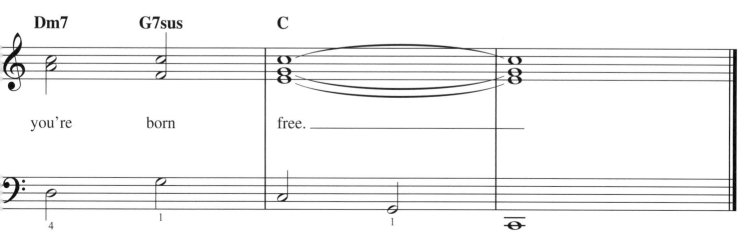

you're born free. _____

BUTTON UP YOUR OVERCOAT

from FOLLOW THRU

Words and Music by B.G. DeSYLVA,
LEW BROWN and RAY HENDERSON

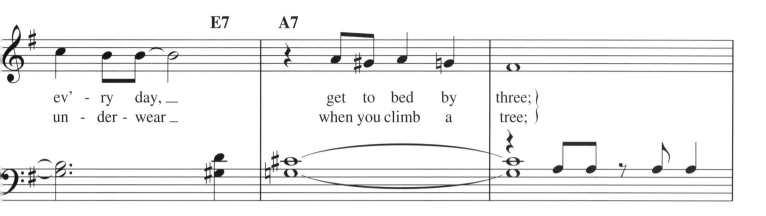

ev' - ry day, __
un - der - wear __

get to bed by three;)
when you climb a tree;)

take good __ care of your-self, you be long to me. __

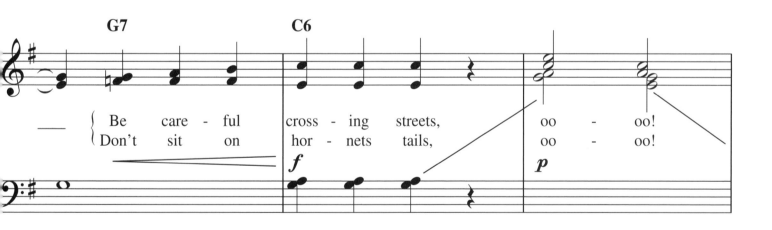

__ { Be care - ful
{ Don't sit on

cross - ing streets,
hor - nets tails,

oo - oo!
oo - oo!

f

p

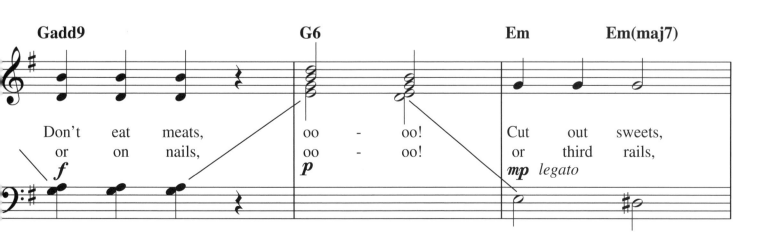

Don't eat meats,
or on nails,

oo - oo!
oo - oo!

Cut out sweets,
or third rails,

f

p

mp *legato*

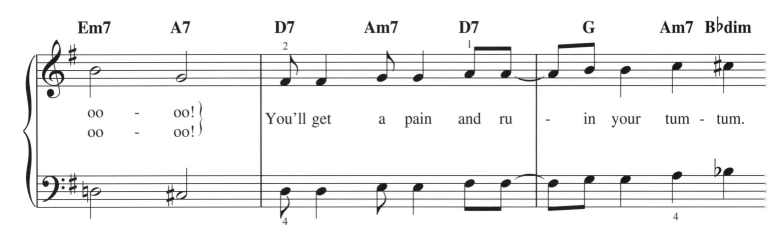

oo - oo!
oo - oo!
You'll get a pain and ru - in your tum - tum.

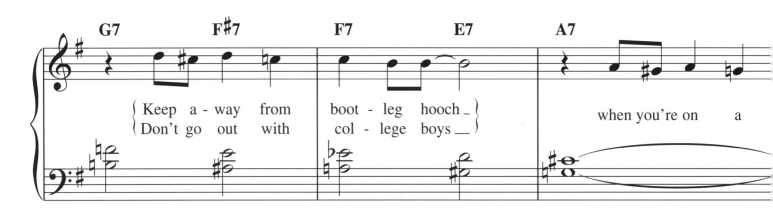

Keep a - way from
Don't go out with
boot - leg hooch
col - lege boys
when you're on a

spree; take good care of your - self, you be -

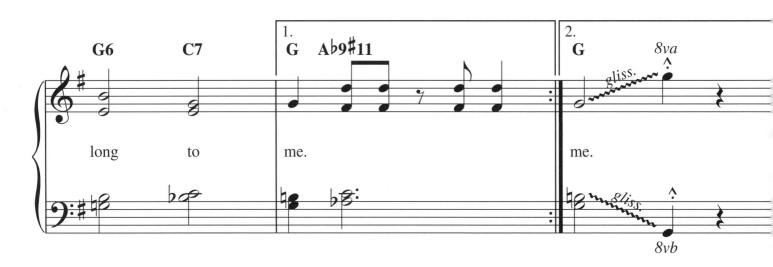

long to me.
me.

BY THE TIME I GET TO PHOENIX

Words and Music by
JIMMY WEBB

1. **Gm7** ... **E♭** ... **C7**

left that girl___ so man-y times___ be - fore._____ By the

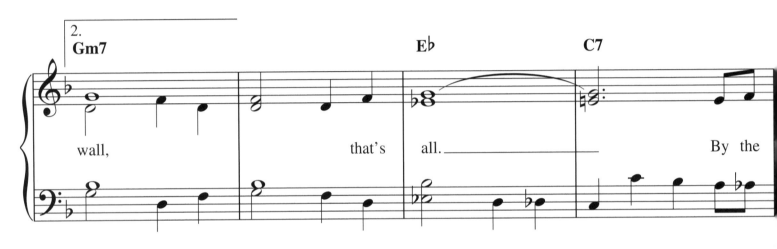

2. **Gm7** ... **E♭** ... **C7**

wall, that's all._____ By the

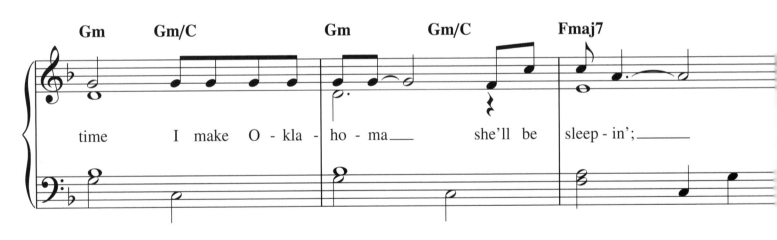

Gm **Gm/C** **Gm** **Gm/C** **Fmaj7**

time I make O - kla - ho - ma___ she'll be sleep-in';_____

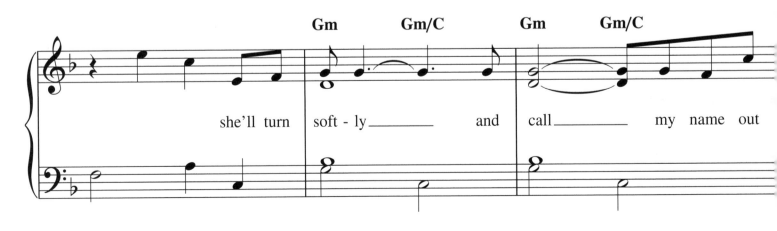

Gm **Gm/C** **Gm** **Gm/C**

she'll turn soft - ly_____ and call_____ my name out

low.　　　　　　　　　　And she'll　cry　　　just　to

think_____ I'd real - ly　leave her,_____　　　　　　　　though_

time　and　time_____　I've tried__ to tell her　so;

she just did-n't　know_____　　　I would real - ly　go.
rit.

BYE BYE BLACKBIRD

from PETE KELLY'S BLUES

Lyric by MORT DIXON
Music by RAY HENDERSON

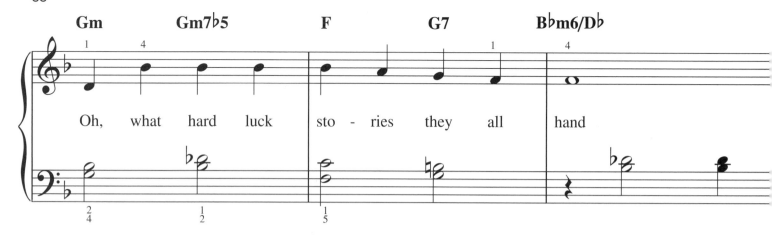

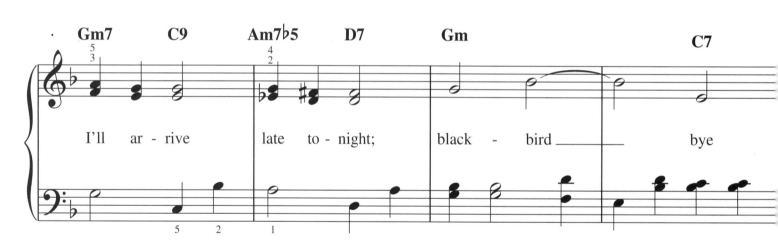

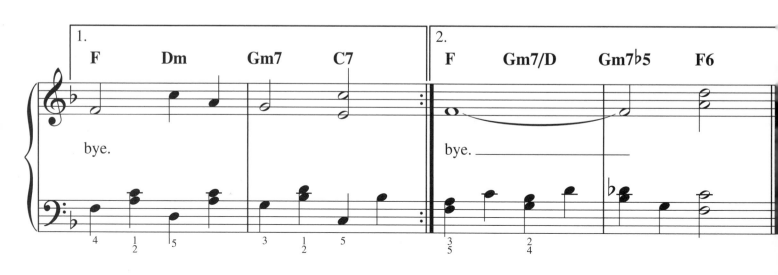

THE CANDY MAN

from WILLY WONKA AND THE CHOCOLATE FACTORY

Words and Music by LESLIE BRICUSSE
and ANTHONY NEWLEY

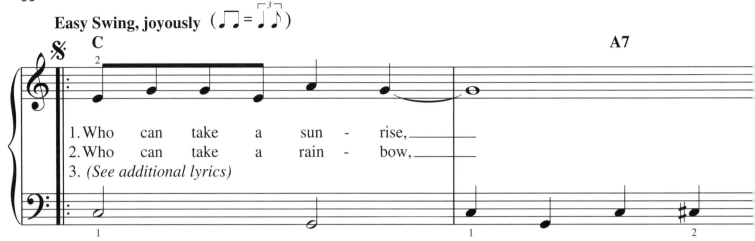

Easy Swing, joyously

1. Who can take a sun - rise,___
2. Who can take a rain - bow,___
3. *(See additional lyrics)*

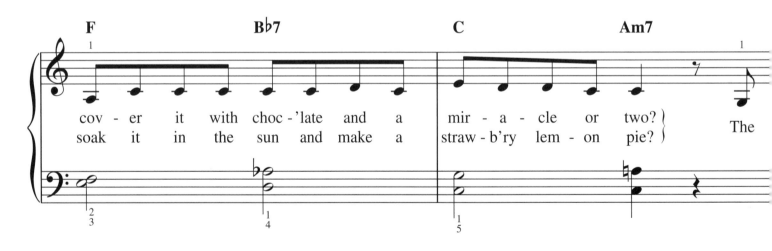

sprin - kle it with dew,___
wrap it in a sigh,___

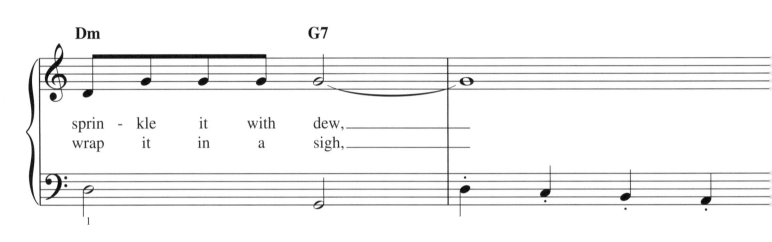

cov - er it with choc -'late and a mir - a - cle or two? } The
soak it in the sun and make a straw - b'ry lem - on pie? }

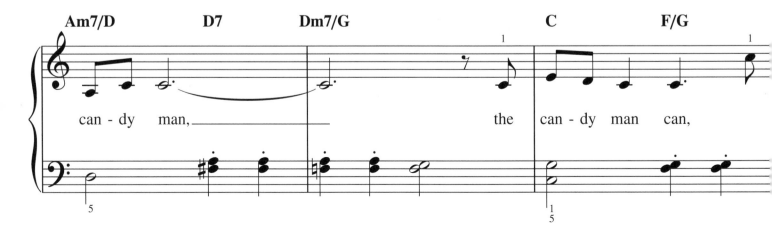

can - dy man,___   the can - dy man can,

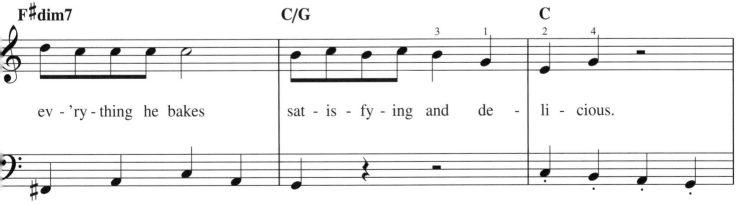

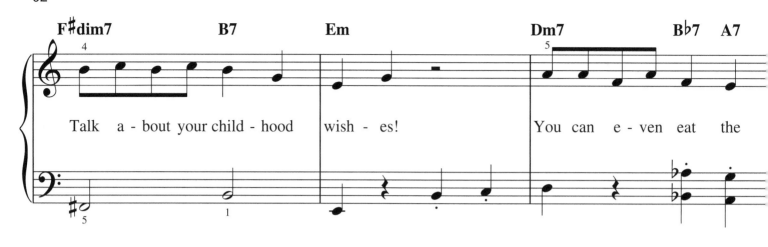

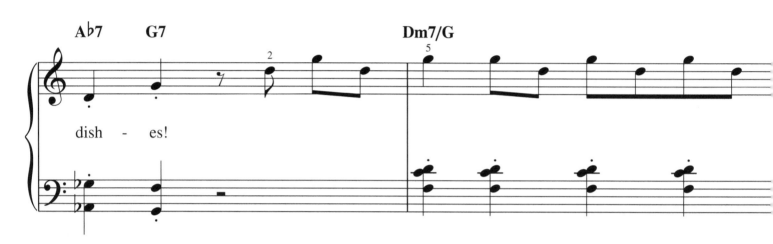

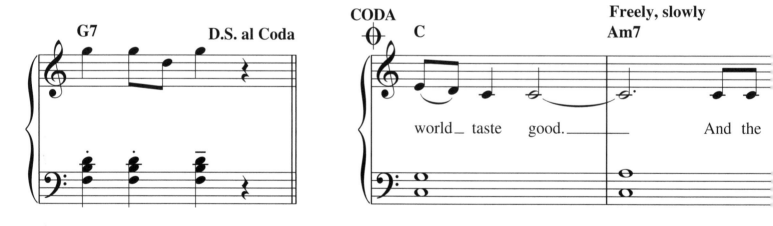

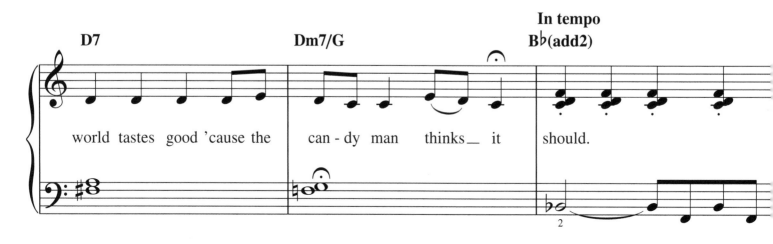

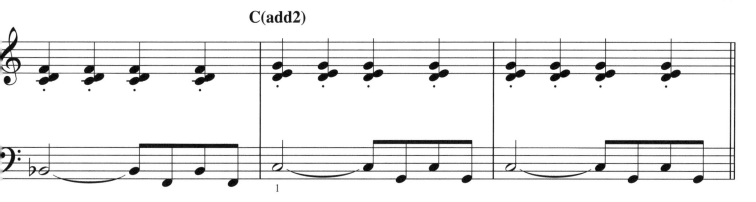

C(add2)

B♭(add2)

C(add2)   **Repeat and Fade**

Additional Lyrics

3. Who can take tomorrow, dip it in a dream,
   Separate the sorrow and collect up all the cream?
   The candy man, the candy man can.
   The candy man can 'cause he mixes it with love
   And makes the world taste good.

CAN'T HELP LOVIN' DAT MAN

from SHOW BOAT

Lyrics by OSCAR HAMMERSTEIN
Music by JEROME KERN

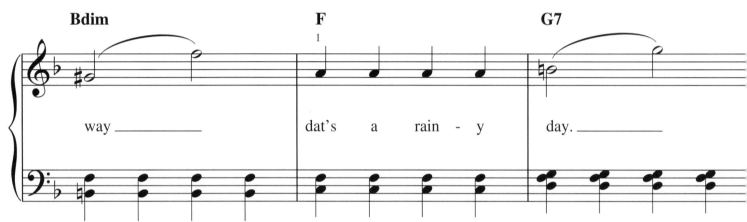

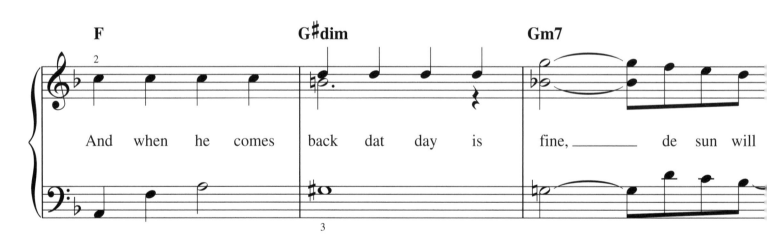

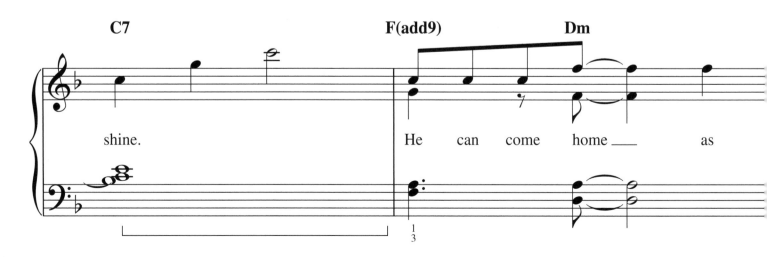

97

CAN'T SMILE WITHOUT YOU

Words and Music by CHRIS ARNOL
DAVID MARTIN and GEOFF MORRO

feel sad when you're sad. I feel glad when

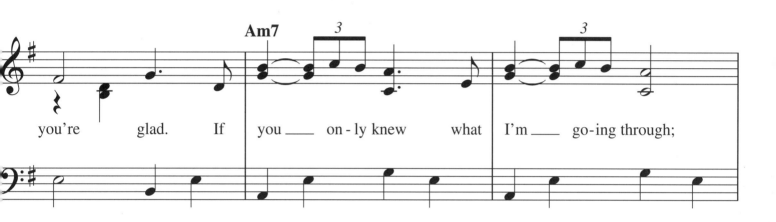

you're glad. If you ___ on-ly knew what I'm ___ go-ing through;

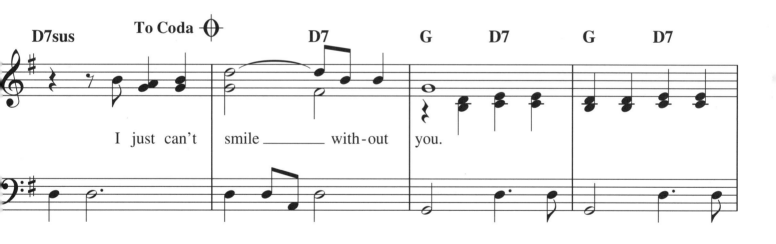

I just can't smile _____ with-out you.

You come a-long ___ just like a song ___ and bright-ened my day. ___

Who'd-a be-lieved that you were part of a dream. Now it all seems

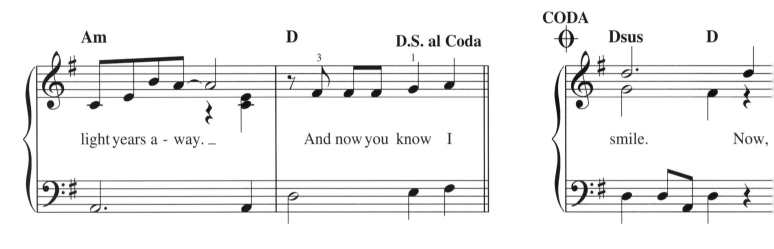

light years a - way. And now you know I smile. Now,

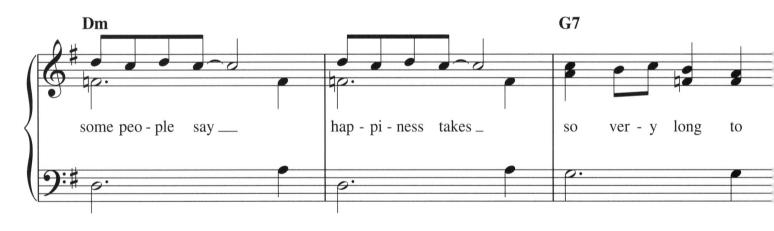

some peo - ple say hap - pi - ness takes so ver - y long to

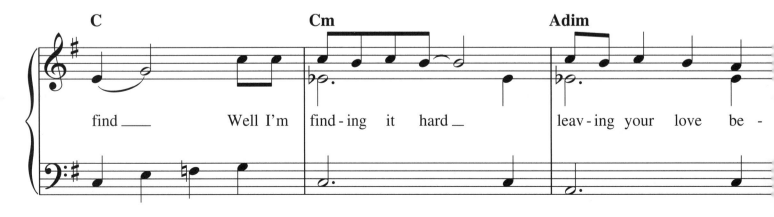

find Well I'm find - ing it hard leav - ing your love be -

hind   me.   You see, I   can't   smile   with-

out   you.   I can't smile with-   out   you,   if   you __ on-ly knew   what

I'm __ go-ing through;   I   just can't   smile   with-out   you. ____

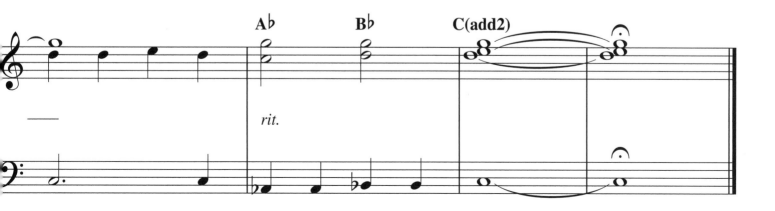

____   rit.

CANDLE ON THE WATER

from Walt Disney's PETE'S DRAGON

Words and Music by AL KASHA
and JOEL HIRSCHHORN

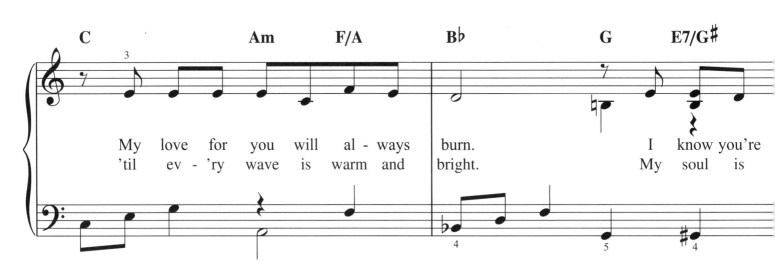

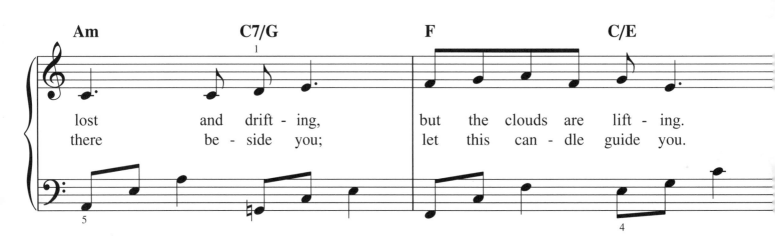

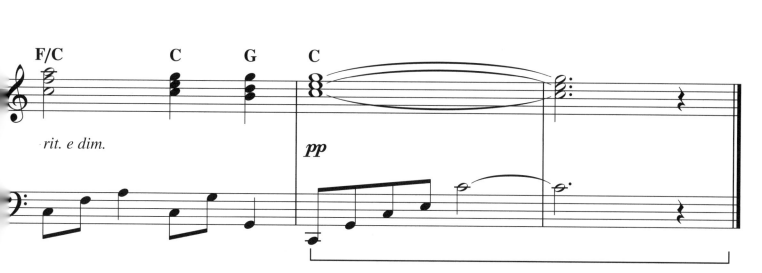

CHEROKEE
(Indian Love Song)

Words and Music by
RAY NOBLE

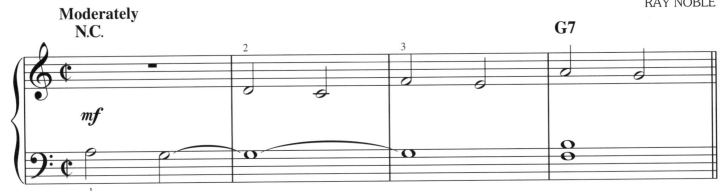

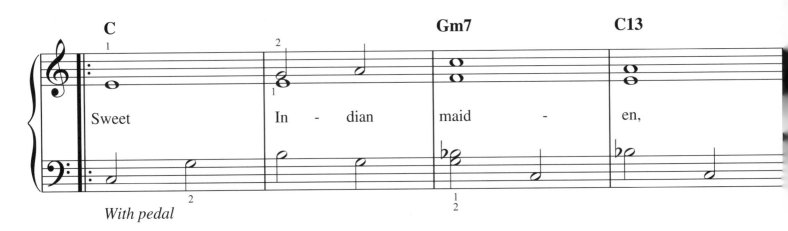

Sweet In - dian maid - en,

With pedal

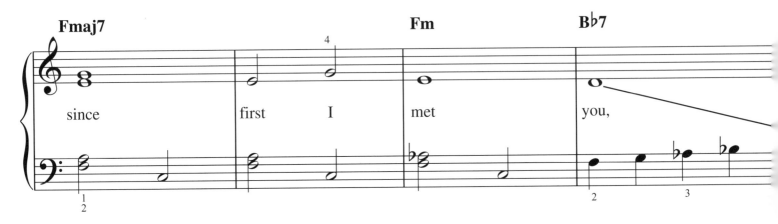

since first I met you,

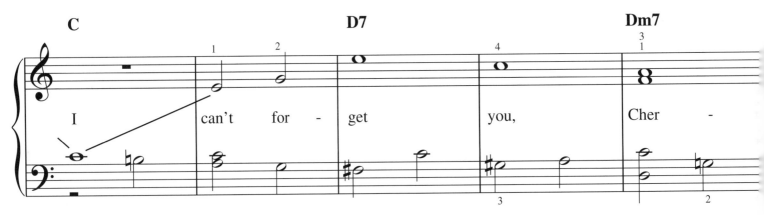

I can't for - get you, Cher -

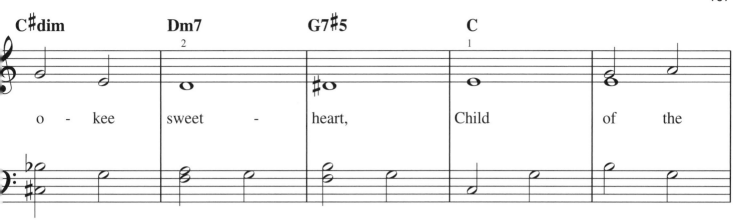

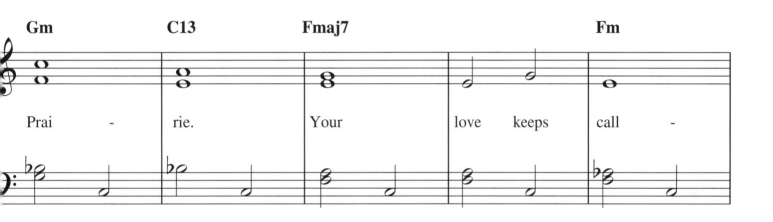

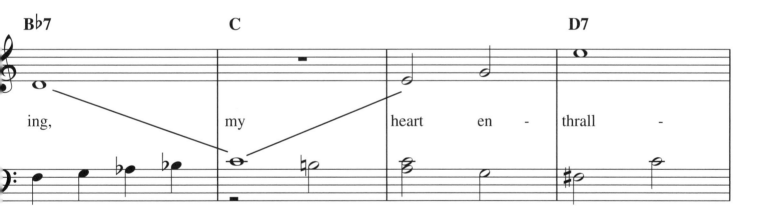

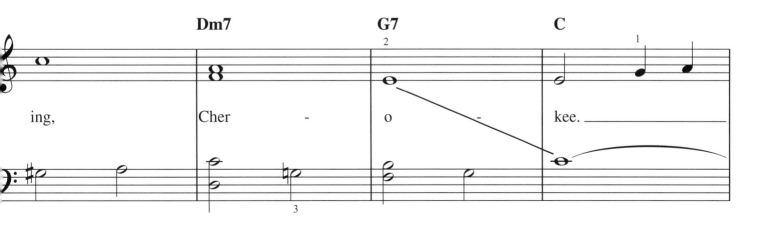

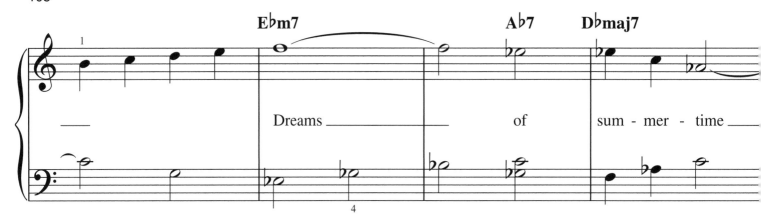

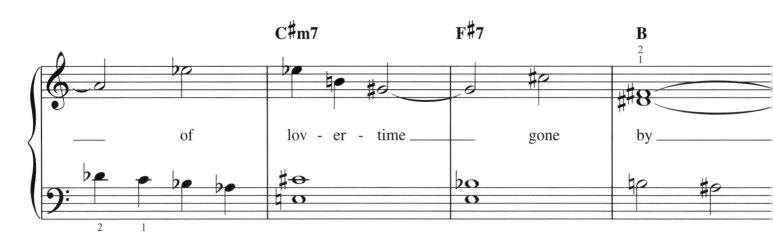

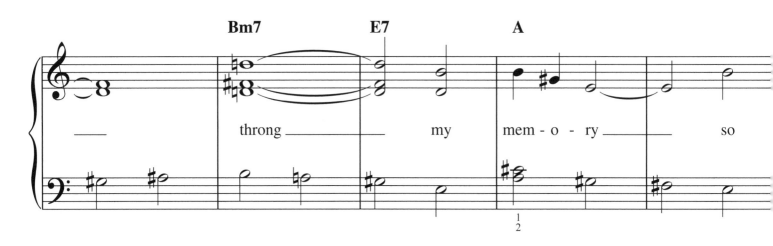

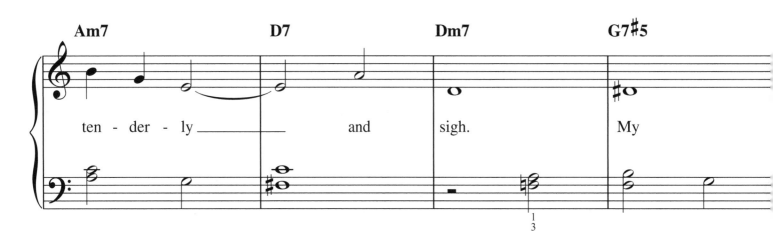

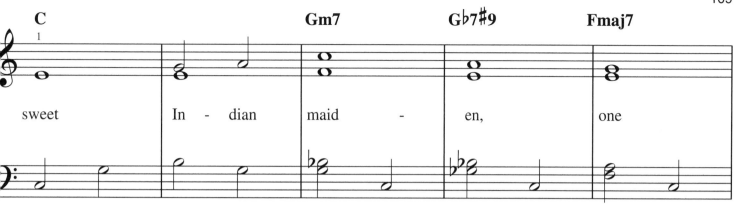

C   Gm7   Gb7#9   Fmaj7

sweet   In - dian   maid -   en,   one

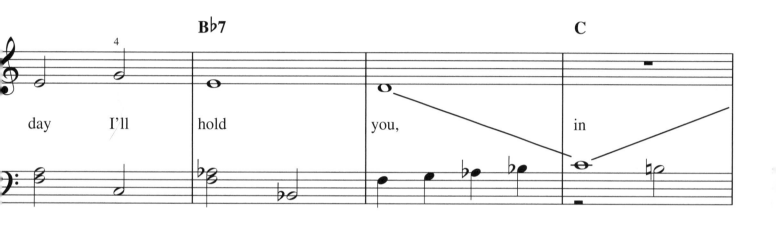

Bb7   C

day   I'll   hold   you,   in

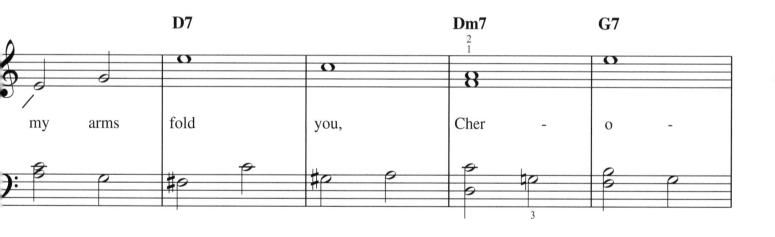

D7   Dm7   G7

my   arms   fold   you,   Cher -   o -

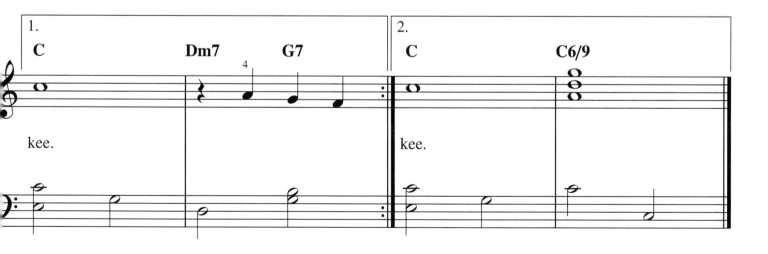

1.
C   Dm7   G7

kee.

2.
C   C6/9

kee.

CHIM CHIM CHER-EE

from Walt Disney's MARY POPPINS

Words and Music by RICHARD M. SHERMAN
and ROBERT B. SHERMAN

Lightly, with gusto

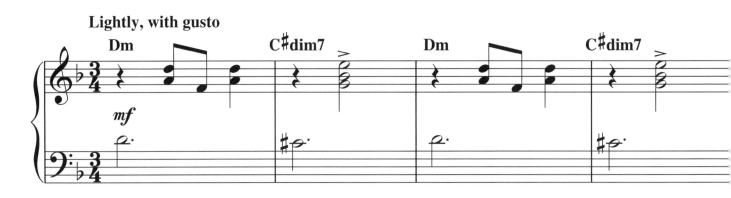

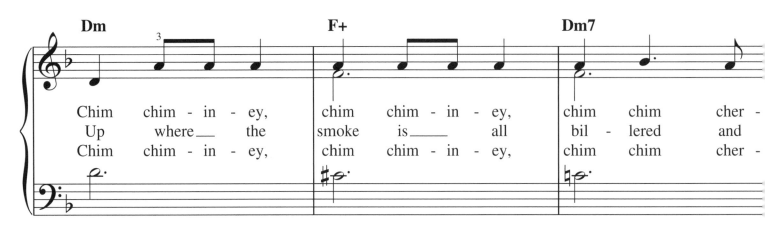

Chim chim-in-ey, chim chim-in-ey, chim chim cher-
Up where the smoke is all bil-lered and
Chim chim-in-ey, chim chim-in-ey, chim chim cher-

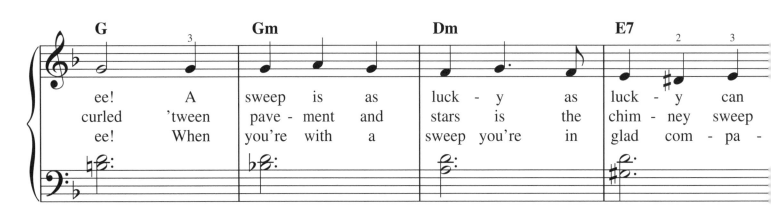

ee! A sweep is as luck-y as luck-y can
curled 'tween pave-ment and stars is the chim-ney sweep
ee! When you're with a sweep you're in glad com-pa-

be. When there's Chim chim-in-ey, chim chim-in-ey,
world. 'ard-ly no day nor
ny. No-where is there a more

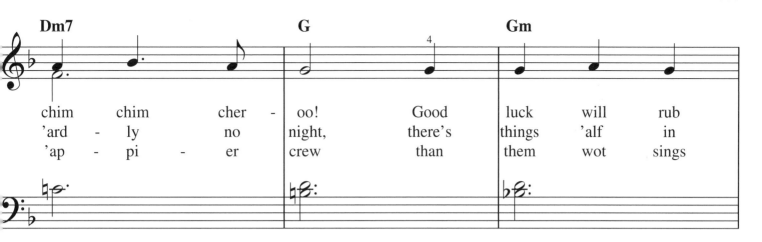

Dm7 / **G** / **Gm**

chim chim cher - oo! Good luck will rub
'ard - ly no night, there's things 'alf in
'ap - pi - er crew than them wot sings

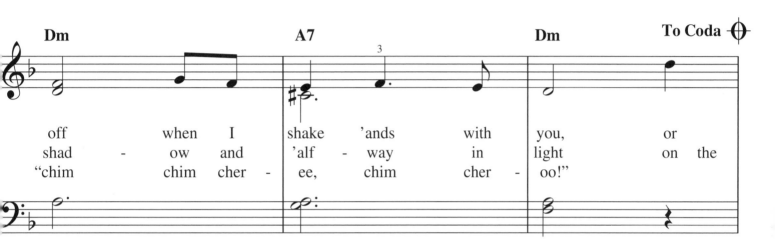

Dm / **A7** / **Dm** **To Coda**

off when I shake 'ands with you, or
shad - ow and 'alf - way in light on the
"chim chim cher - ee, chim cher - oo!"

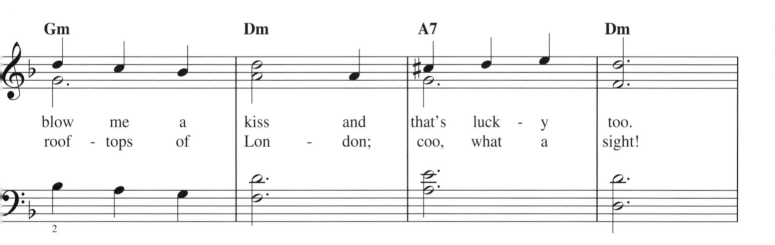

Gm / **Dm** / **A7** / **Dm**

blow me a kiss and that's luck - y too.
roof - tops of Lon - don; coo, what a sight!

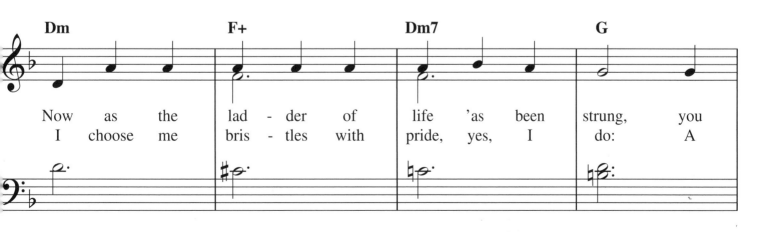

Dm / **F+** / **Dm7** / **G**

Now as the lad - der of life 'as been strung, you
I choose me bris - tles with pride, yes, I do: A

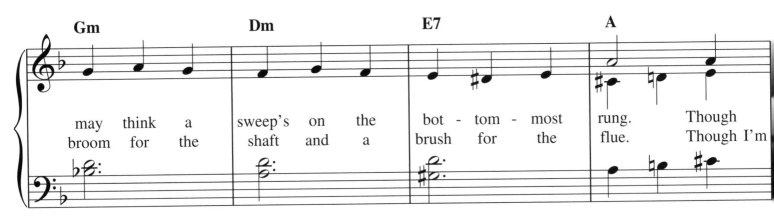

Gm | **Dm** | **E7** | **A**

may think a | sweep's on the | bot - tom - most | rung. Though
broom for the | shaft and a | brush for the | flue. Though I'm

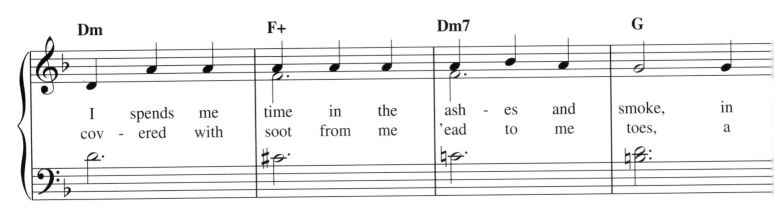

Dm | **F+** | **Dm7** | **G**

I spends me | time in the | ash - es and | smoke, in
cov - ered with | soot from me | 'ead to me | toes, a

1st time: D.C
2nd time: D.C. al Coda

Gm | **Dm** | **A7** | **Dm**

this 'ole wide | world there's no | 'ap - pi - er | bloke.
sweep knows 'e's | wel - come wher - | ev - er 'e | goes.

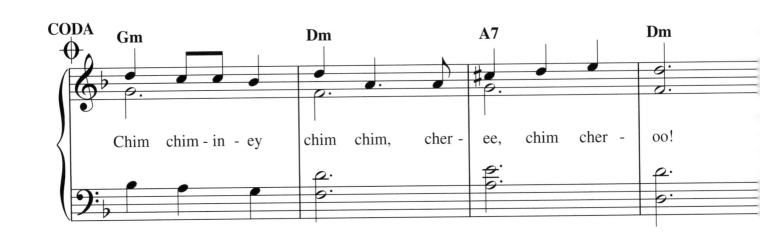

CODA

Gm | **Dm** | **A7** | **Dm**

Chim chim - in - ey | chim chim, cher - | ee, chim cher - | oo!

(They Long to Be)
CLOSE TO YOU

Lyric by HAL DAVID
Music by BURT BACHARACH

Fmaj7   **C6**   **Cmaj7**

Just like me,   they long to be   close to   you. _____

C6   **C7**   **F**

_____ On the day that you were born the an-gels got to-geth-er and de-

mf

Em7   **A7**   **F**

cid-ed to cre-ate a dream come true.   So, they sprin-kled moon-dust in your hair of

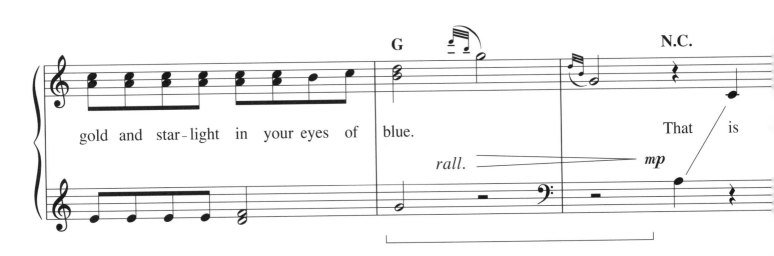

                                    G   **N.C.**

gold and star-light in your eyes of blue.   That is

rall. _____ *mp*

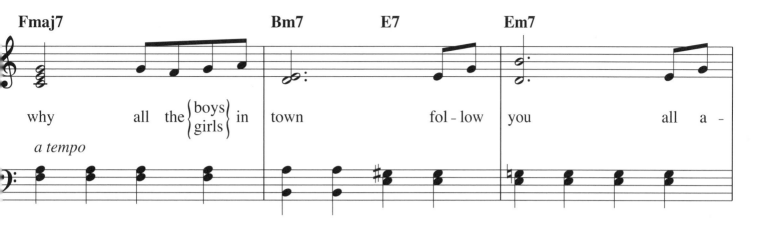

why   all   the { boys / girls } in   town   fol - low   you   all   a -

a tempo

round.   Just / like   me,   they / long   to   be

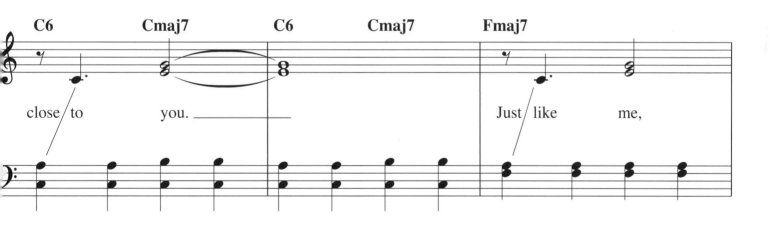

close / to   you. ___   Just / like   me,

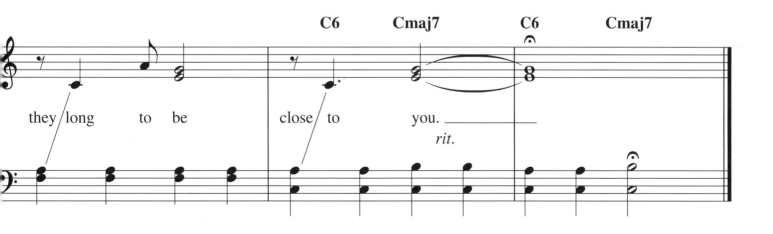

they / long   to   be   close / to   you. ___

COME RAIN OR COME SHINE

from ST. LOUIS WOMAN

Words by JOHNNY MERCER
Music by HAROLD ARLEN

Slowly

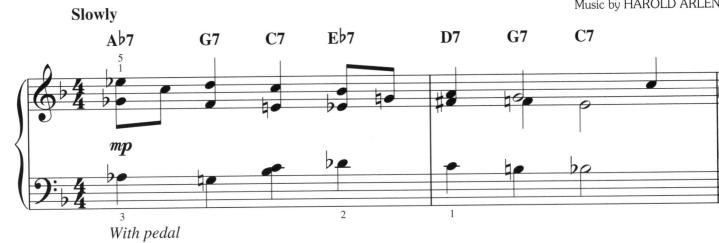

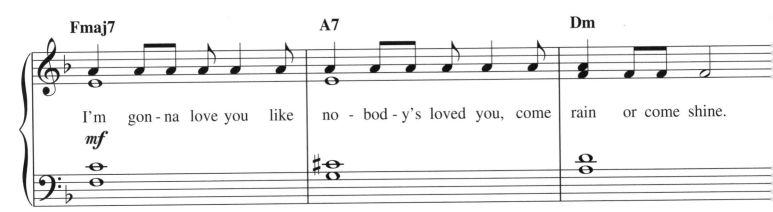

I'm gon-na love you like no-bod-y's loved you, come rain or come shine.

High as a moun-tain and deep as a riv-er, come

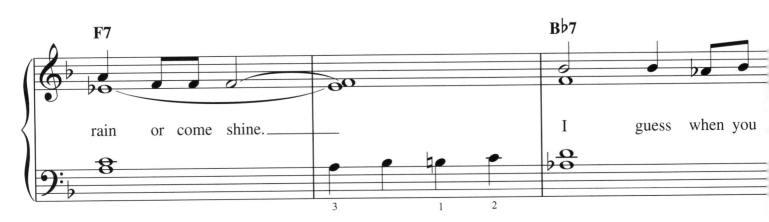

rain or come shine._____ I guess when you

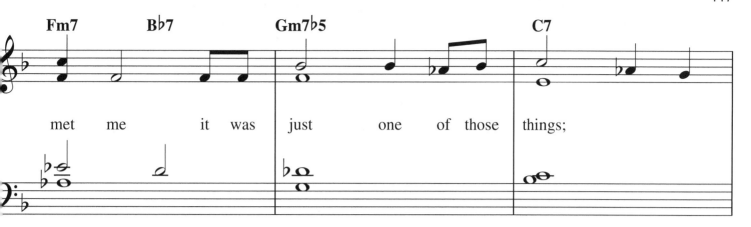

met me it was just one of those things;

but don't ev - er bet me, 'cause I'm gon - na be true if you

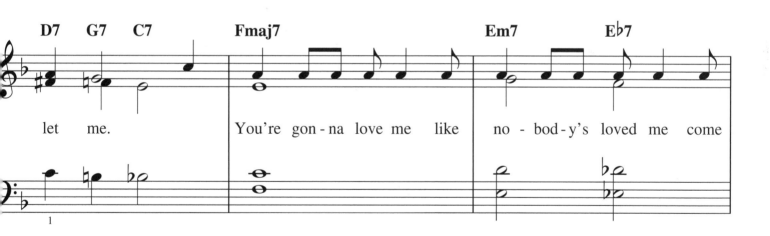

let me. You're gon - na love me like no - bod - y's loved me come

rain or come shine. Hap - py to - geth - er, un -

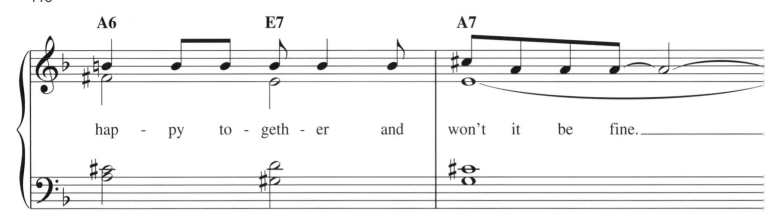

hap - py to - geth - er and won't it be fine._____

_____ Days may be cloud - y or sun - ny, we're

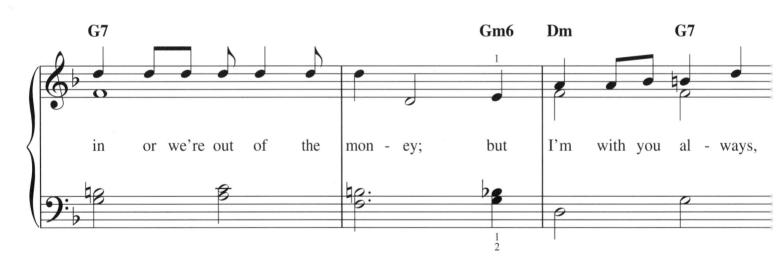

in or we're out of the mon - ey; but I'm with you al - ways,

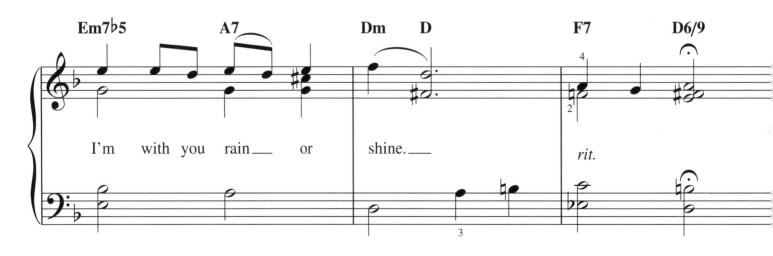

I'm with you rain__ or shine.__ *rit.*

CRAZY

Words and Music by
WILLIE NELSON

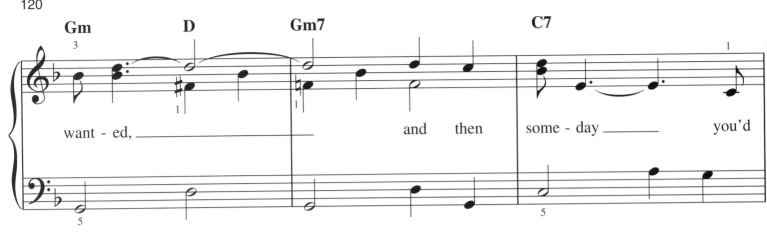

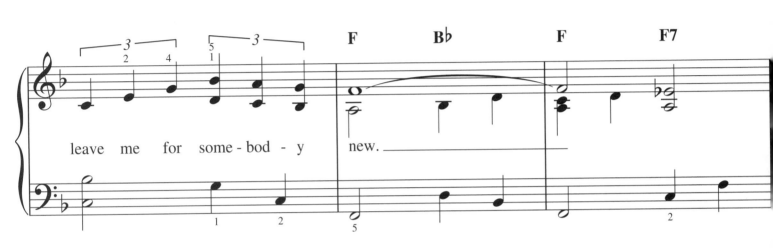

CRY ME A RIVER

Words and Music by
ARTHUR HAMILTON

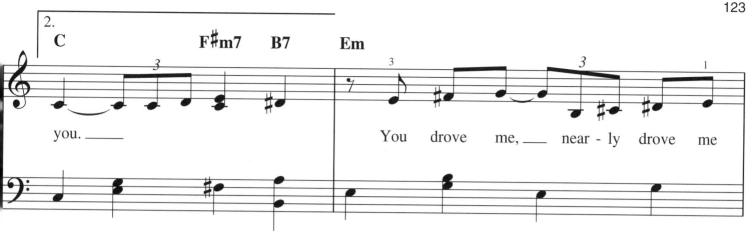

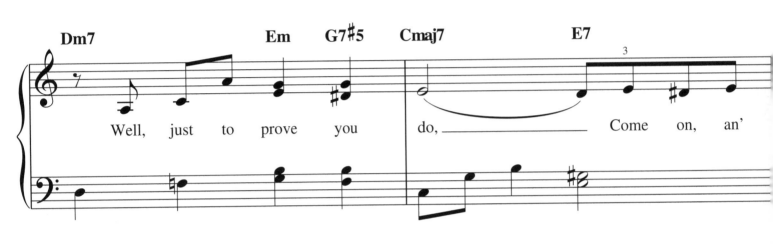

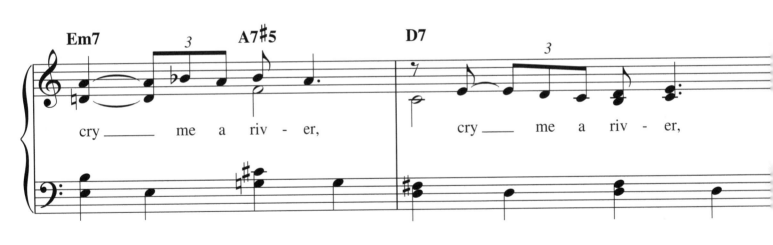

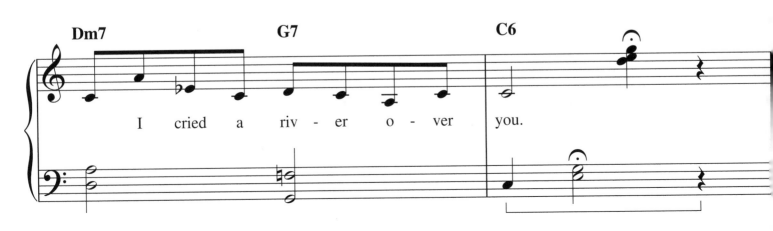

DARN THAT DREAM

Lyric by EDDIE DeLANGE
Music by JIMMY VAN HEUSEN

Darn that dream I dream each night, you say you love me and you hold me tight, but when I a-wake you're out of sight, oh darn that dream.

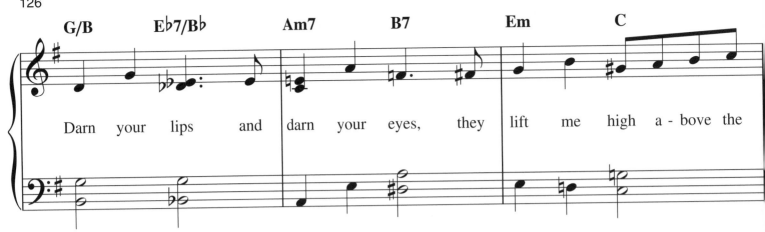

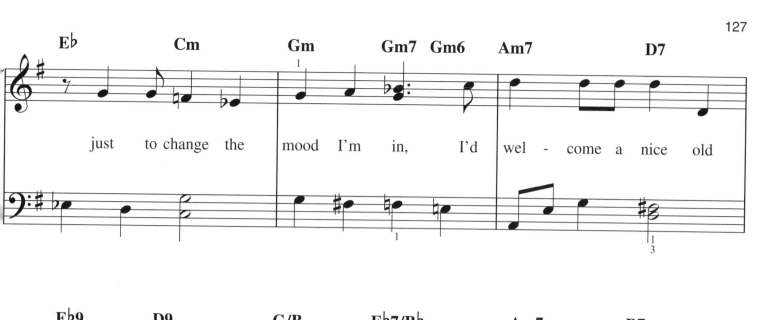

just to change the mood I'm in, I'd wel - come a nice old

night - mare. Darn that dream and bless it too, with -

out that dream, I nev - er would have you. But it haunts me and it

won't come true, oh darn that dream.

rit.

DADDY'S LITTLE GIRL

Words and Music by BOBBY BURKE
and HORACE GERLACH

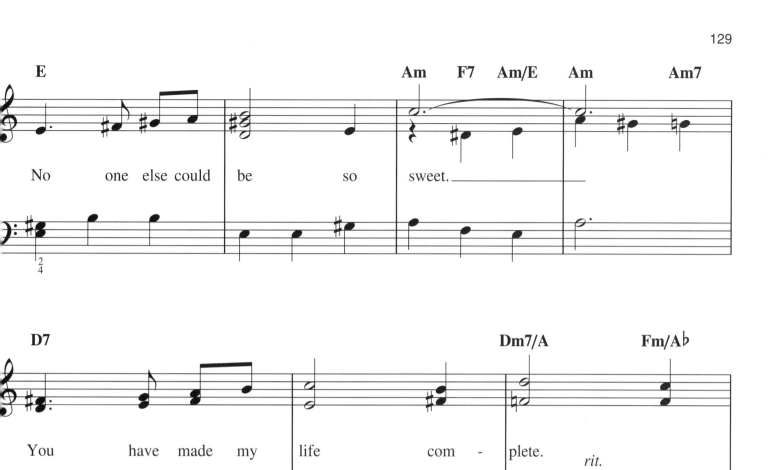

No one else could be so sweet.

You have made my life com - plete. *rit.*

a tempo You're the end of the rain - bow, my

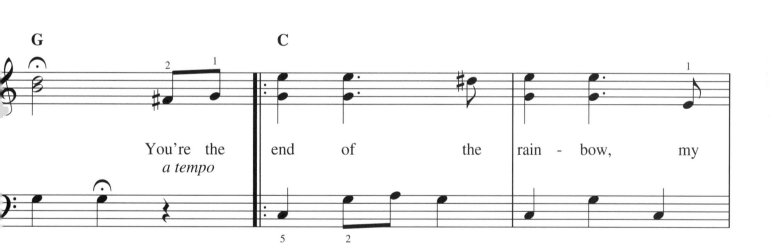

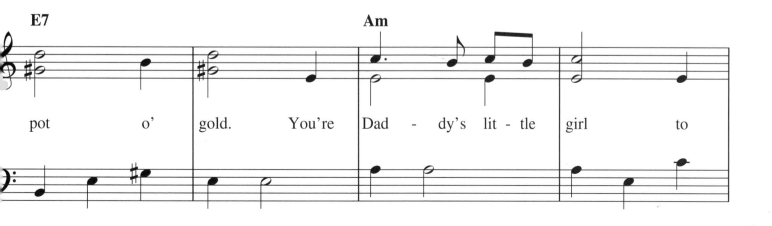

pot o' gold. You're Dad - dy's lit - tle girl to

E7 ... F ... F#dim7

have and hold. A pre - cious gem is

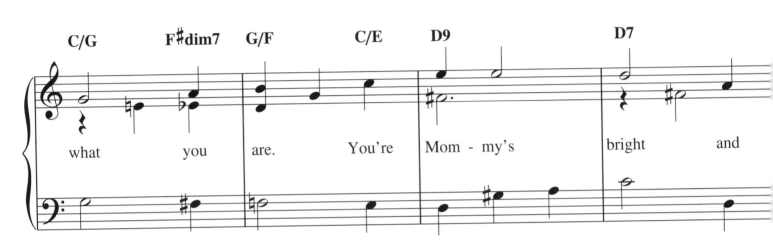

C/G ... F#dim7 ... G/F ... C/E ... D9 ... D7

what you are. You're Mom - my's bright and

G7 ... Dm7/A ... G7 ... C

shin - ing star. {You're the spir - it of Christ - mas, my
{You're the treas - ure I cher - ish, so

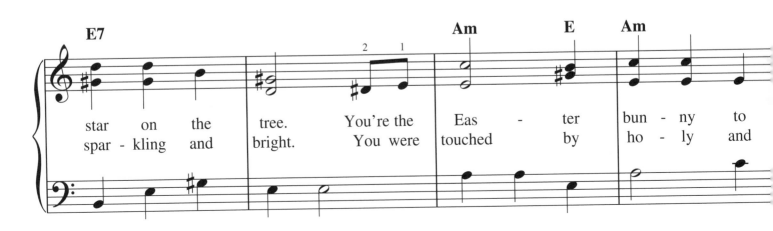

E7 ... Am ... E ... Am

star on the tree. You're the Eas - ter bun - ny to
spar - kling and bright. You were touched by ho - ly and

DEARLY BELOVED
from YOU WERE NEVER LOVELIER

Music by JEROME KERN
Words by JOHNNY MERCER

An - gel eyes _____ knew you. _____

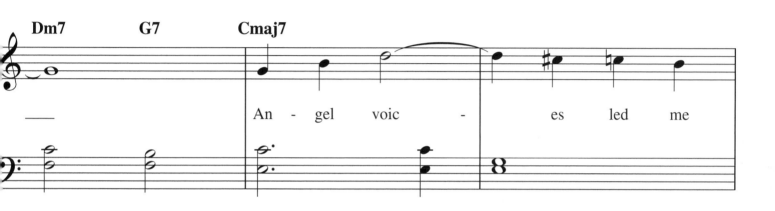

_____ An - gel voic - es led me

to you. _____ Noth - ing could

save me. Fate gave me a sign.

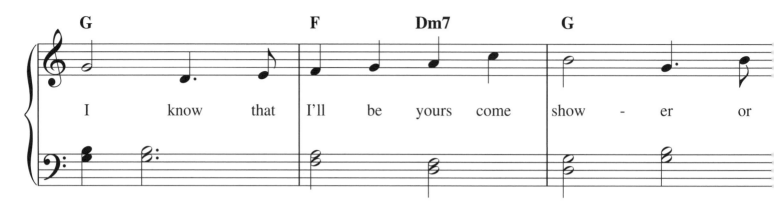

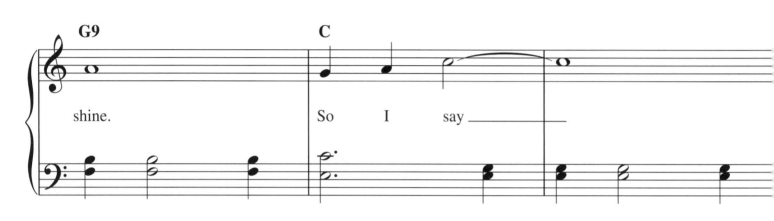

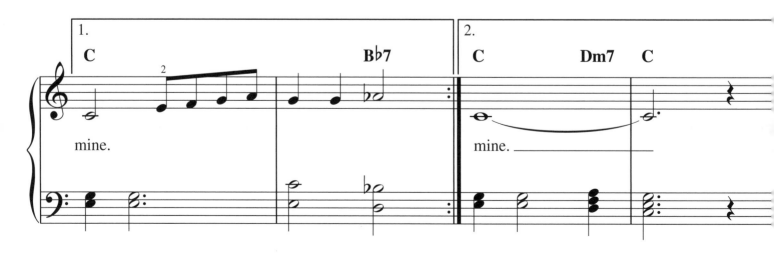

DO-RE-MI

from THE SOUND OF MUSIC

Lyrics by OSCAR HAMMERSTEIN II
Music by RICHARD RODGERS

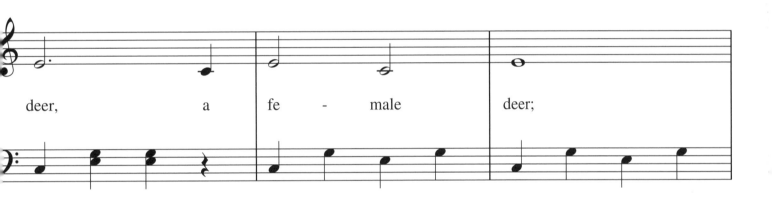

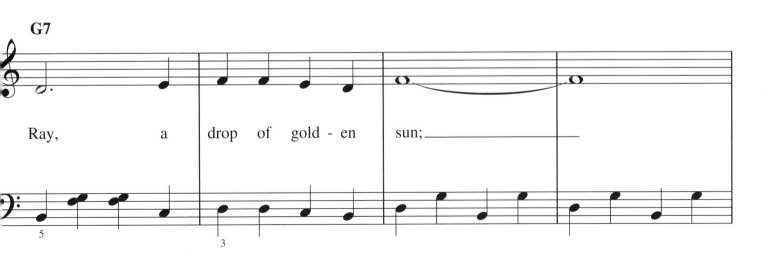

C

Me, a name I call my -

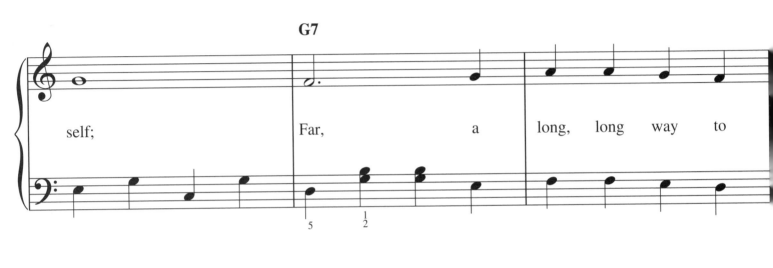

G7

self; Far, a long, long way to

C7

run; Sew, a

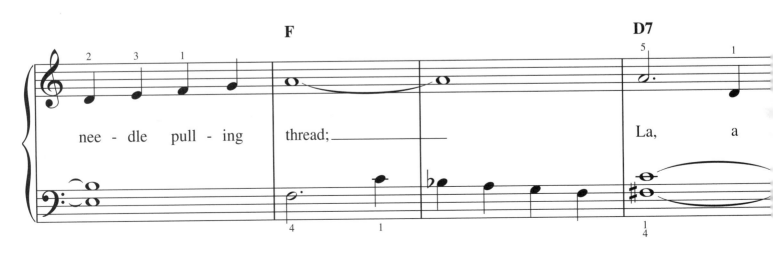

F **D7**

nee - dle pull - ing thread; La, a

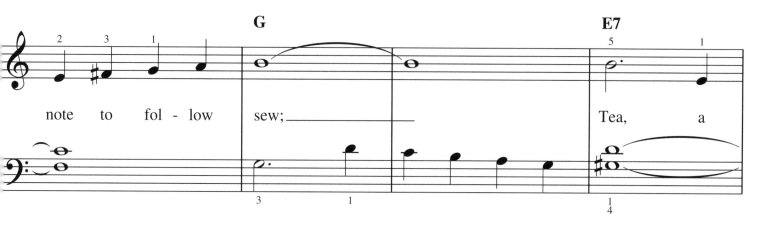

note to fol - low sew;_____ Tea, a

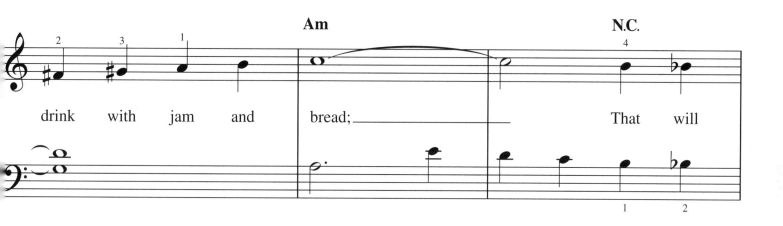

drink with jam and bread;_____ That will

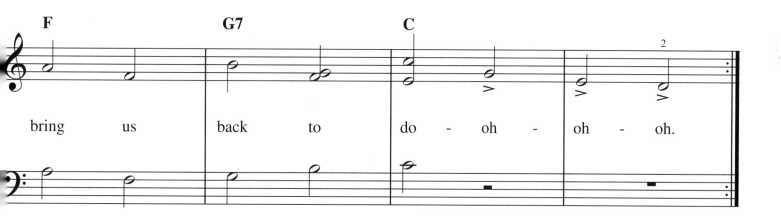

bring us back to do - oh - oh - oh.

oh!

DO NOTHIN' TILL YOU HEAR FROM ME

Words and Music by DUKE ELLINGTON
and BOB RUSSELL

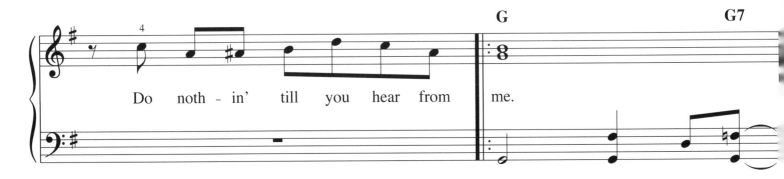

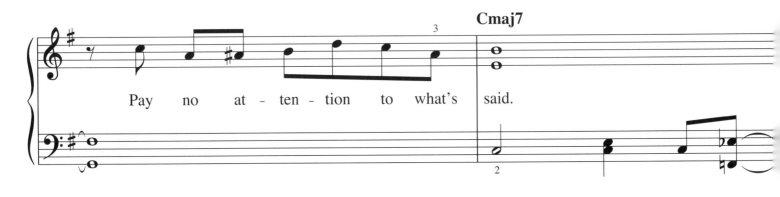

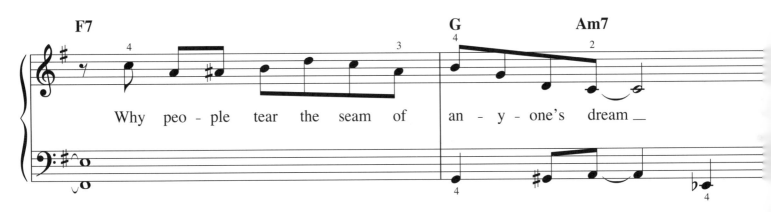

is o - ver my head.

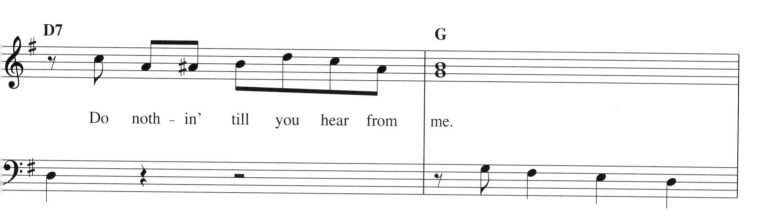

Do noth - in' till you hear from me.

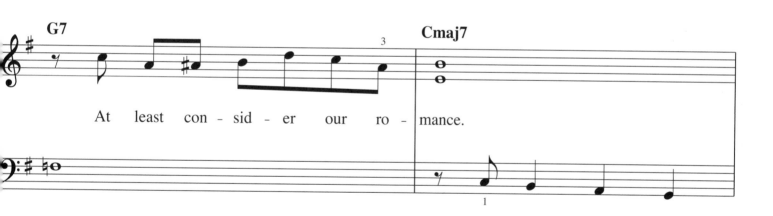

At least con - sid - er our ro - mance.

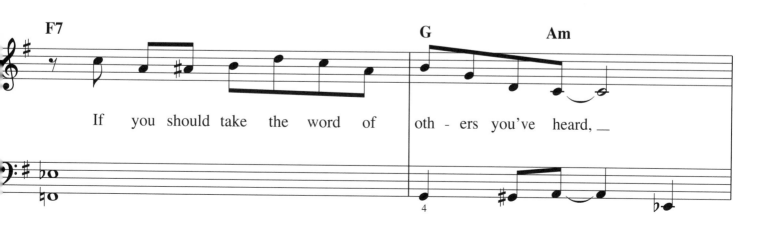

If you should take the word of oth - ers you've heard, __

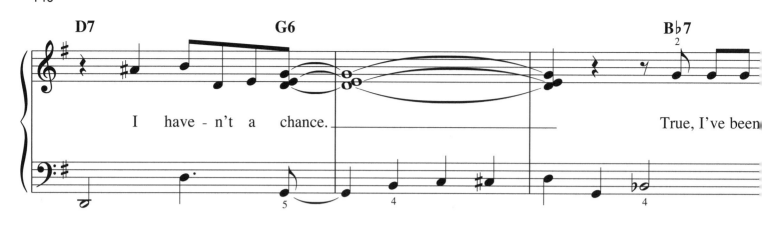

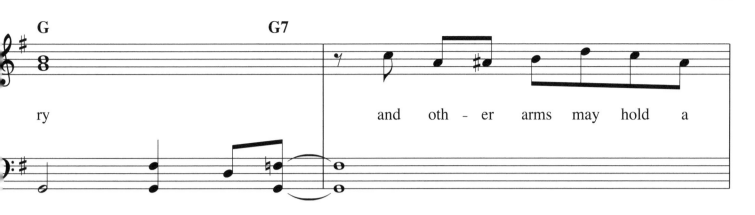

ry

thrill.

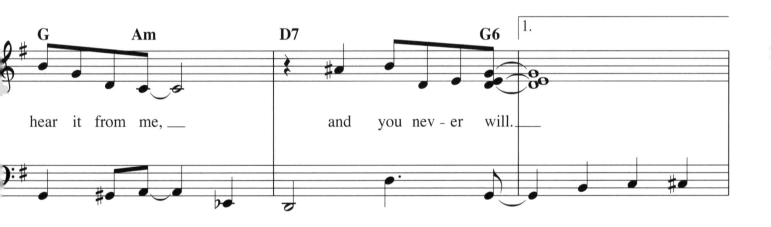

hear it from me, ___

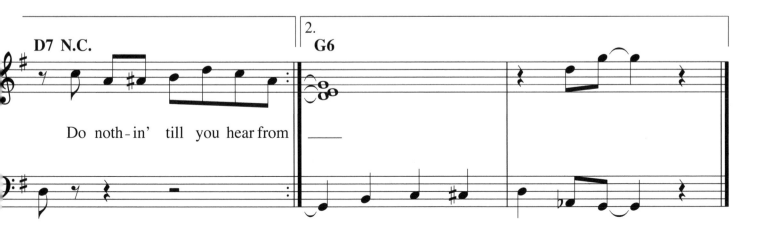

Do noth - in' till you hear from ___

DO YOU KNOW THE WAY TO SAN JOSE

Lyric by HAL DAVID
Music by BURT BACHARACH

Moderately

Do you know the way to San __ Jo - se?
You can real - ly breathe in San __ Jo - se.

I've been a - way so long, I may go wrong and lose __ my way.
They've got a lot of space, there'll be a place where I _____ can stay.

Do you know the way to San __ Jo - se? I'm go - ing back to
I was born and raised in San __ Jo - se. I'm go - ing back to

and all the stars that nev-er were are park-ing
and there you are with-out a friend. You pack your

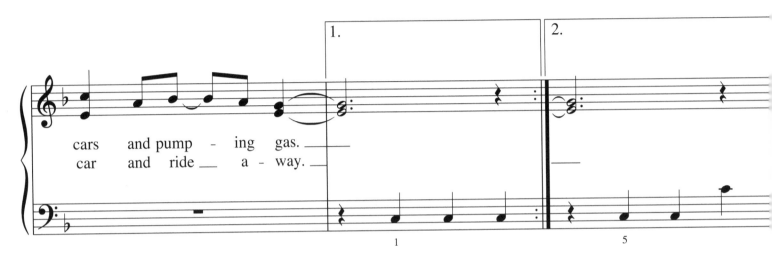

1.

2.

cars and pump-ing gas.
car and ride a-way.

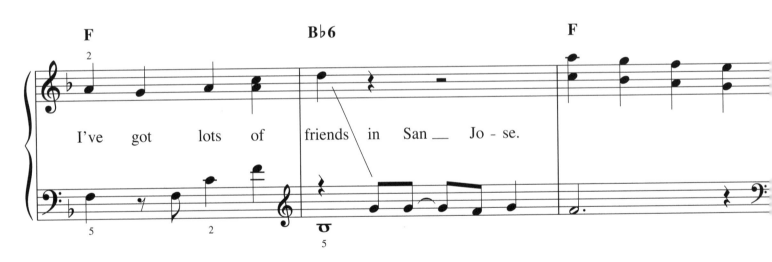

F   B♭6   F

I've got lots of friends in San Jo-se.

B♭6

Do you know the way to San Jo-se?

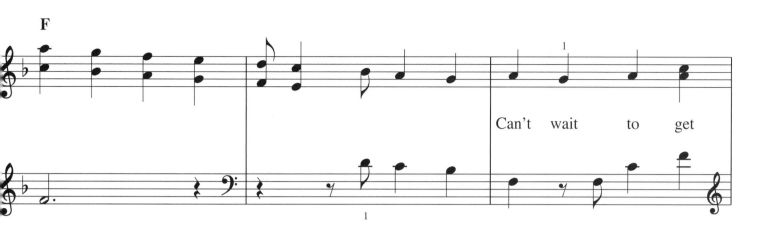

F

Can't wait to get

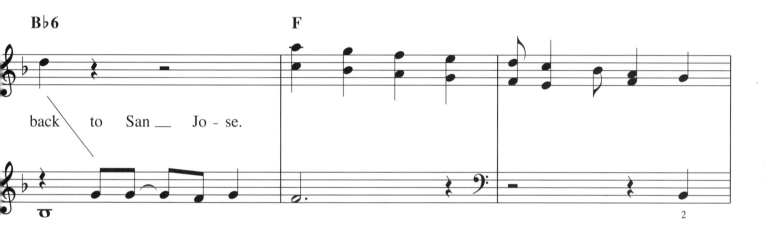

Bb6   **F**

back to San — Jo - se.

Fmaj7

gradually softer

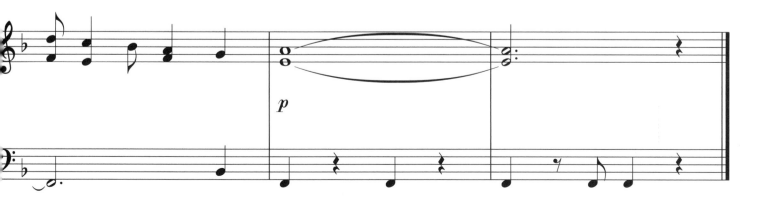

p

EASTER PARADE

from AS THOUSANDS CHEER

Words and Music
IRVING BERL

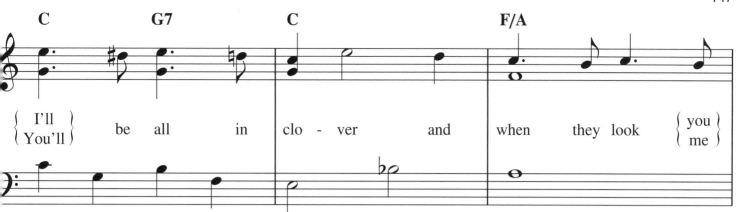

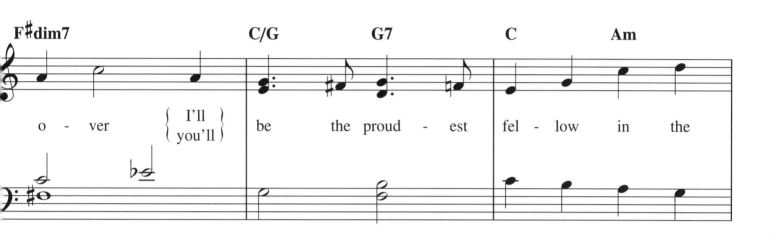

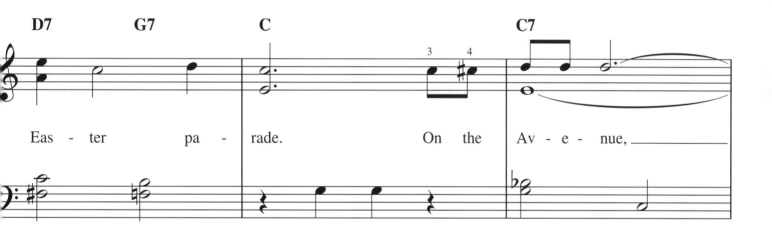

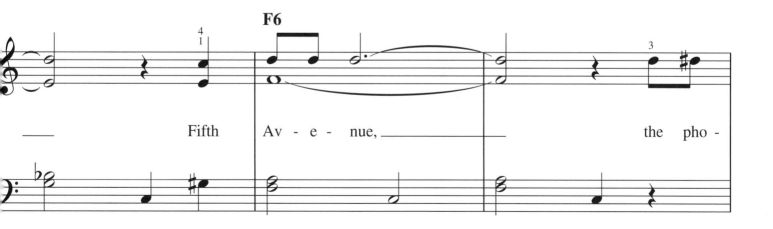

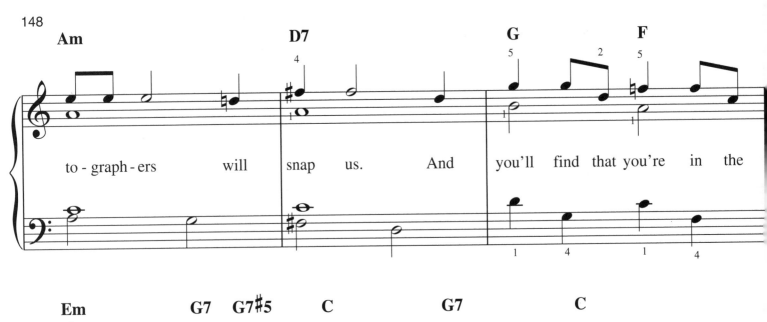

to - graph - ers   will   snap   us.   And   you'll   find   that   you're   in   the

ro - to - gra - vure.   Oh,   { I   could }   write   a   son - net   a-
                                    { you   may }

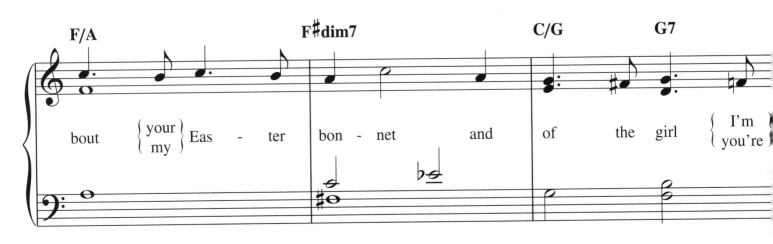

bout   { your }   Eas - ter   bon - net   and   of   the   girl   { I'm
        { my }   { you're

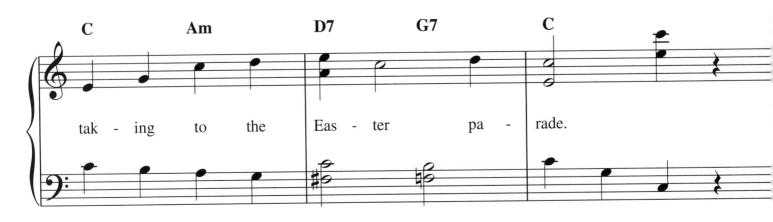

tak - ing   to   the   Eas - ter   pa - rade.

EVERYBODY'S TALKIN'
(Echoes)
from MIDNIGHT COWBOY

Words and Music by
FRED NEIL

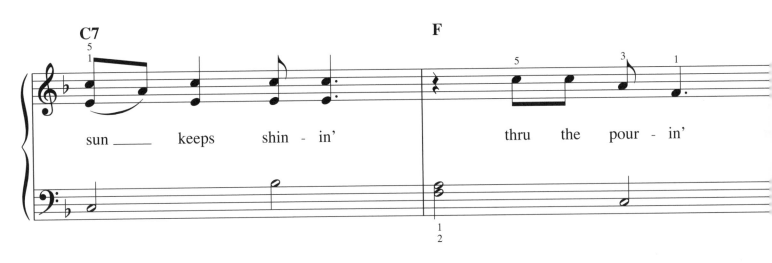

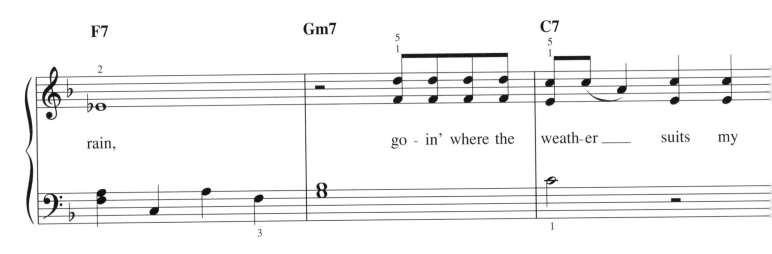

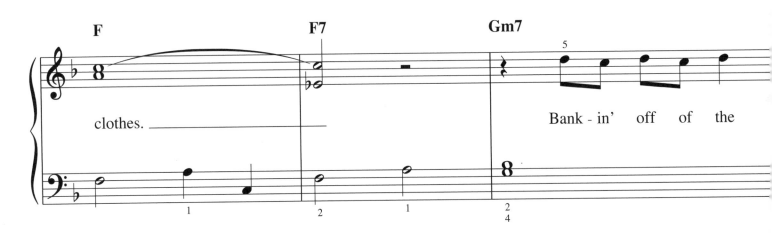

north-east wind, sail - in' on a sum - mer breeze,

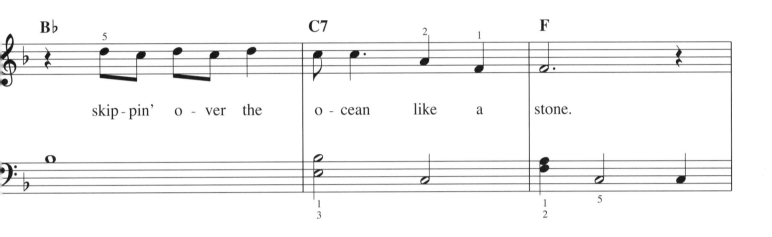

skip - pin' o - ver the o - cean like a stone.

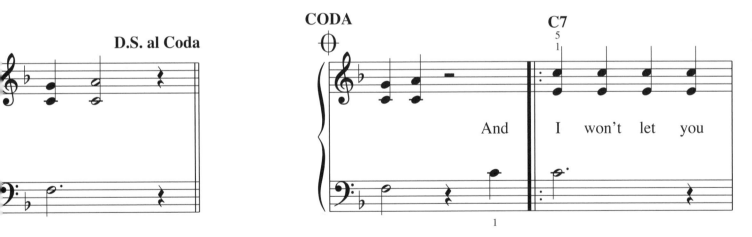

D.S. al Coda

CODA

And I won't let you

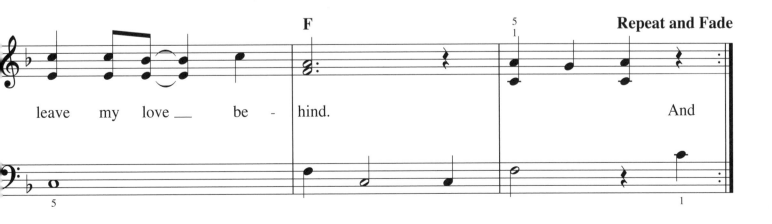

Repeat and Fade

leave my love ___ be - hind. And

EASY LIVING
Theme from the Paramount Picture EASY LIVING

Words and Music by LEO ROBIN
and RALPH RAINGER

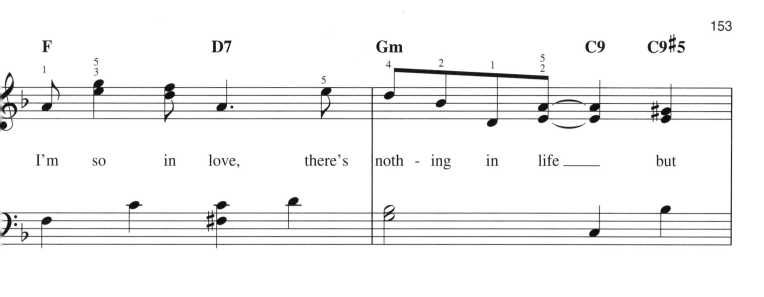

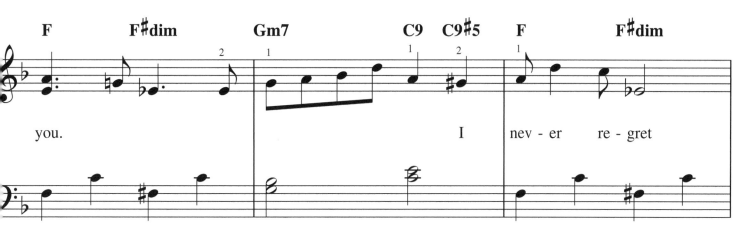

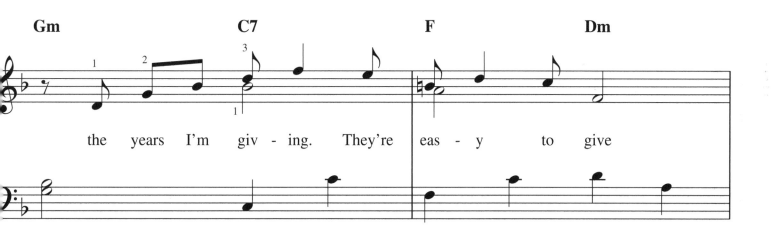

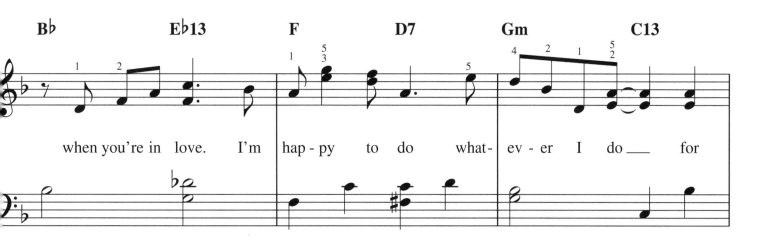

154

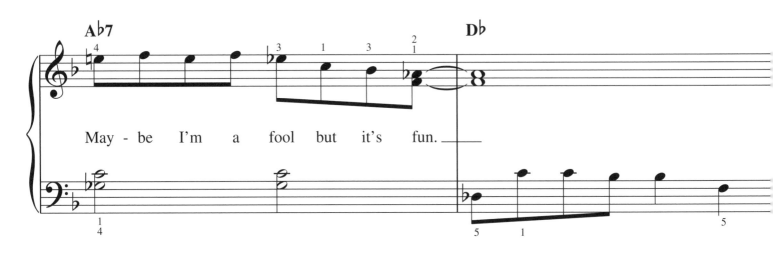

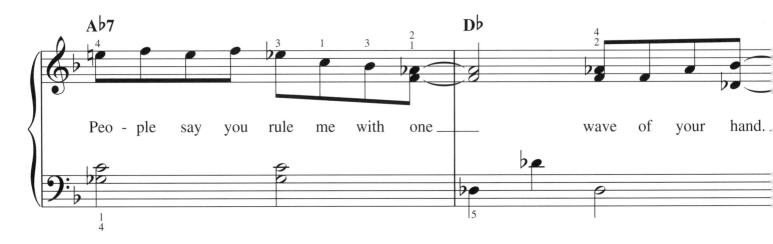

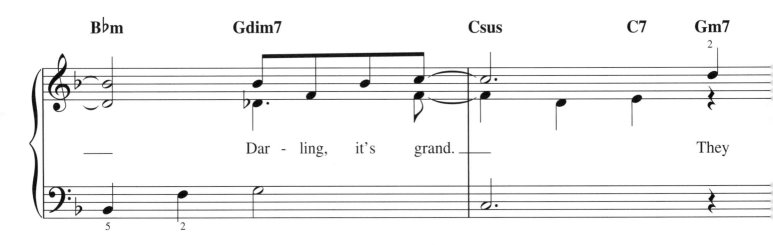

just don't un - der - stand. Liv - ing for you is eas - y liv - ing. It's

eas - y to live when you're in love, and I'm so in love, there's

noth - ing in life __ but you.

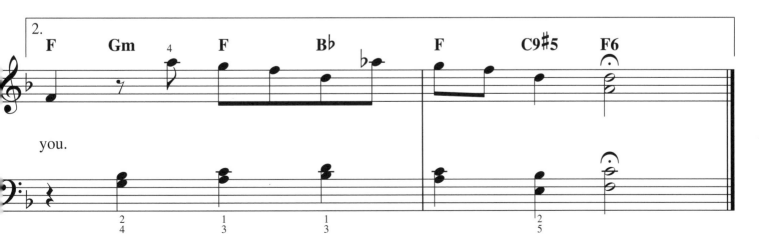

you.

EASY TO LOVE
(You'd Be So Easy to Love)
from BORN TO DANCE

Words and Music by
COLE PORTER

Slowly, with expression

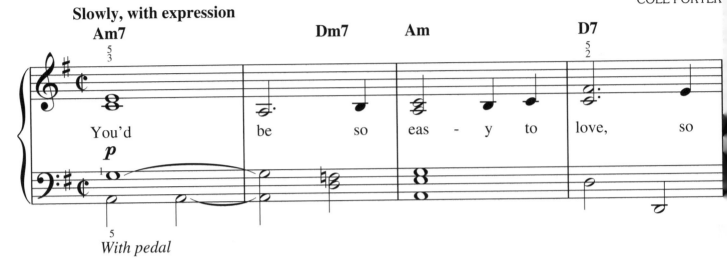

You'd be so eas - y to love, so

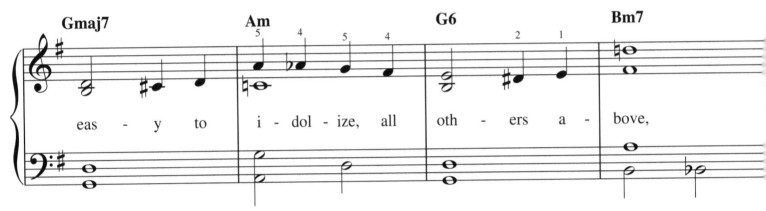

eas - y to i - dol - ize, all oth - ers a - bove,

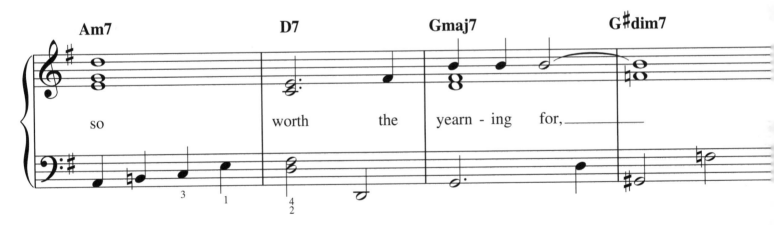

so worth the yearn - ing for,___

so swell to keep ev - 'ry home fire burn - ing for.___

FEELINGS
(¿Dime?)

English Words and Music by MORRIS ALBER
and LOUIS GAST
Spanish Words by THOMAS FUNDOR

Slowly, with expression

Both hands 8va (1st time only)

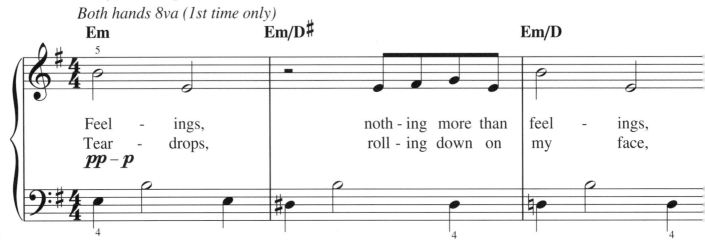

Feel - ings,   noth - ing more than   feel - ings,
Tear - drops,   roll - ing down on   my   face,

pp - p

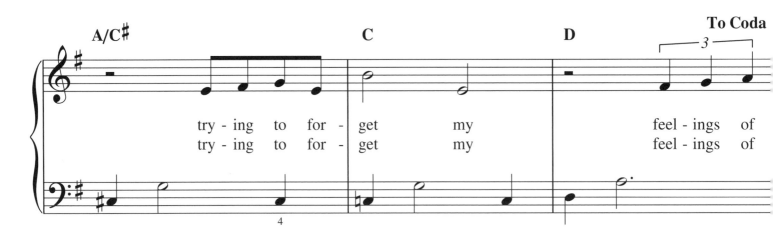

To Coda

try - ing   to   for - get   my   feel - ings   of
try - ing   to   for - get   my   feel - ings   of

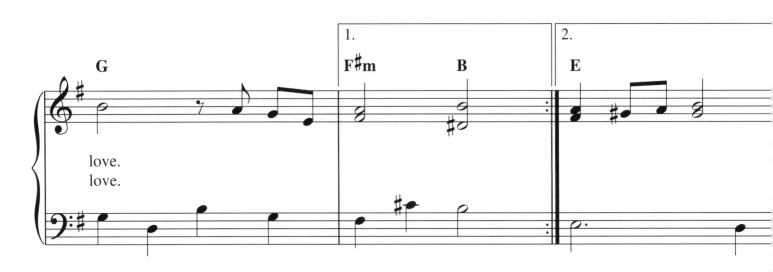

love.
love.

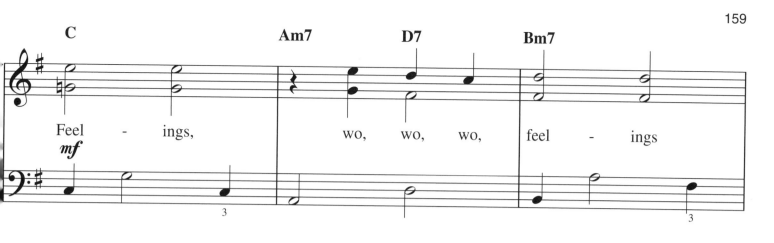

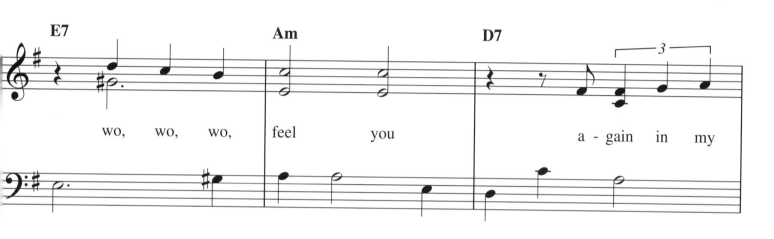

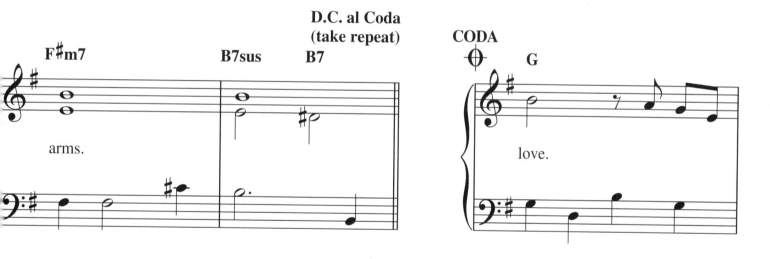

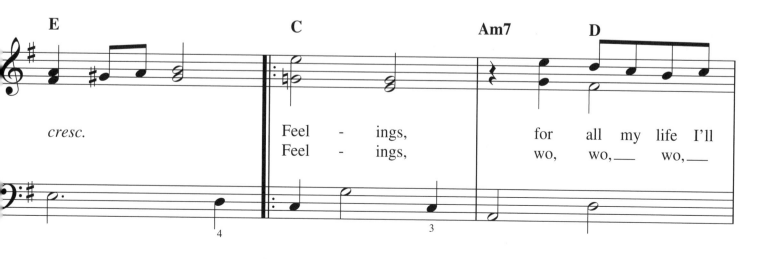

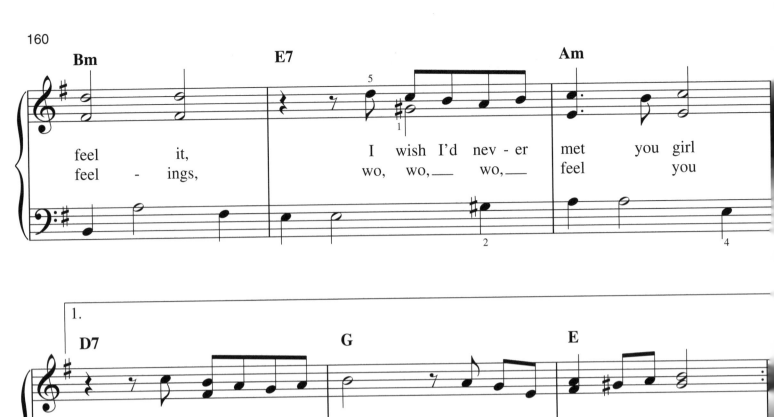

feel it,
feel - ings,
I wish I'd nev - er met you girl
wo, wo,— wo,— feel you

1.
you'll nev - er come a - gain.

2.
a - gain in my arms.
dim.
poco rit.

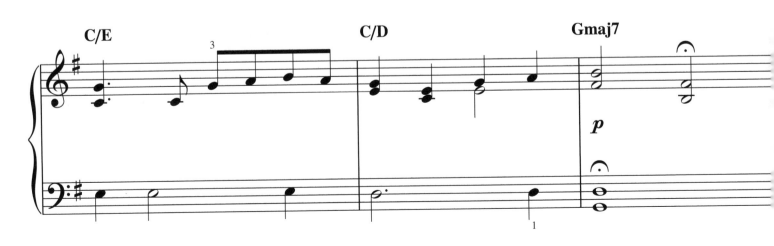

GENTLE ON MY MIND

Words and Music by
JOHN HARTFORD

Bright tempo

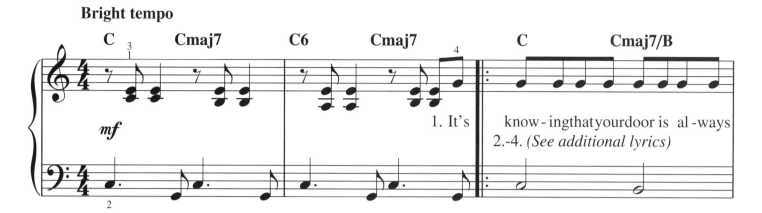

1. It's know-ingthatyourdoor is al-ways
2.-4. *(See additional lyrics)*

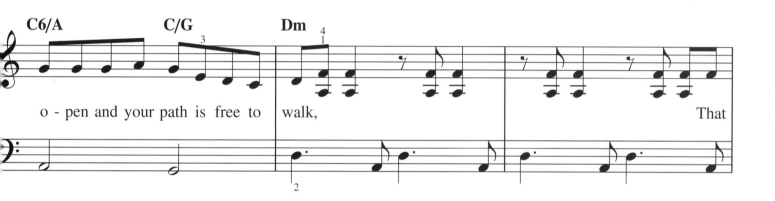

o - pen and your path is free to walk, That

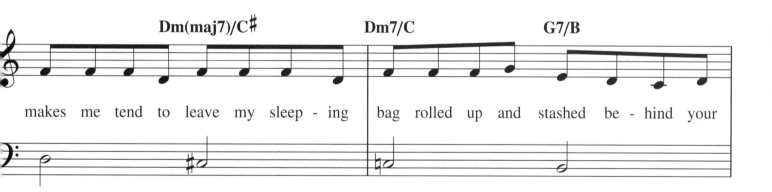

makes me tend to leave my sleep - ing bag rolled up and stashed be - hind your

couch, And it's know - ing I'm not shack - led by for-

got - ten words and bonds_ And the ink stains that have dried up - on some

line, That keeps you in the back - roads by the

riv - ers of my mem - 'ry that keeps you ev - er gen - tle on my

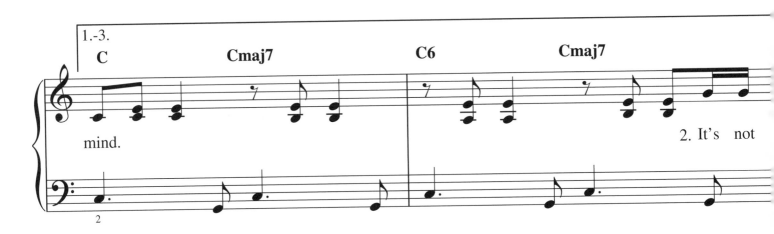

mind. 2. It's not

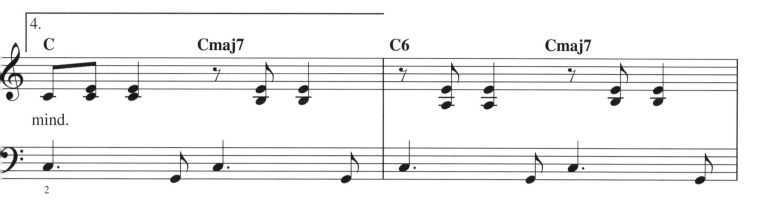

mind.

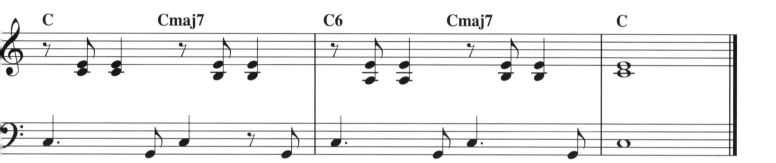

Additional Lyrics

2. It's not clinging to the rocks and ivy planted on their columns now that binds me
   Or something that somebody said because they thought we fit together walkin'.
   It's just knowing that the world will not be cursing or forgiving when I walk along some
       railroad track and find
   That you're moving on the backroads by the rivers of my memory and for hours you're just
       gentle on my mind.

3. Though the wheat fields and the clotheslines and junkyards and the highways come between us
   And some other woman crying to her mother 'cause she turned away and I was gone.
   I still run in silence, tears of joy might stain my face and summer sun might burn me 'til I'm blind.
   But not to where I cannot see you walkin' on the backroads by the rivers flowing gentle on my mind.

4. I dip my cup of soup back from the gurglin' cracklin' caldron in some train yard
   My beard, a rough'ning coal pile and a dirty hat pulled low across my face.
   Through cupped hands 'round a tin can I pretend I hold you to my breast and find
   That you're waving from the backroads by the rivers of my memory ever smilin' ever
       gentle on my mind.

A FINE ROMANCE
from SWING TIME

Words by DOROTHY FIELDS
Music by JEROME KERN

Moderate bounce

mp lightly

(He:) A fine fine ro - mance! ro - mance, With my

no good kiss - es! fel - low! A You fine take

ro - mance, ro - mance, my I'll friend take this is! Jel - lo! We You're

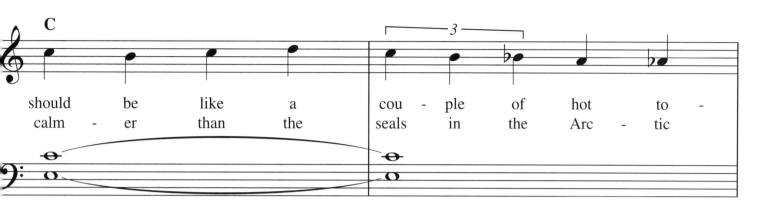

should be like a | cou - ple of hot to -
calm - er than the | seals in the Arc - tic

ma - toes, _____ | but | you're as cold as
O - cean, _____ | at | least they flap their

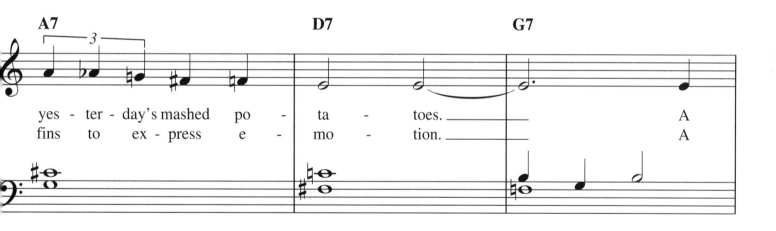

yes - ter - day's mashed po - ta - toes. _____ | A
fins to ex - press e - mo - tion. _____ | A

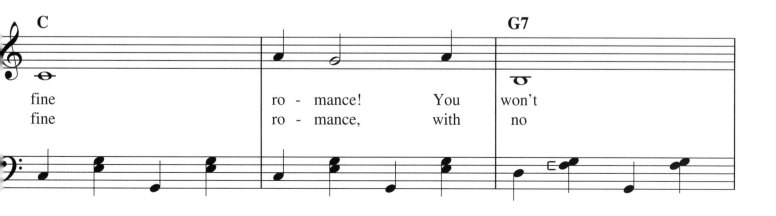

fine | | |
fine | ro - mance! You | won't
  | ro - mance, with | no

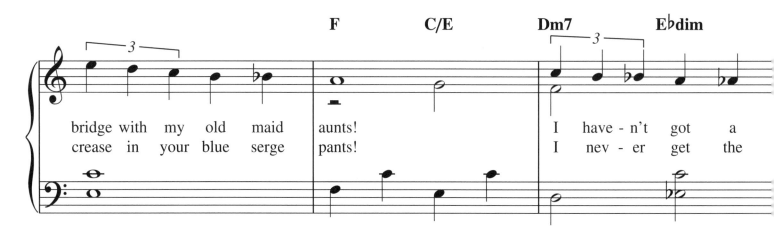

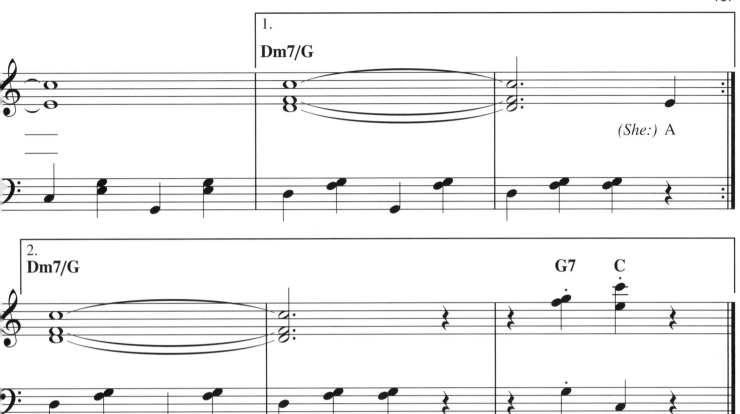

Additional Lyrics

She:
A fine romance,
With no kisses!
A fine romance,
My friend, this is!
We two should be like clams in a dish of chowder;
But we just fizz like parts of a Seidlitz Powder.
A fine romance
With no clinches,
A fine romance
With no pinches.
You're just as hard to land as the "Ile de France!"
I haven't got a chance.
This is a fine romance!

He:
A fine romance,
My dear duchess!
Two old fogies
Who need crutches!
True love should have the thrills that a healthy crime has!
We don't have half the thrills that the March of Time has!
A fine romance,
My good woman,
My strong "aged in the wood" woman!
You never give the orchids I sent a glance!
No, you like cactus plants!
This is a fine romance.

FOR ALL WE KNOW
from the Motion Picture LOVERS AND OTHER STRANGERS

Words by ROBB WILSON and ARTHUR JAME
Music by FRED KARLI

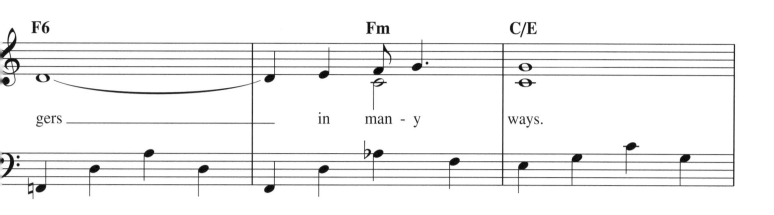

gers _____ in man - y ways.

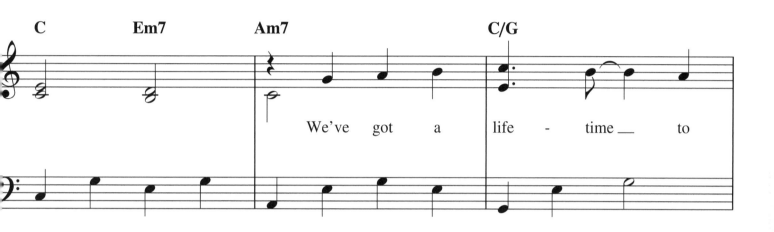

We've got a life - time __ to

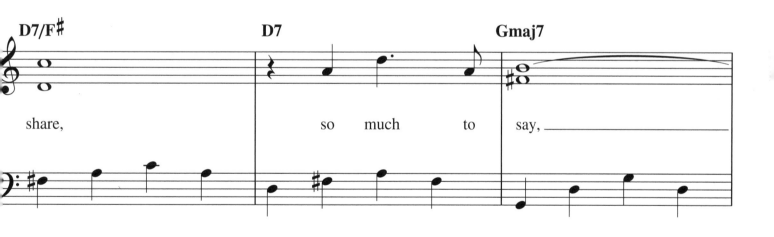

share, so much to say, _____

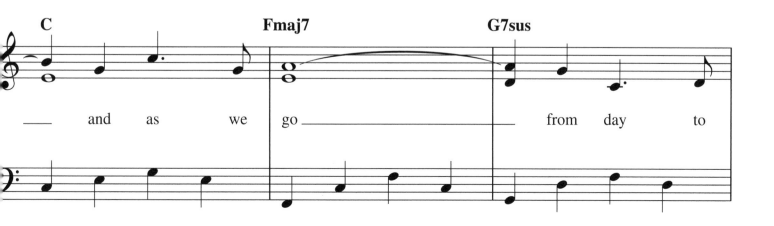

__ and as we go _____ from day to

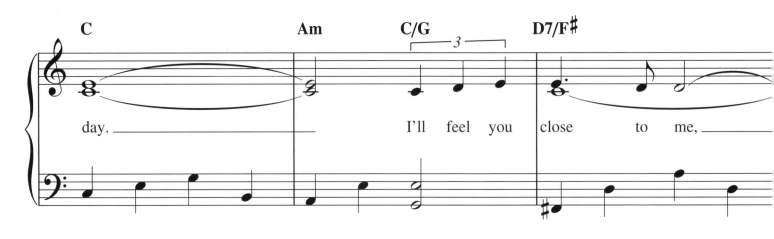

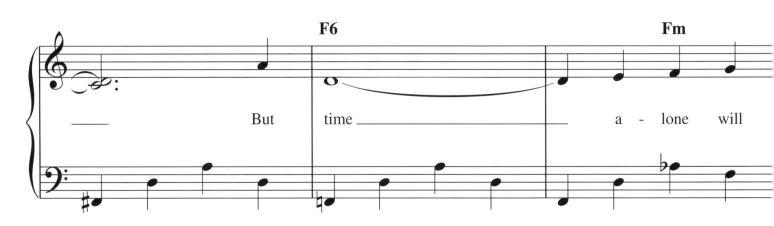

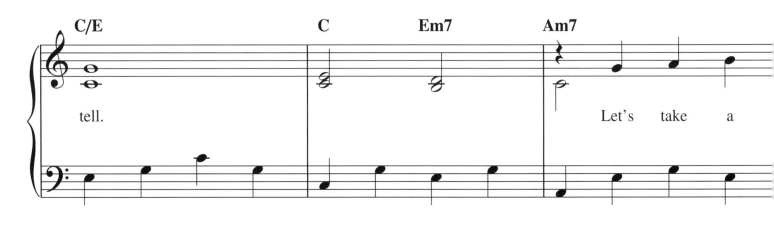

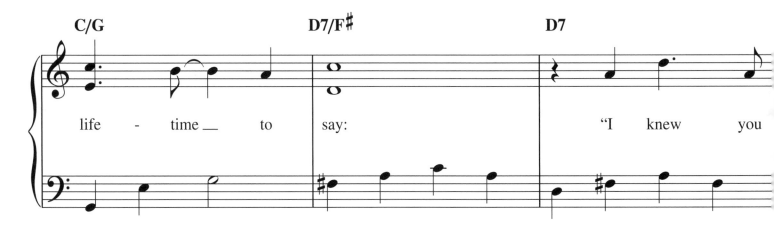

GETTING TO KNOW YOU
from THE KING AND I

Lyrics by OSCAR HAMMERSTEIN II
Music by RICHARD RODGERS

Moderately (*gracefully and not fast*)

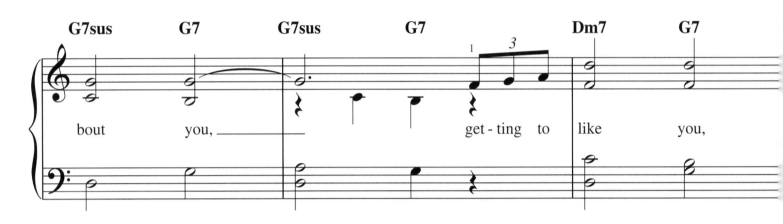

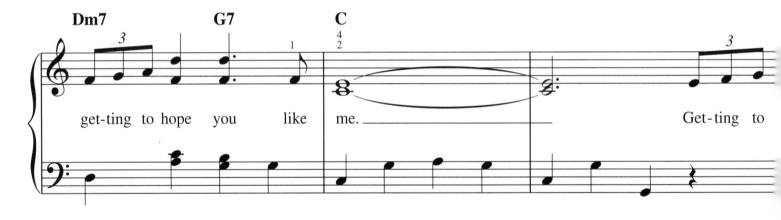

you are pre - cise - ly _____ my cup of
cresc.

tea! _____ Get - ting to know you,
f *p*

get-ting to feel free and eas - y. _____ When I am

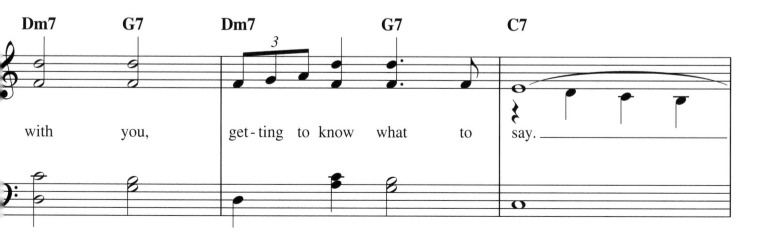

with you, get-ting to know what to say. _____

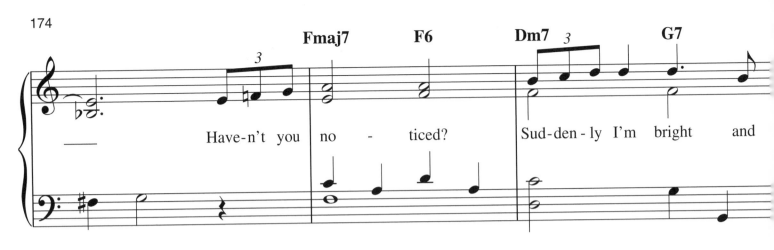

Have-n't you no - ticed? Sud-den-ly I'm bright and

breez - y, be - cause of all the

beau-ti - ful and new things I'm learn-ing a-bout you

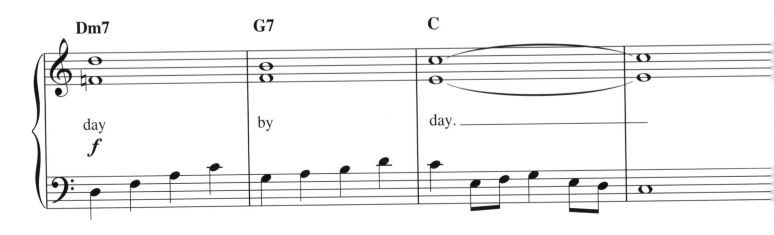

day by day.

GIRL TALK

from the Paramount Picture HARLOW

Words by BOBBY TROUP
Music by NEAL HEFTI

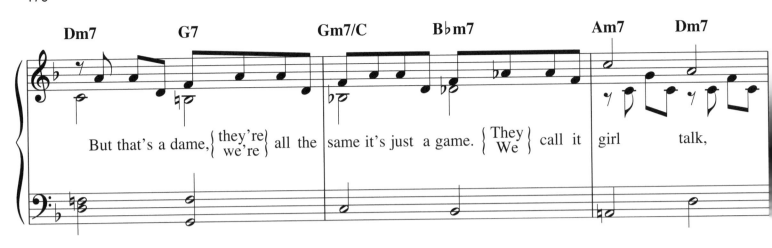

But that's a dame, {they're / we're} all the same it's just a game. {They / We} call it girl talk,

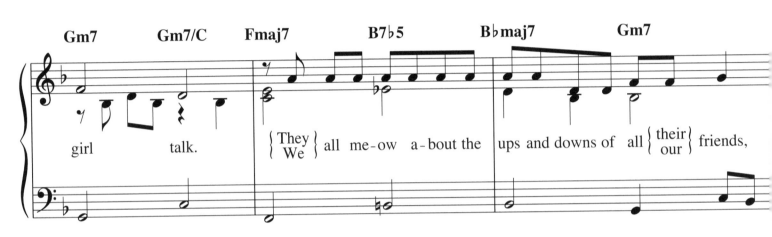

girl talk. {They / We} all me-ow a-bout the ups and downs of all {their / our} friends,

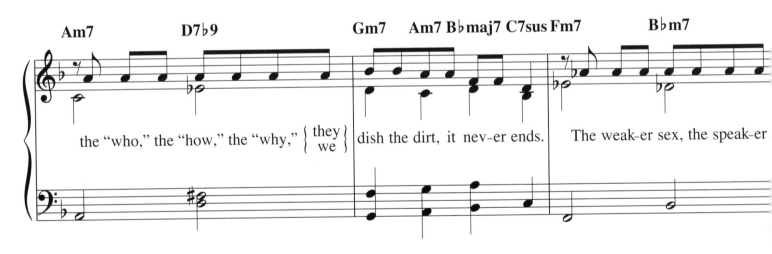

the "who," the "how," the "why," {they / we} dish the dirt, it nev-er ends. The weak-er sex, the speak-er

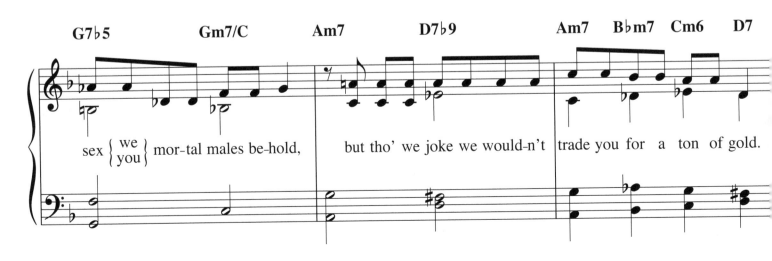

sex {we / you} mor-tal males be-hold, but tho' we joke we would-n't trade you for a ton of gold.

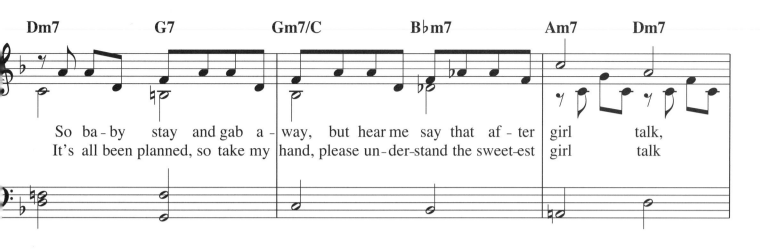

So ba-by stay and gab a-way, but hear me say that af-ter girl talk,
It's all been planned, so take my hand, please un-der-stand the sweet-est girl talk

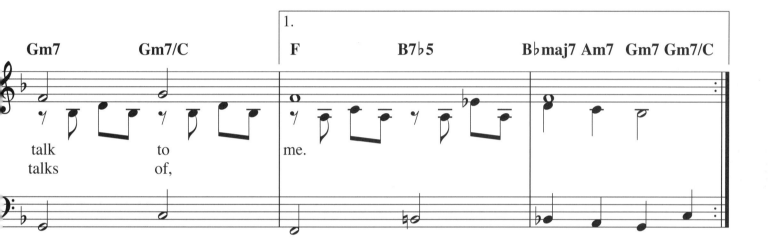

talk to me.
talks of,

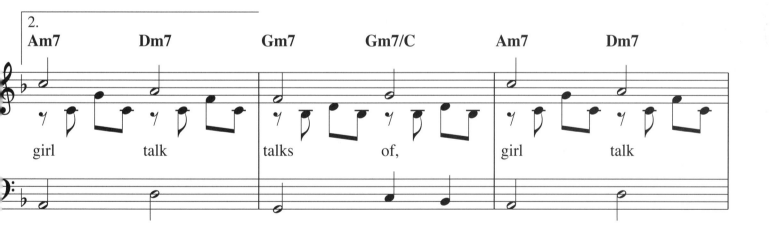

girl talk talks of, girl talk

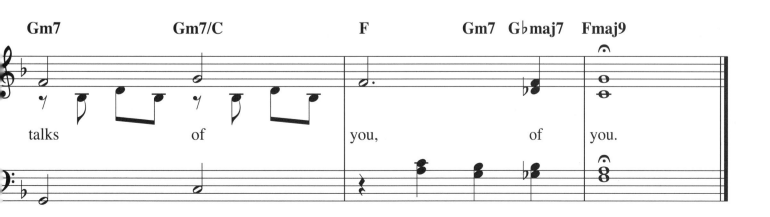

talks of you, of you.

GLAD TO BE UNHAPPY

from ON YOUR TOES

Words by LORENZ HART
Music by RICHARD RODGERS

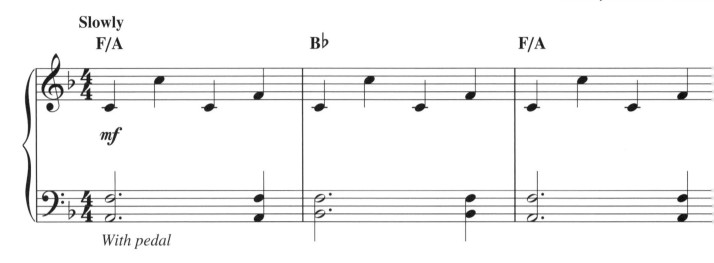

Fools rush in, so here I am

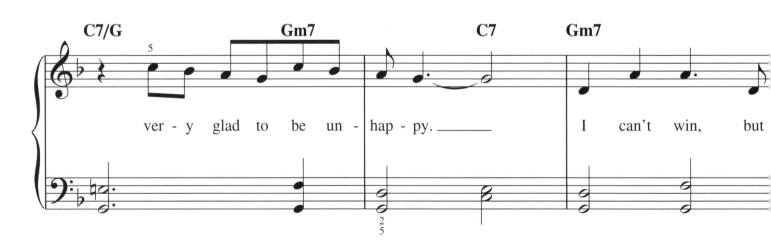

ver - y glad to be un - hap - py. _____ I can't win, but

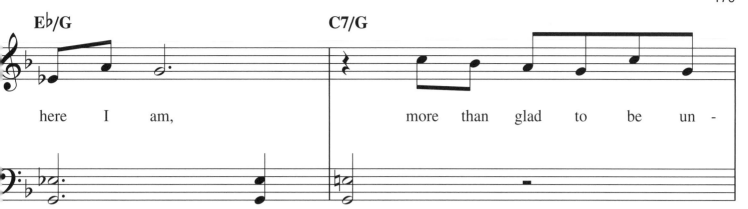

here I am, more than glad to be un-

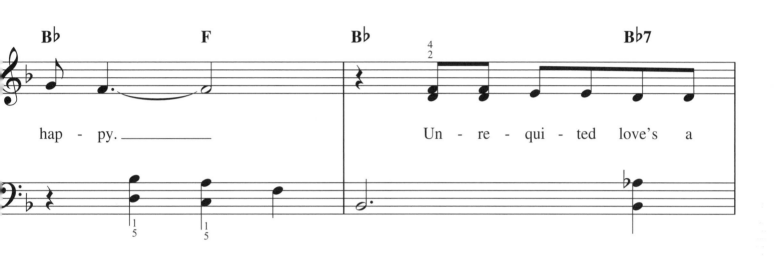

hap - py. _____ Un - re - qui - ted love's a

bore. And I've got it pret - ty bad,

but for some - one you a - dore,

THE GLORY OF LOVE

from GUESS WHO'S COMING TO DINNER

Words and Music by
BILLY HILL

You've got to give a lit-tle, take a lit-tle and let your poor heart break a lit-tle. That's the sto-ry of, that's the glo-ry of love. You've got to laugh a lit-tle, cry a lit-tle

be - fore the clouds roll by a lit - tle. That's the sto - ry of,

that's the glo - ry of love. As

long as there's the two of us we've got the world and all its

No pedal

charms. And when the world is through with us

GOIN' OUT OF MY HEAD

Words and Music by TEDDY RANDAZZO
and BOBBY WEINSTEIN

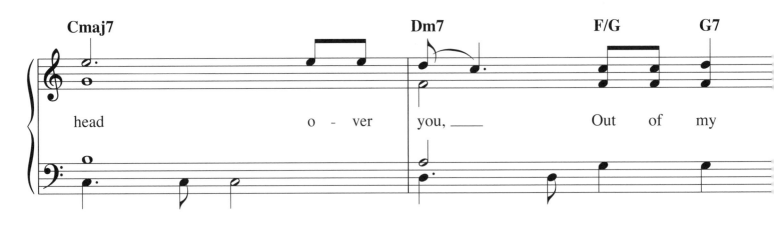

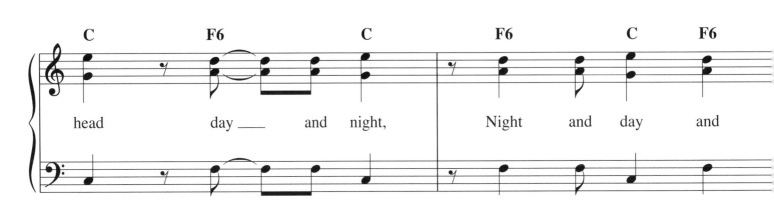

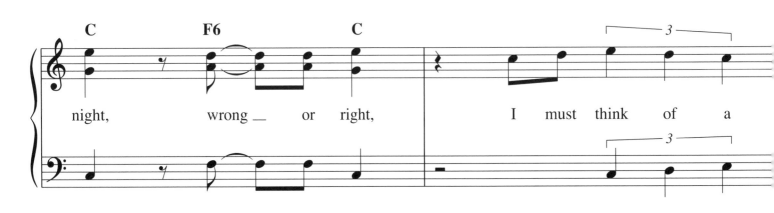

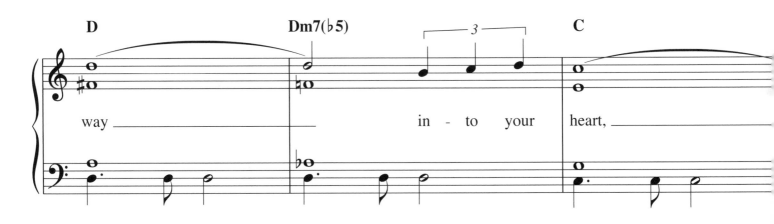

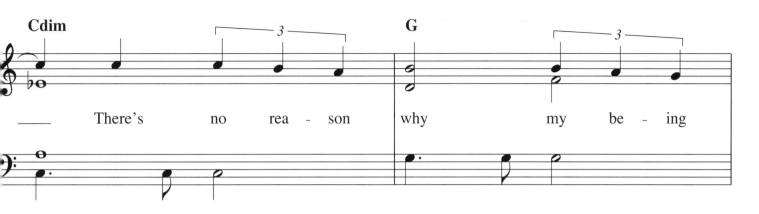

There's no rea - son why my be - ing

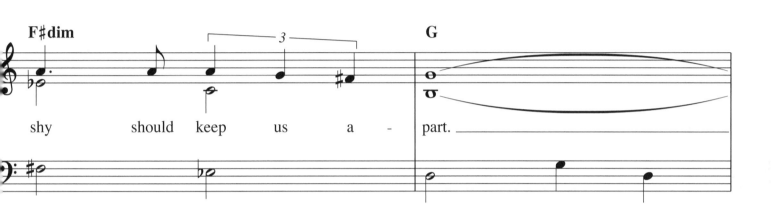

shy should keep us a - part. _____

_____ And I think I'm go - ing out of my head. Yes, I

Repeat ad lib.

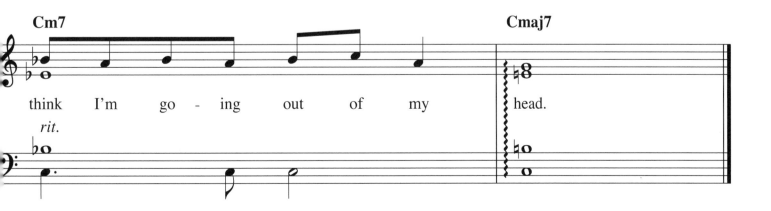

think I'm go - ing out of my head.

rit.

GOOD NIGHT

Words and Music by JOHN LENNON
and PAUL McCARTNEY

Slowly and dreamily

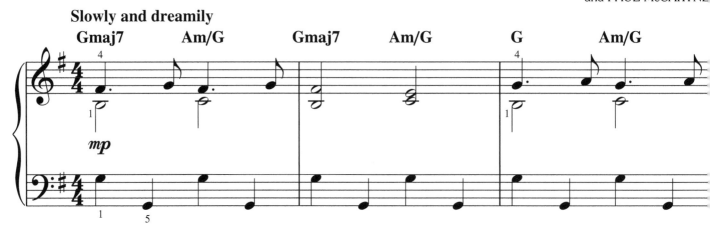

Now it's time to say good night. Good night,

Close your eyes and I'll close mine.

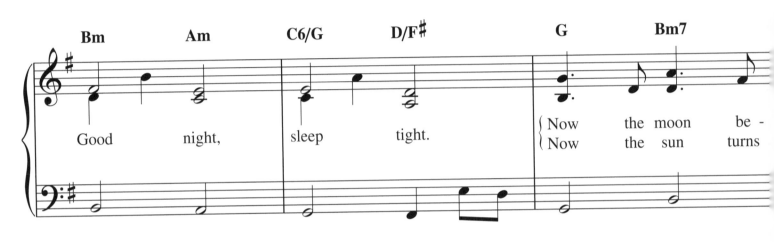

Good night, sleep tight. Now the moon be-
Now the sun turns

gins to shine.
out his light. Good night, sleep tight.

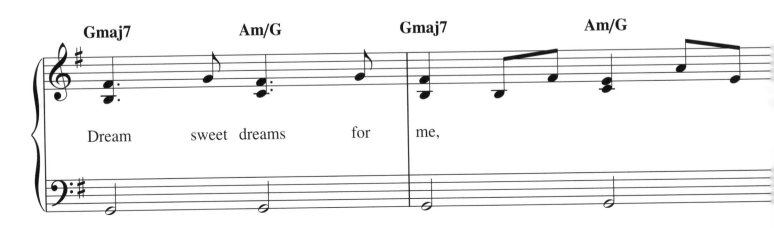

Dream sweet dreams for me,

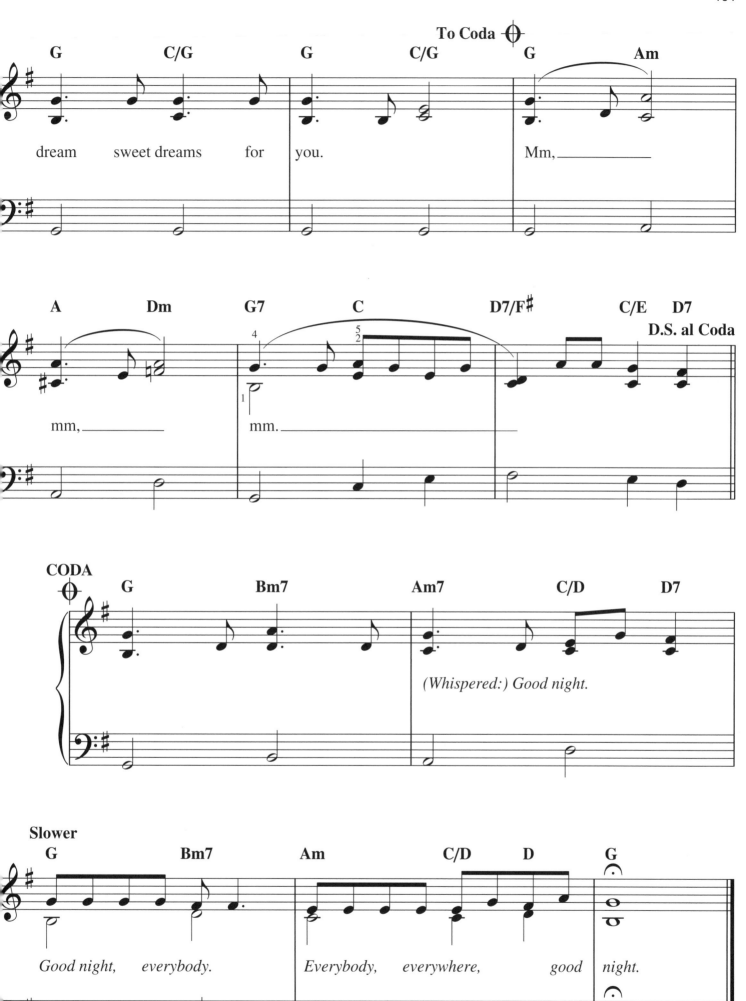

HAPPY TRAILS

from the Television Series THE ROY ROGERS SHOW

Words and Music
DALE EVAN

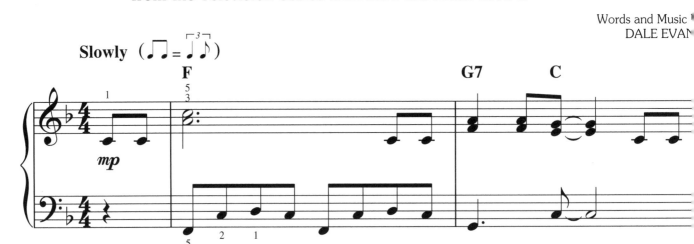

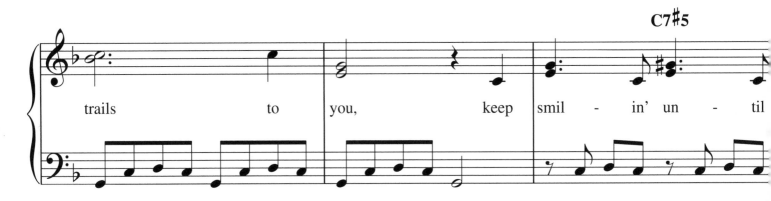

HARLEM NOCTURNE

Words by DICK ROGERS
Music by EARLE HAGEN

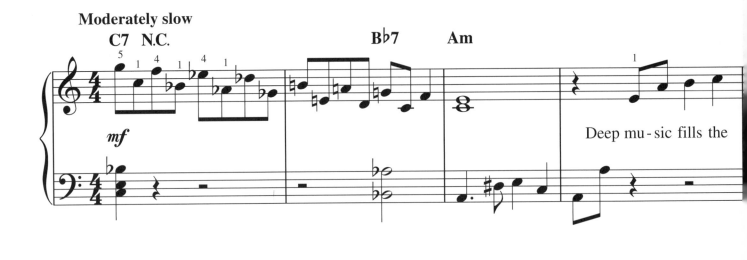

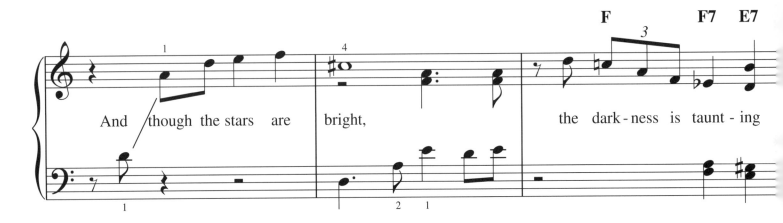

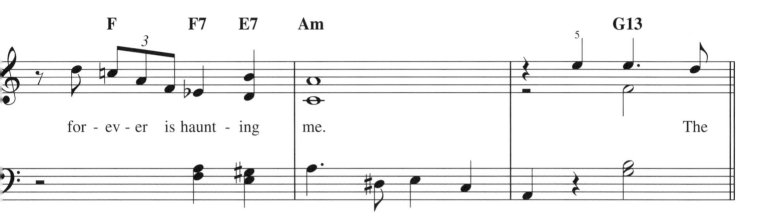

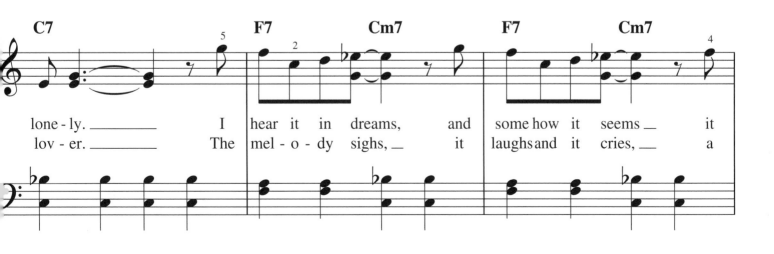

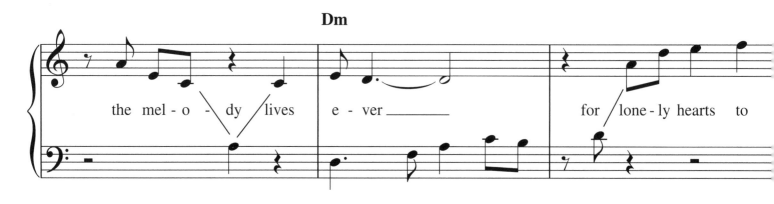

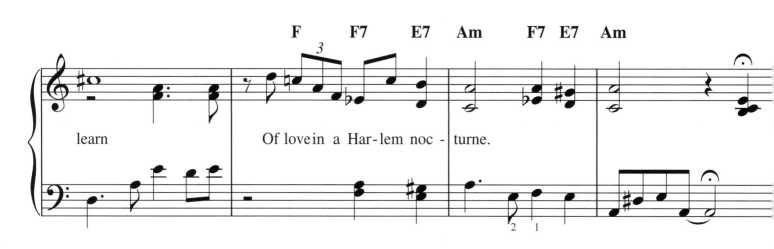

HELLO, DOLLY!

from HELLO, DOLLY!

Music and Lyrics by
JERRY HERMAN

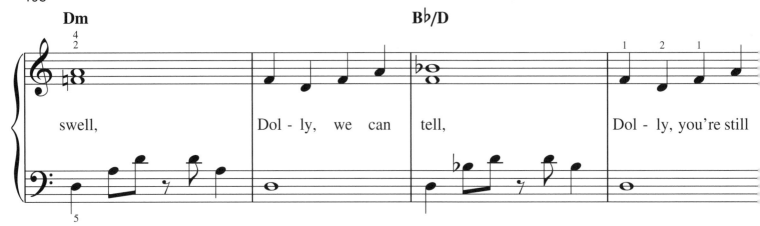

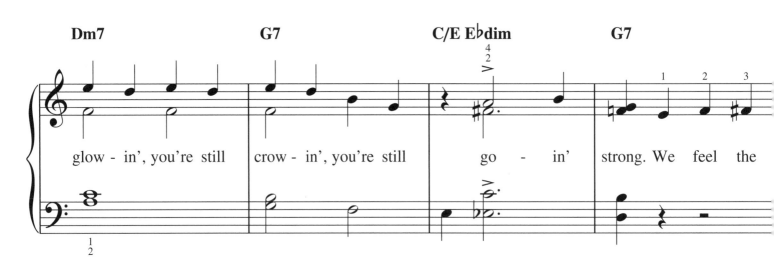

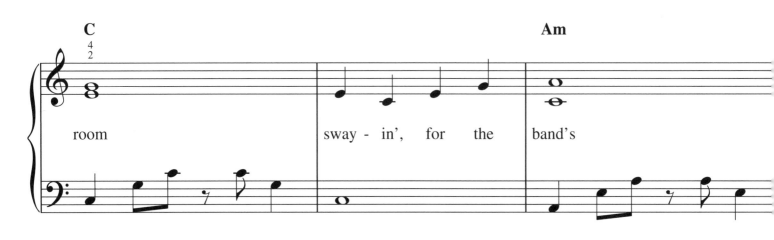

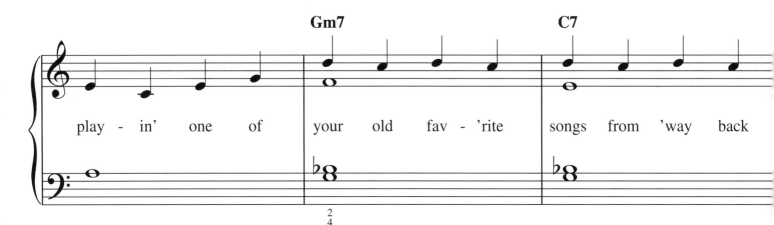

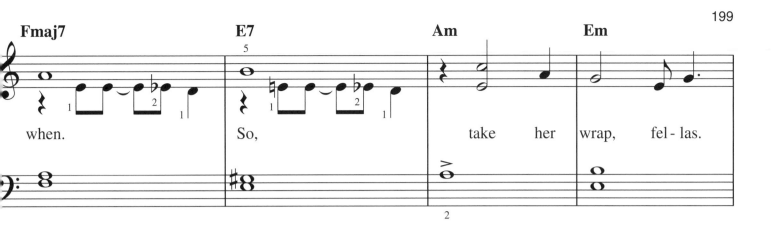

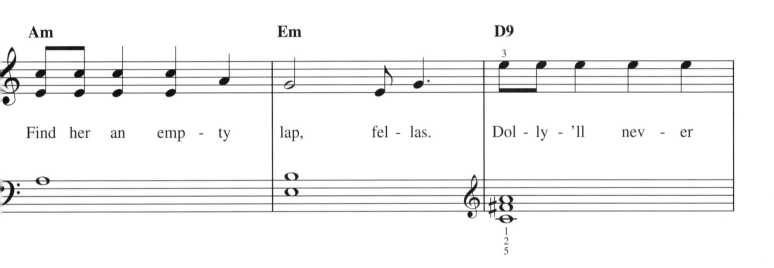

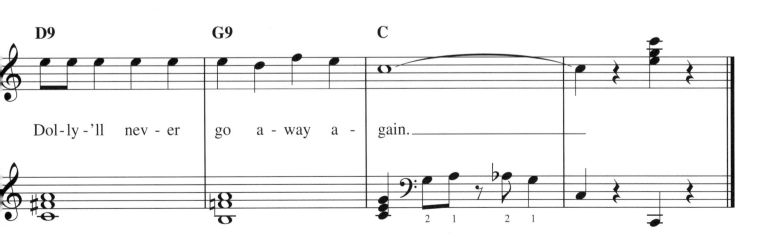

HEART AND SOUL
from the Paramount Short Subject A SONG IS BORN

Words by FRANK LOESSER
Music by HOAGY CARMICHAEL

HEY, LOOK ME OVER

from WILDCAT

Lyric by CAROLYN LEIGH
Music by CY COLEMAN

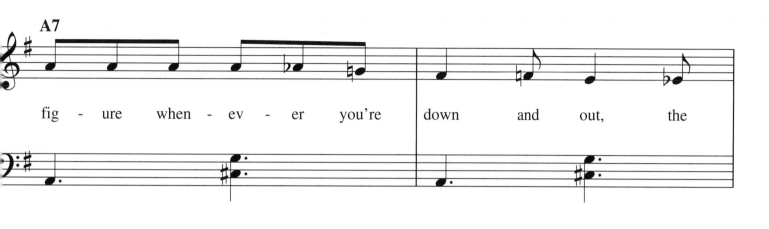

fig - ure when - ev - er you're down and out, the

on - ly way is up! And I'll be up like a

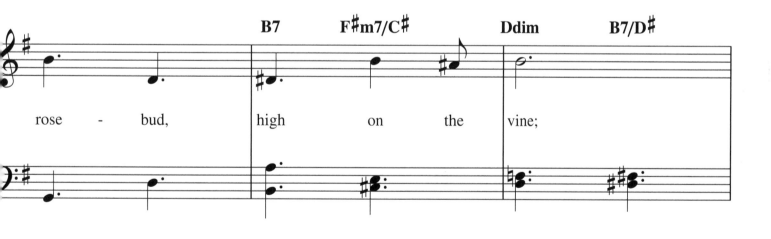

rose - bud, high on the vine;

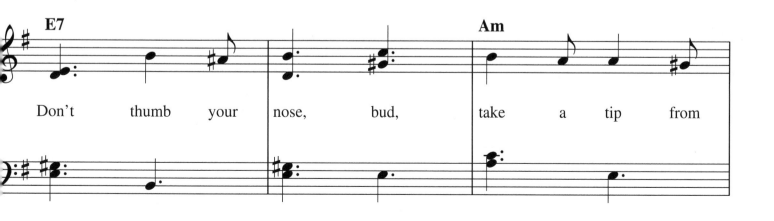

Don't thumb your nose, bud, take a tip from

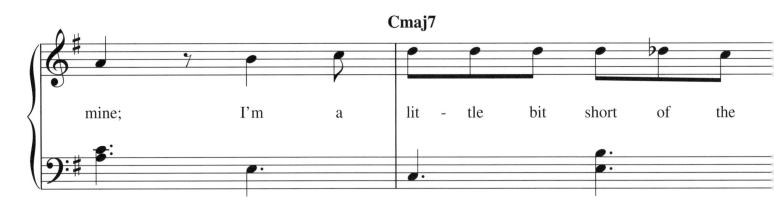

mine; I'm a lit - tle bit short of the

F9 el - bow room, but **G** let me get me **E7** some. { And look / Hear me

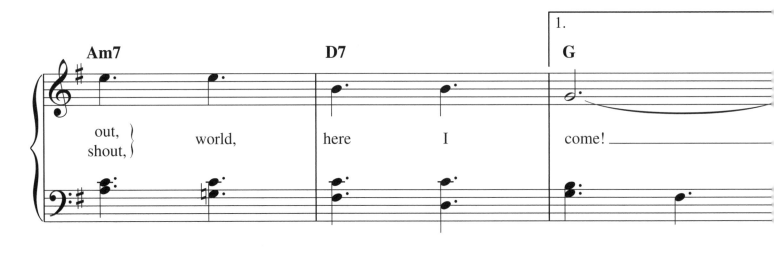

Am7 { out, / shout, } world, **D7** here I **1.** **G** come! _____

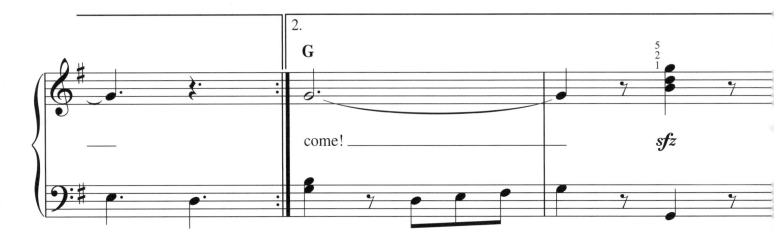

_____ **2.** **G** come! _____

HILL STREET BLUES THEME

from the Television Series

By MIKE POST

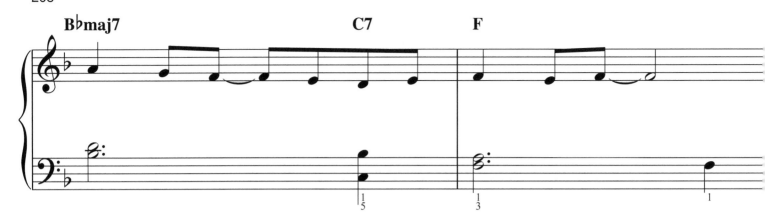

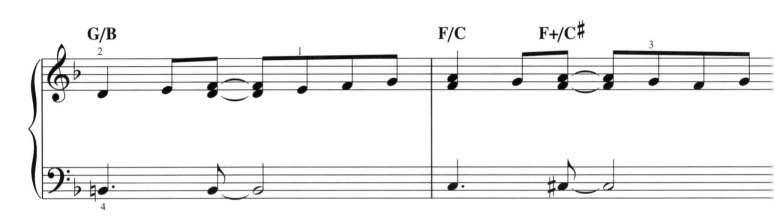

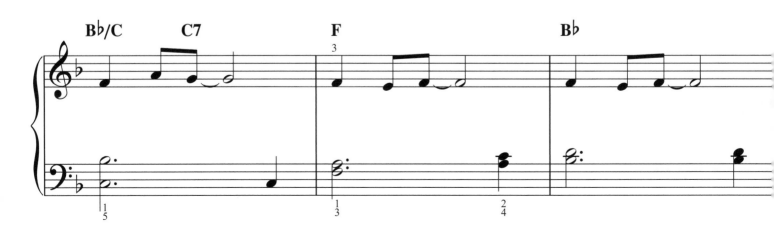

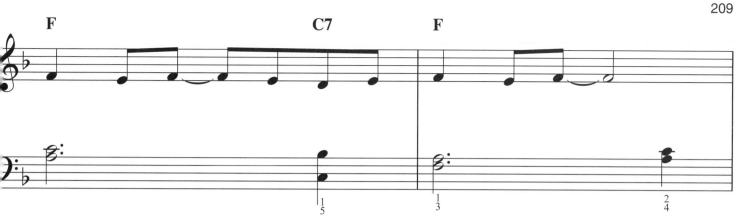

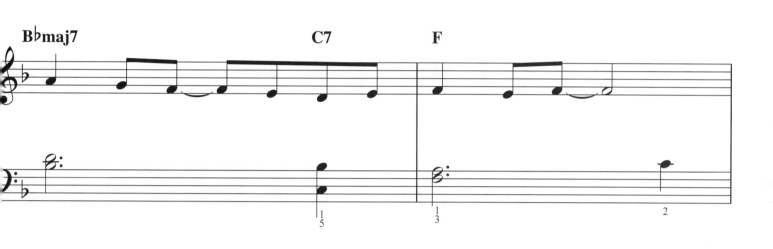

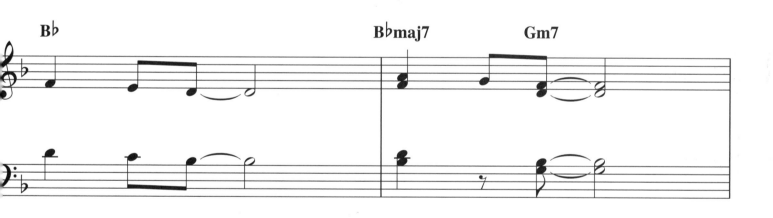

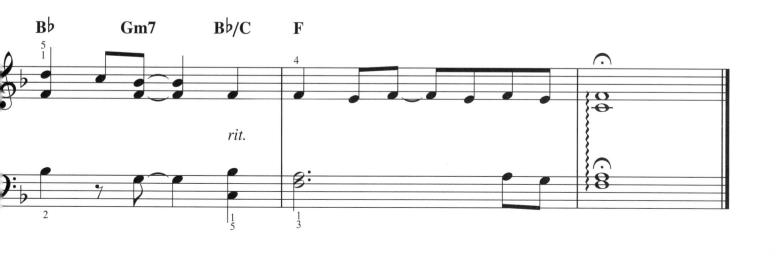

HONEYSUCKLE ROSE

from AIN'T MISBEHAVIN'
from TIN PAN ALLEY

Words by ANDY RAZAF
Music by THOMAS "FATS" WALLER

With an easy Swing

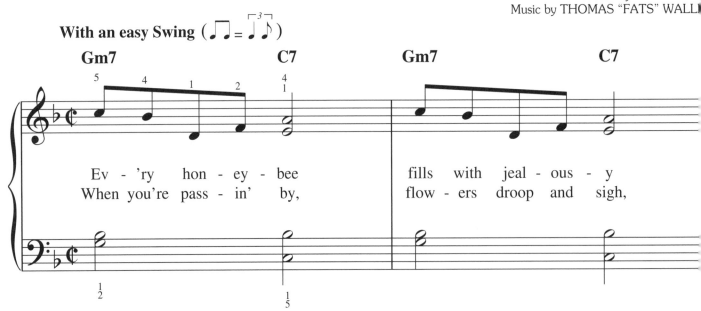

Ev - 'ry hon - ey - bee
When you're pass - in' by,

fills with jeal - ous - y
flow - ers droop and sigh,

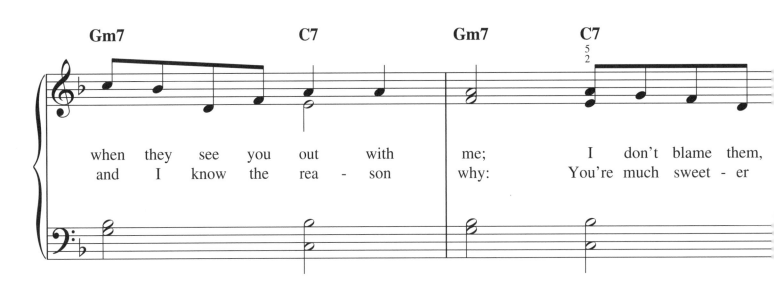

when they see you out with
and I know the rea - son

me;
why:

I don't blame them,
You're much sweet - er

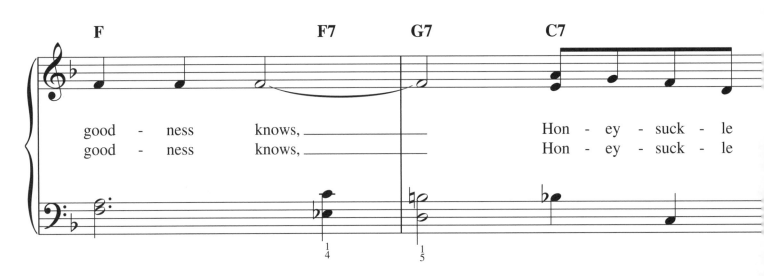

good - ness knows, _____
good - ness knows, _____

Hon - ey - suck - le
Hon - ey - suck - le

Rose. _____

Rose. _____

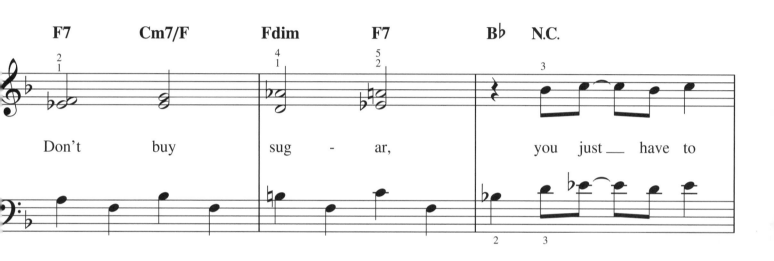

Don't buy sug - ar, you just __ have to

touch my cup. __ You're my sug - ar,

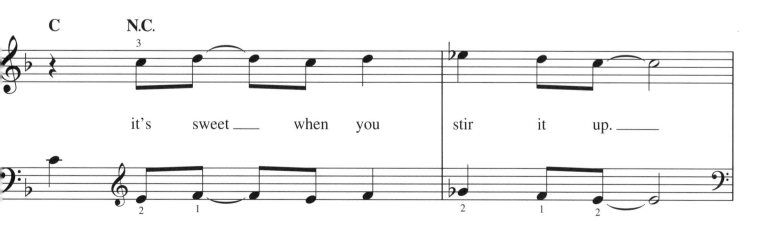

it's sweet __ when you stir it up. _____

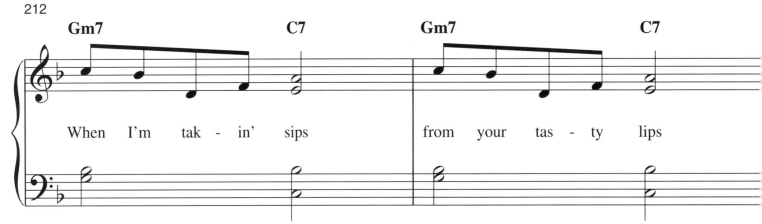

When I'm tak - in' sips   from your tas - ty lips

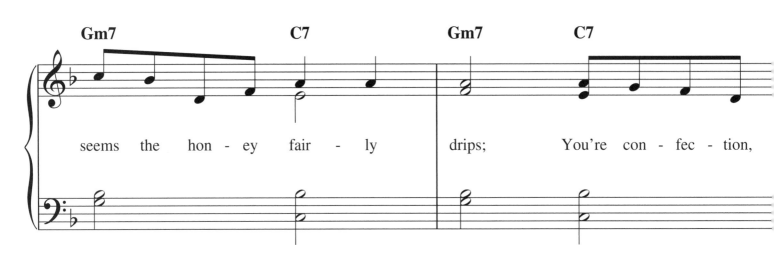

seems the hon - ey fair - ly   drips;   You're con - fec - tion,

good - ness knows,_____   Hon - ey - suck - le

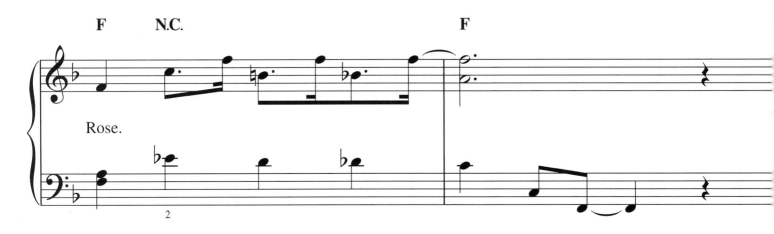

Rose.

I BELIEVE IN YOU

from HOW TO SUCCEED IN BUSINESS WITHOUT REALLY TRYING

Words and Music by
FRANK LOESSER

214

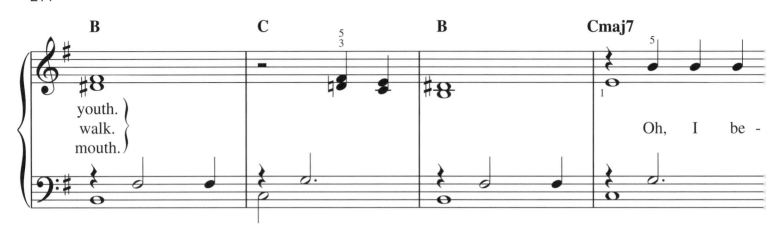

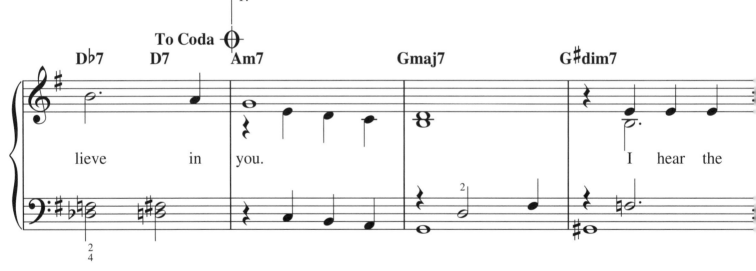

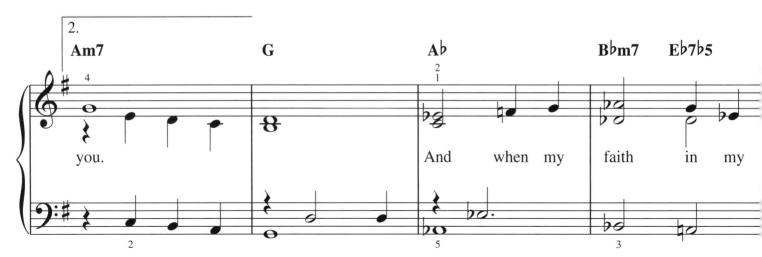

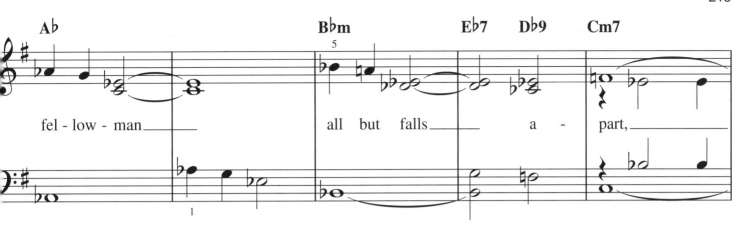

fel - low - man_____ all but falls_____ a - part,_____

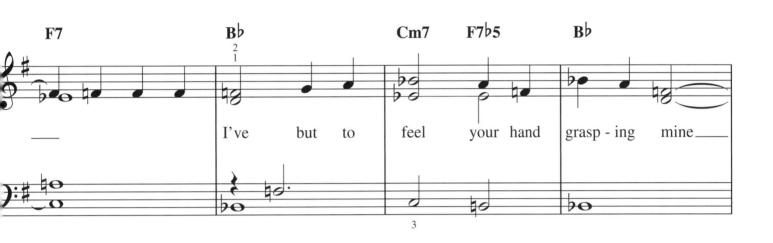

____ I've but to feel your hand grasp - ing mine____

____ and I take heart,_____ I take heart

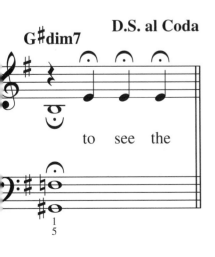

to see the

you.

I COULD HAVE DANCED ALL NIGHT

from MY FAIR LADY

Words by ALAN JAY LERNER
Music by FREDERICK LOEWE

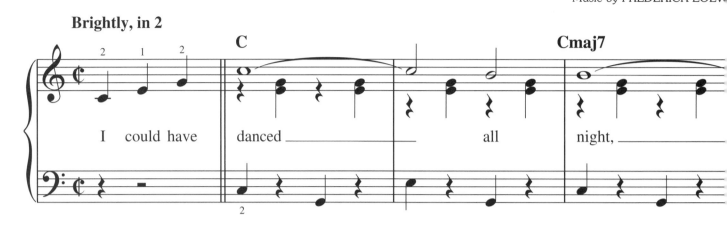

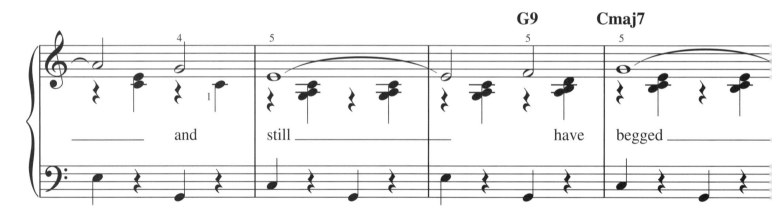

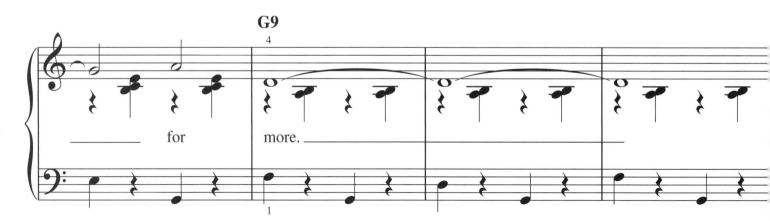

I could have spread _____ my wings, _____

_____ and done a thou - sand things _____

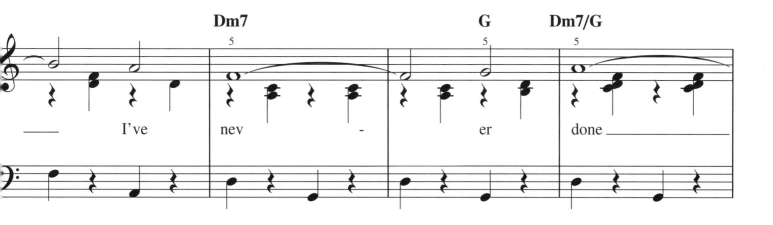

_____ I've nev - er done _____

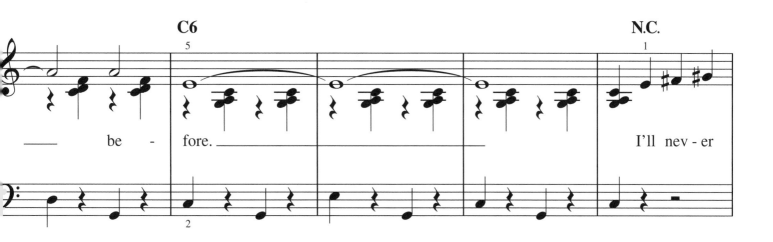

_____ be - fore. _____ I'll nev - er

know _____ what made it so _____ ex -

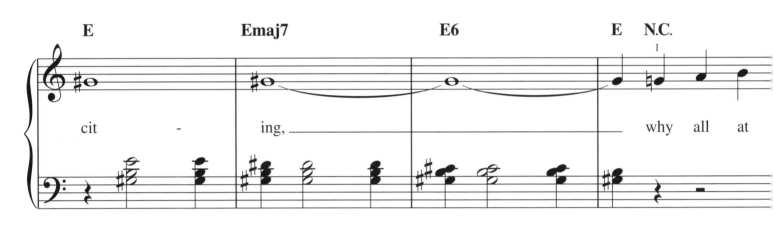

cit - ing, _____ why all at

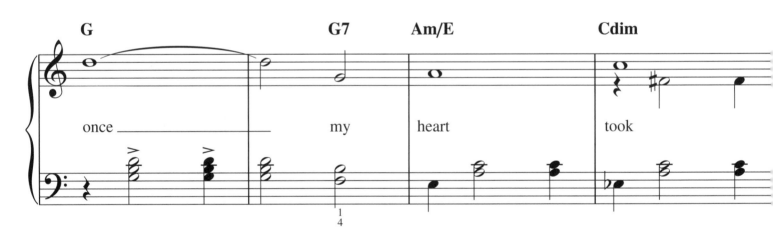

once _____ my heart took

flight. _____ I on - ly

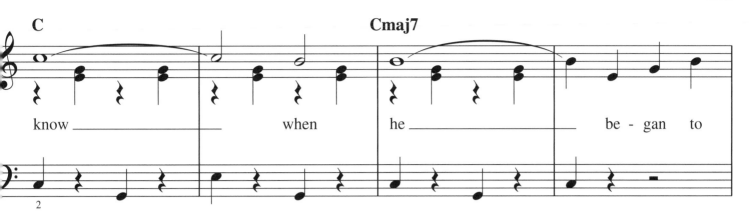

know _____ when he _____ be - gan to

dance _____ with me, _____ I could have

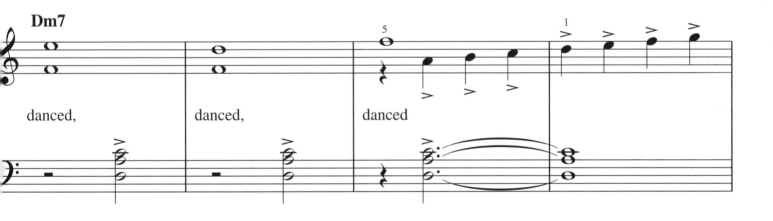

danced, danced, danced

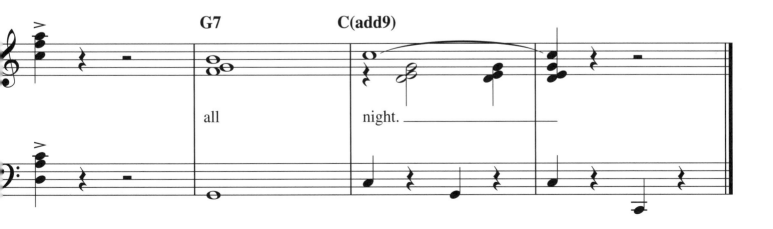

all night. _____

I COULD WRITE A BOOK

from PAL JOEY

Words by LORENZ HART
Music by RICHARD RODGERS

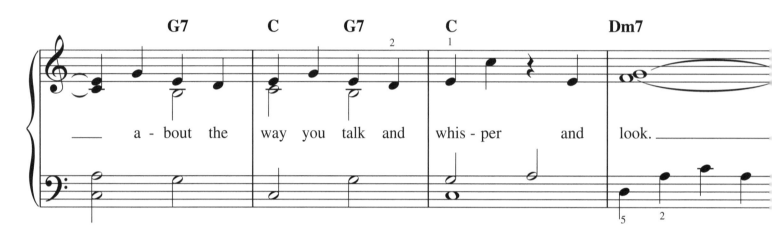

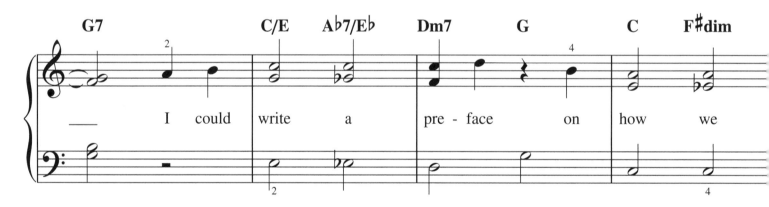

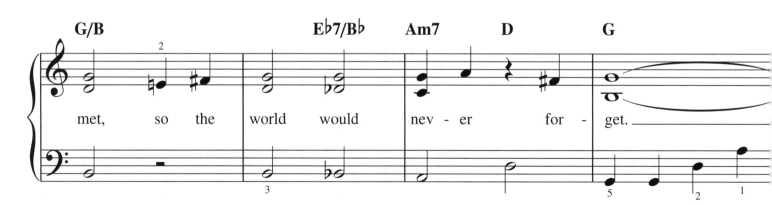

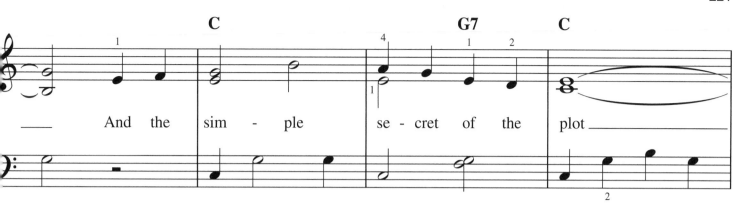

And the sim - ple se - cret of the plot ____

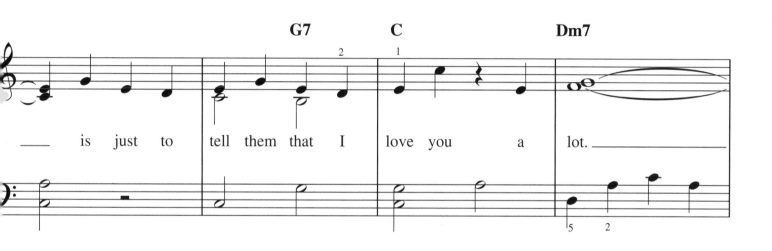

____ is just to tell them that I love you a lot. ____

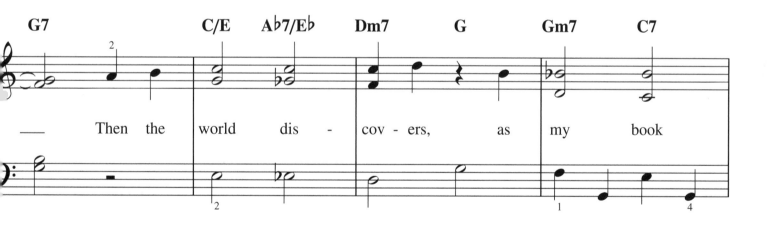

____ Then the world dis - cov - ers, as my book

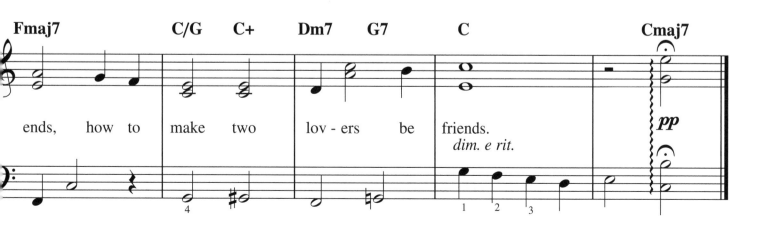

ends, how to make two lov - ers be friends.

dim. e rit.

pp

I DON'T WANT TO WALK WITHOUT YOU

from the Paramount Picture SWEATER GIRL

Words by FRANK LOESSER
Music by JULE STYNE

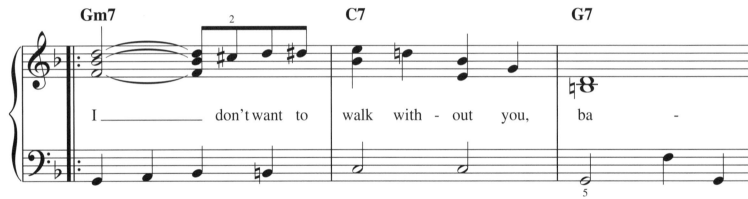

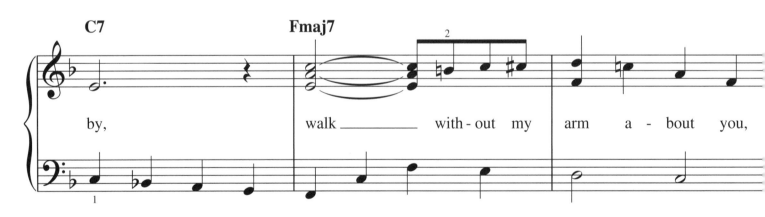

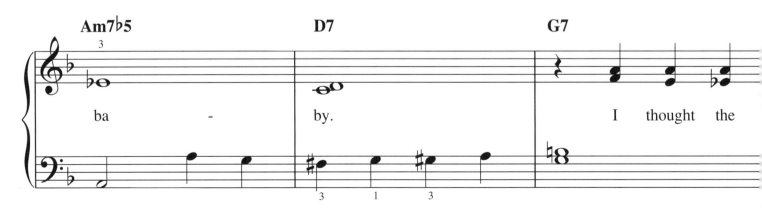

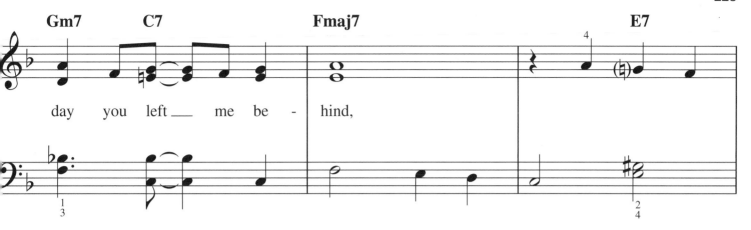

day you left me be - hind,

I'd take a   stroll and get you right   off   my   mind   but

now   I   find that   I don't want to   walk with - out the

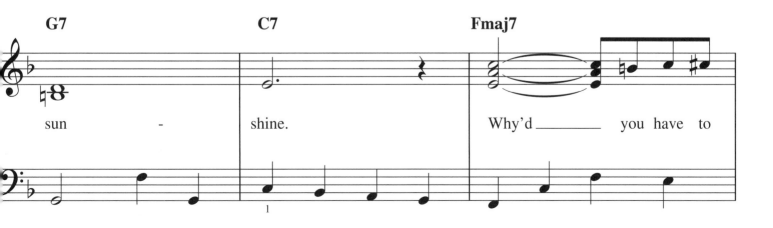

sun -   shine.   Why'd you have to

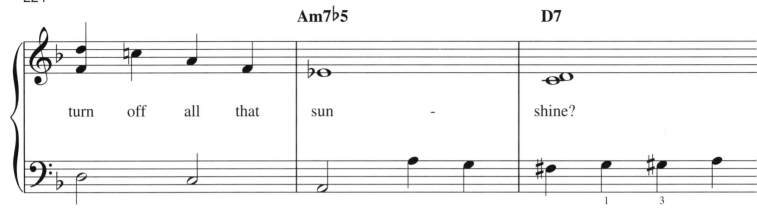

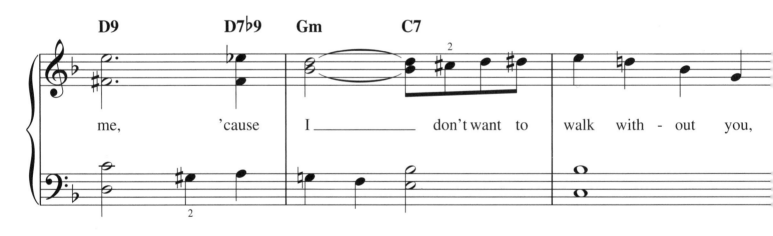

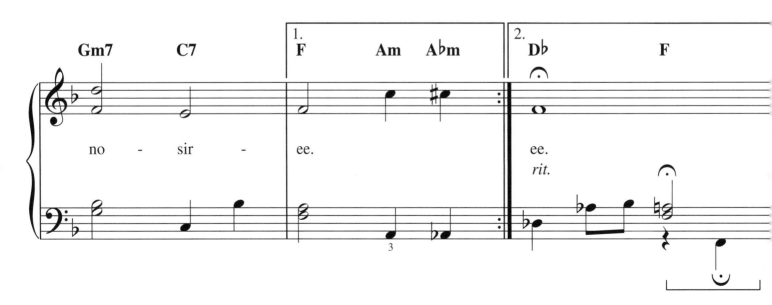

I ENJOY BEING A GIRL
from FLOWER DRUM SONG

Lyrics by OSCAR HAMMERSTEIN II
Music by RICHARD RODGERS

float   as   the   clouds   on   air   do. _____
just   lap   it   up   like   hon - ey. _____

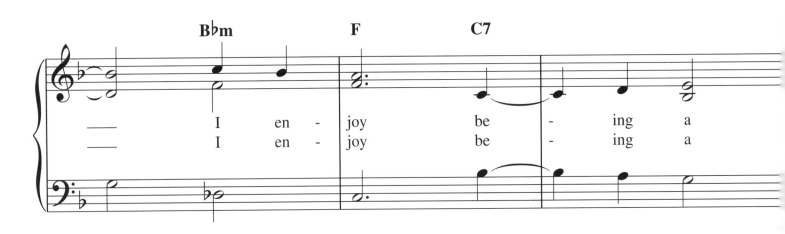

_____ I en - joy   be - ing   a
_____ I en - joy   be - ing   a

1.   2.

girl! _____
girl! _____   When
_____   I

flip   when   a   fel - low   sends   me   flow - ers, _____

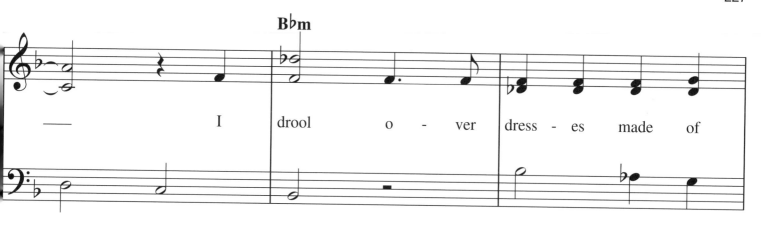

I drool o - ver dress - es made of

lace. I talk on the

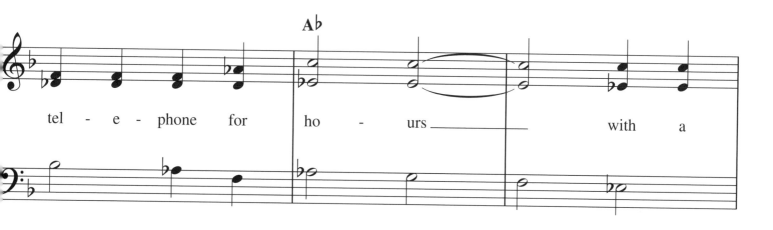

tel - e - phone for ho - urs with a

pound and a half of cream up - on my face!

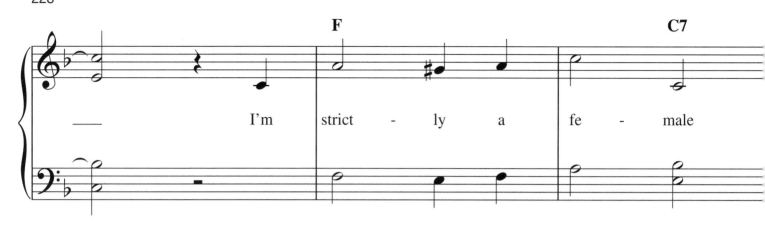

I'm strict - ly a fe - male

fe - male, _____ and my fu - ture I

hope will be _____ in the

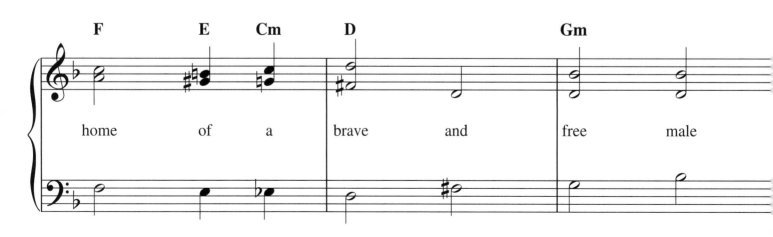

home of a brave and free male

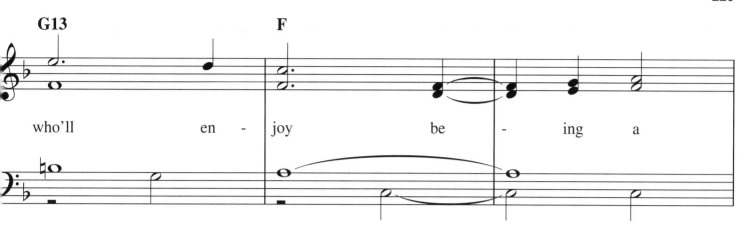

who'll en - joy be - ing a

guy hav - ing a girl _____

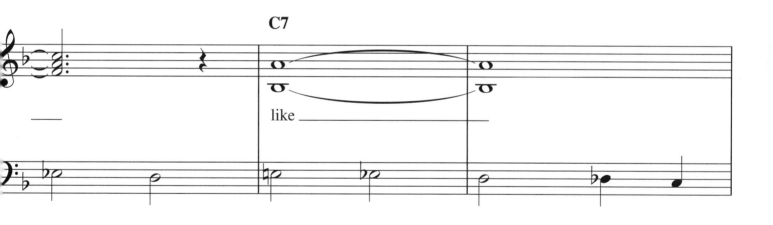

_____ like _____

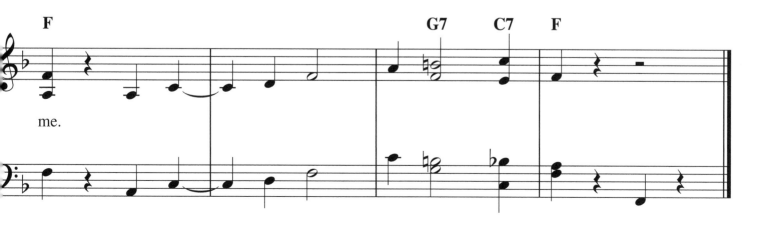

me.

I GET ALONG WITHOUT YOU VERY WELL
(Except Sometimes)

Words and Music by HOAGY CARMICHAE[L]
Inspired by a poem written by J.B. THOMPSO[N]

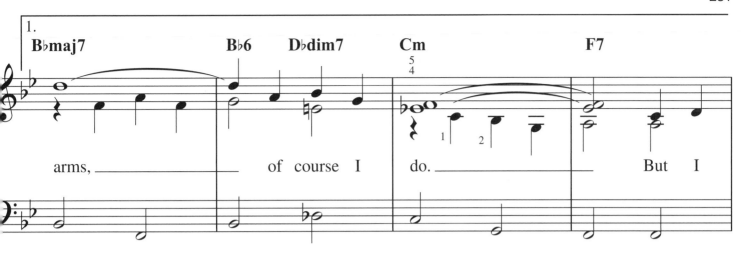

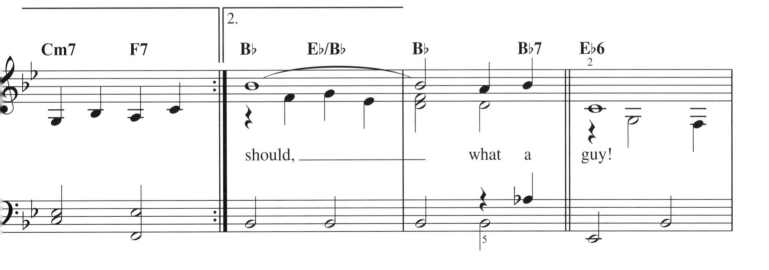

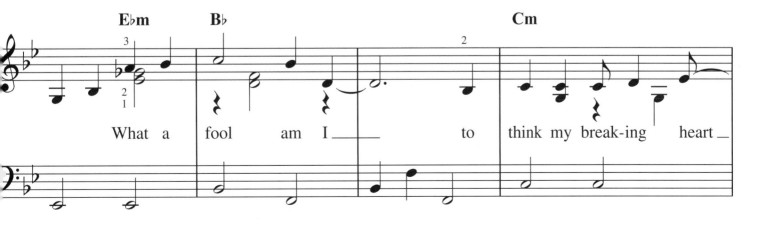

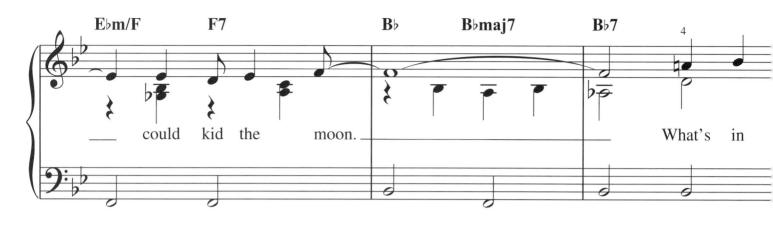

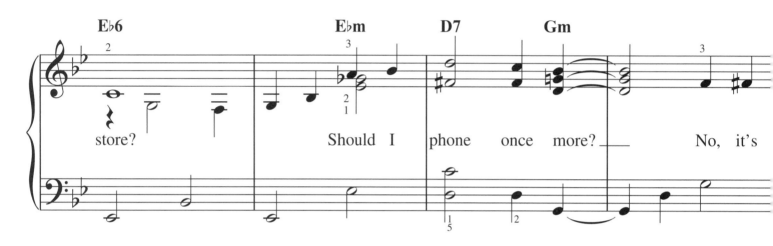

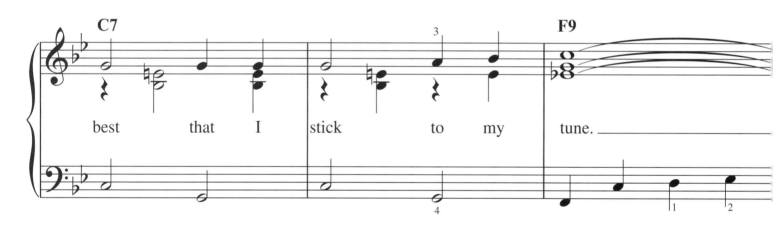

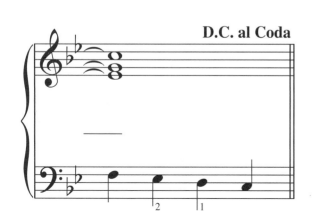

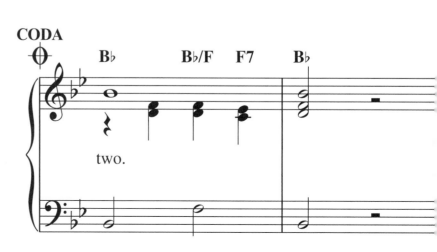

I WHISTLE A HAPPY TUNE

from THE KING AND I

Lyrics by OSCAR HAMMERSTEIN II
Music by RICHARD RODGERS

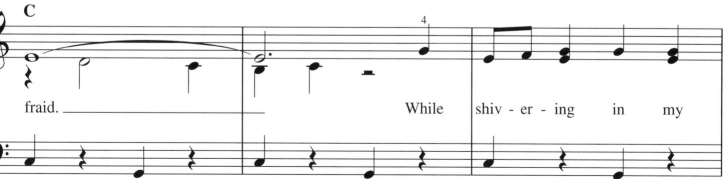

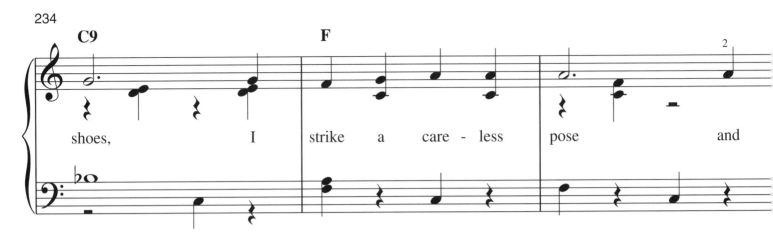

shoes,   I   strike   a   care - less   pose   and

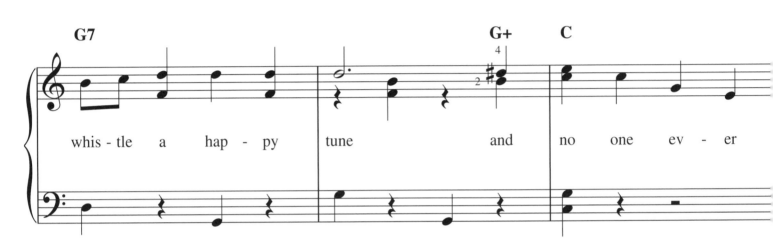

whis - tle   a   hap – py   tune   and   no   one   ev - er

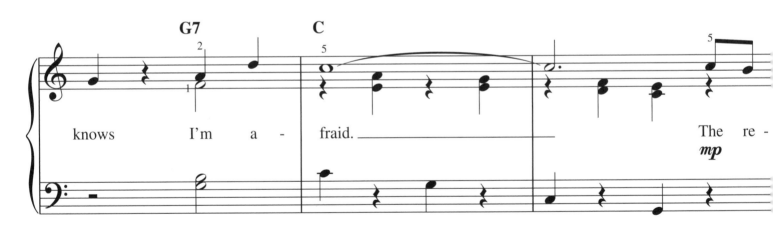

knows   I'm   a -   fraid. _____   The   re -

mp

sult   of   this   de -   cep - tion   is   ver - y   strange   to _____

G7   **Gm6**

tell,   for   when   I   fool   the   peo - ple   I   fear,   I

D9   **G7**   **C**

fool   my - self   as   well!   I   whis - tle   a   hap - py

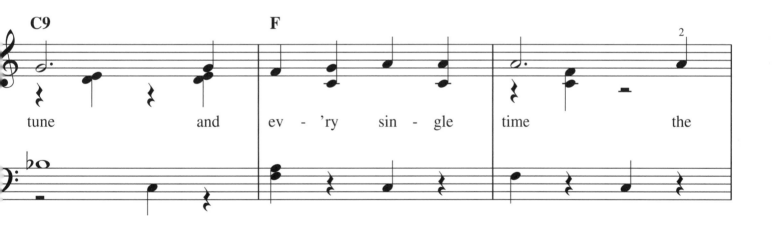

C9   **F**

tune   and   ev - 'ry   sin - gle   time   the

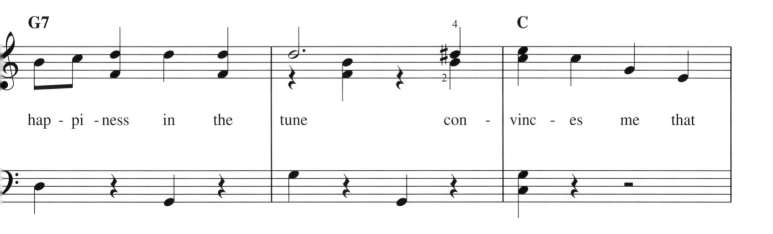

G7   **C**

hap - pi - ness   in   the   tune   con - vinc - es   me   that

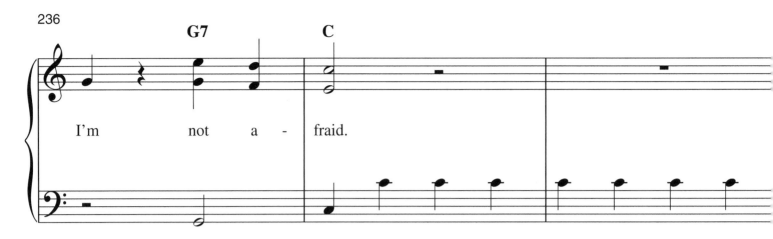

I'm not a - fraid.

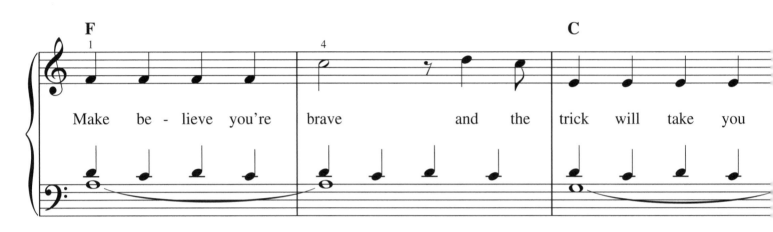

Make be - lieve you're brave and the trick will take you

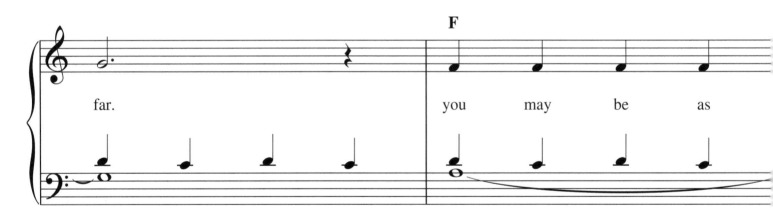

far. you may be as

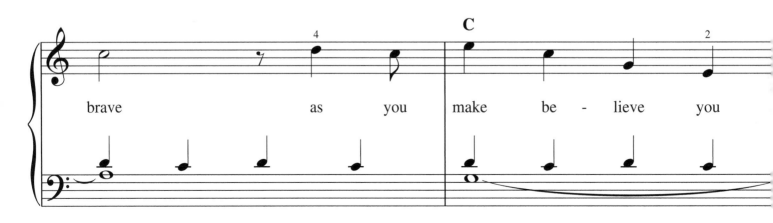

brave as you make be - lieve you

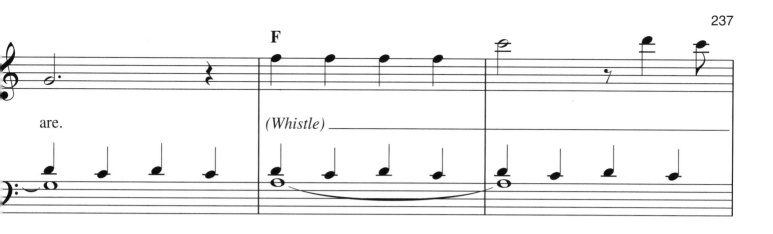

are.

F

(Whistle)

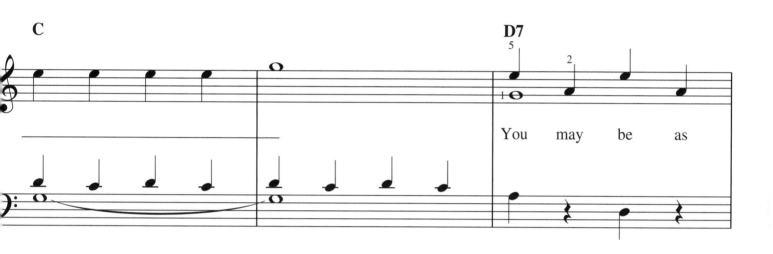

C

D7

You may be as

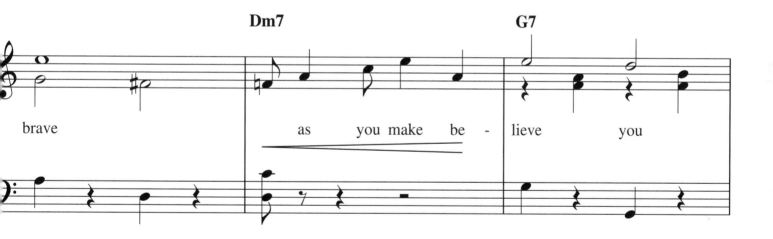

brave

Dm7

as you make be - lieve you

G7

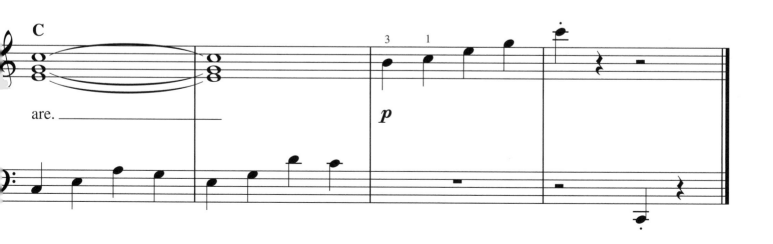

C

are.

p

I LOVE PARIS

from CAN-CAN
from HIGH SOCIETY

Words and Music
COLE PORTE

Slow Fox-trot tempo

I love **Par - is** in the **spring - time,**

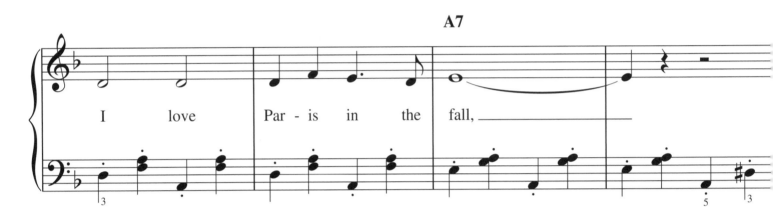

I love **Par - is** in the **fall,**

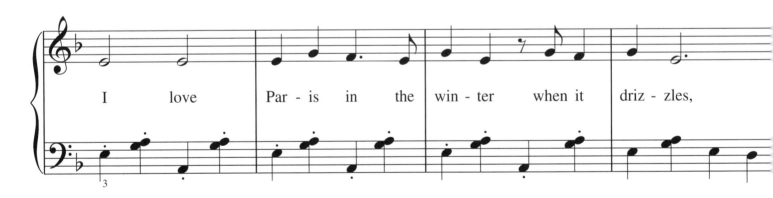

I love **Par - is** in the **win - ter** when it **driz - zles,**

I love **Par - is** in the **sum - mer,** when it **siz - zles.**

With pedal

I love Par - is ev - 'ry mo - ment,

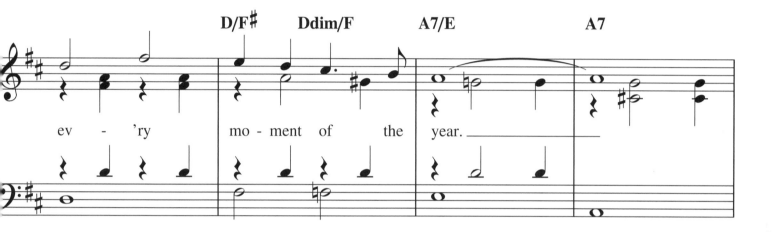

ev - 'ry mo - ment of the year.

I love Par - is, why, oh why do I love Par - is?

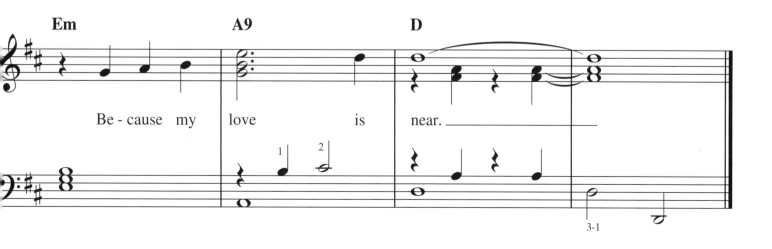

Be - cause my love is near.

I SAY A LITTLE PRAYER

Lyric by HAL DAVID
Music by BURT BACHARAC

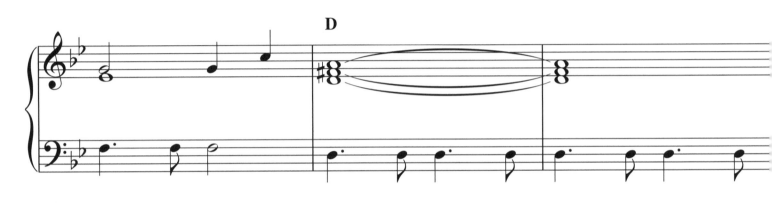

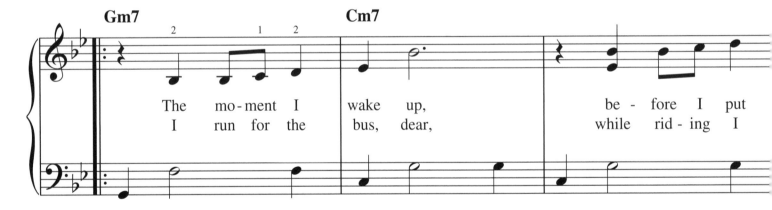

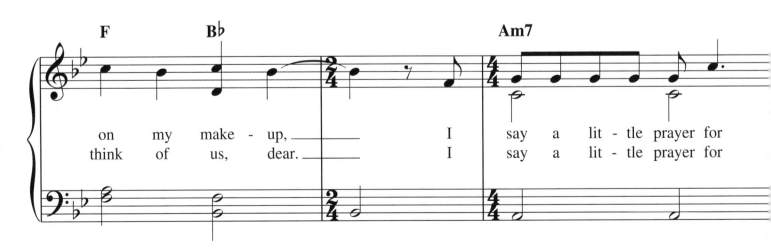

you.
you.

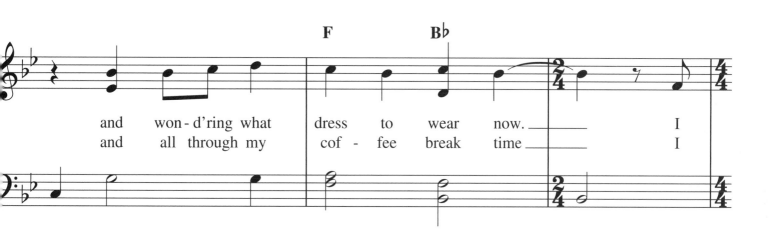

While comb ing my hair now
At work I just take time

and won - d'ring what dress to wear now._____ I
and all through my cof - fee break time _____ I

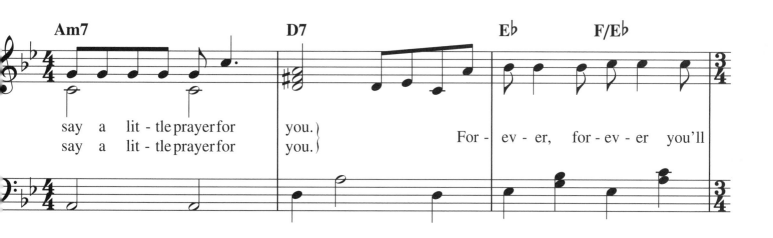

say a lit - tle prayer for you.)
say a lit - tle prayer for you.)

For - ev - er, for - ev - er you'll

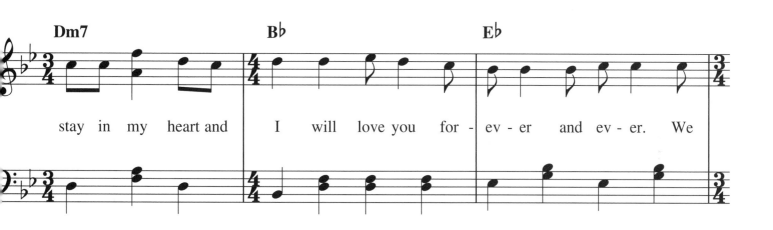

stay in my heart and I will love you for - ev - er and ev - er. We

nev - er will part. Oh, how I'll love you. To - geth - er, to - geth - er, that's

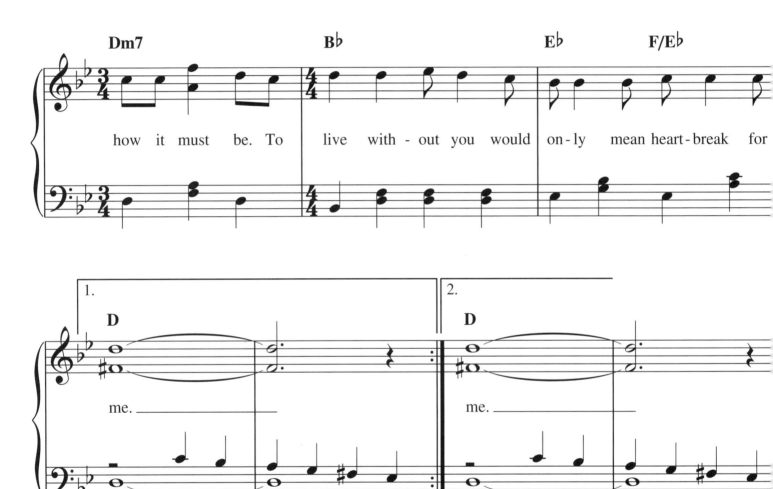

how it must be. To live with - out you would on - ly mean heart - break for

me. ____

me. ____

My dar - ling, be - lieve me, for me there is

no one _____ but you.   Please love me,

too. _____   I'm in love with you. _____

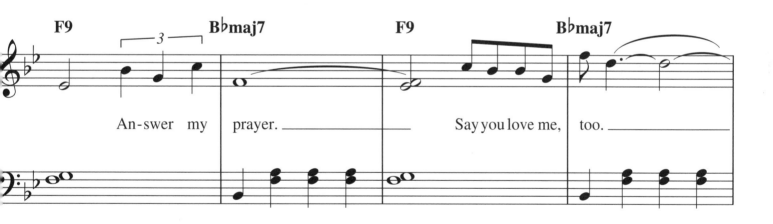

An-swer my   prayer. _____   Say you love me, too. _____

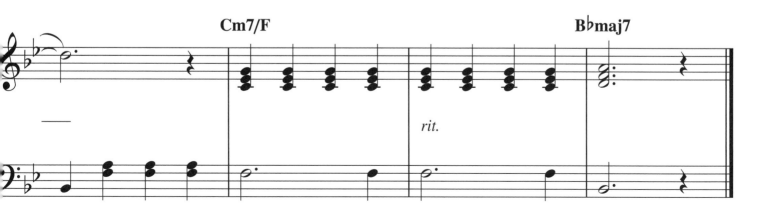

___   *rit.*

I WALK THE LINE

Words and Music
JOHN R. CAS

Bright Country 2-beat

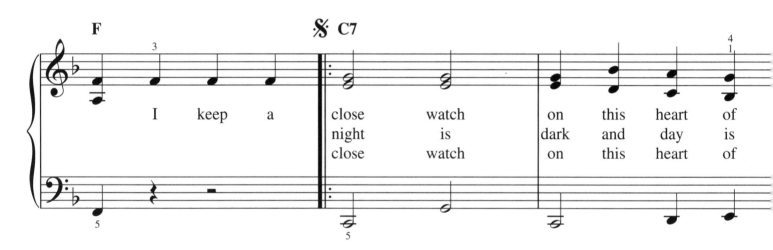

I keep a close watch on this heart of
night is dark and day is
close watch on this day heart of

mine. I keep my eyes wide
light, I keep you on my
mine. I keep my eyes wide

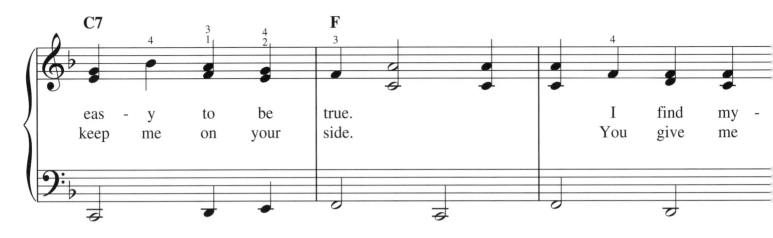

I WISH I WERE IN LOVE AGAIN
from BABES IN ARMS

Words by LORENZ HART
Music by RICHARD RODGERS

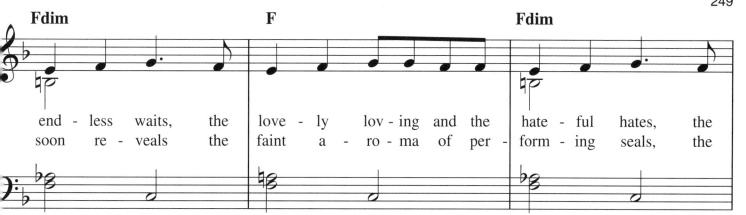

end - less waits, the love - ly lov - ing and the hate - ful hates, the
soon re - veals the faint a - ro - ma of per - form - ing seals, the

con - ver - sa - tion with the fly - ing plates; I wish I were in
dou - ble cross - ing of a pair of heels; I wish I were in

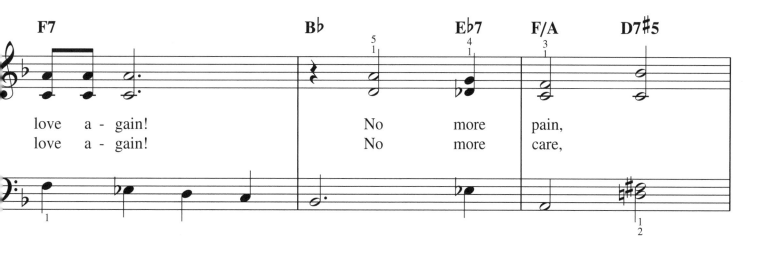

love a - gain! No more pain,
love a - gain! No more care,

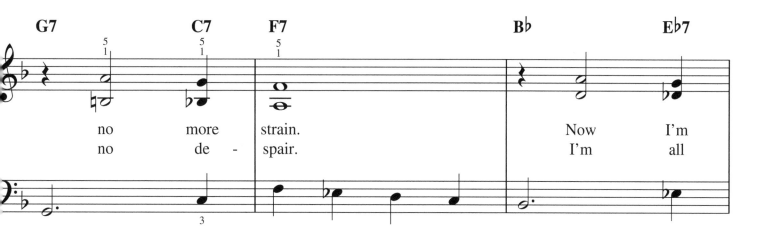

no more strain.
no de - spair.

Now I'm
I'm all

F/A D7#5 G7 C7

sane,   but   I would rath-er be   ga - ga! ___ The
there   now,   but I'd rath-er be   punch-drunk! _ Be-

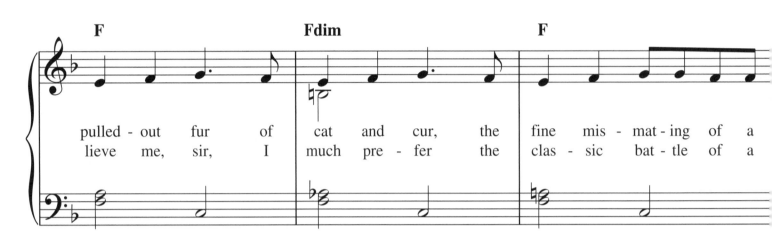

F   Fdim   F

pulled-out fur of   cat and cur, the   fine mis-mat-ing of a
lieve me, sir, I   much pre-fer the   clas-sic bat-tle of a

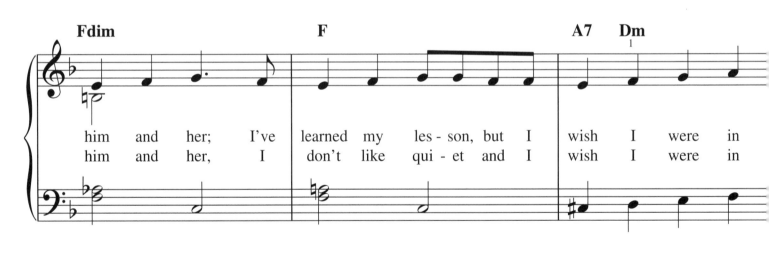

Fdim   F   A7   Dm

him and her; I've   learned my les-son, but I   wish I were in
him and her, I   don't like qui-et and I   wish I were in

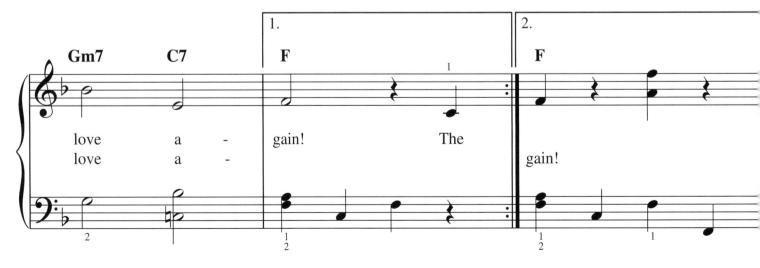

Gm7   C7   1. F   2. F

love a - gain!   The
love a - gain!

IF

Words and Music by
DAVID GATES

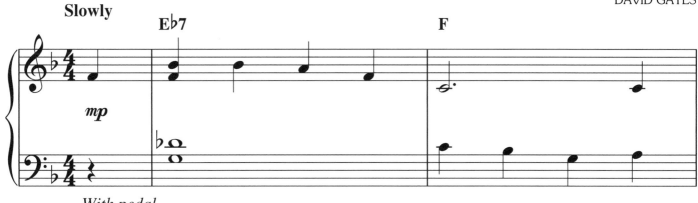

With pedal

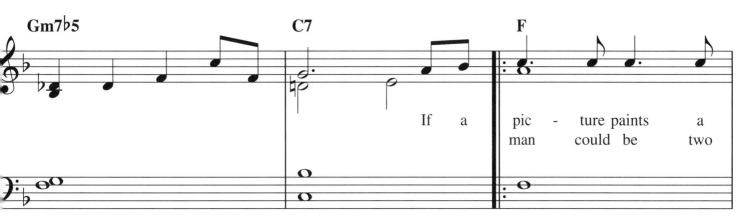

If a pic - ture paints a
man could be two

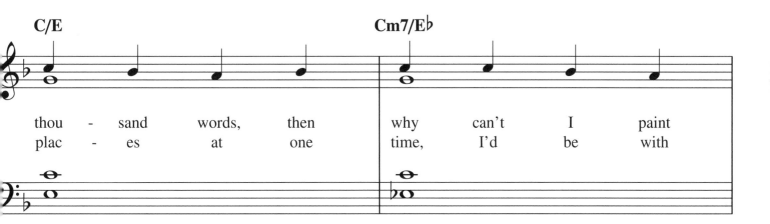

thou - sand words, then why can't I paint
plac - es at one time, I'd be paint with

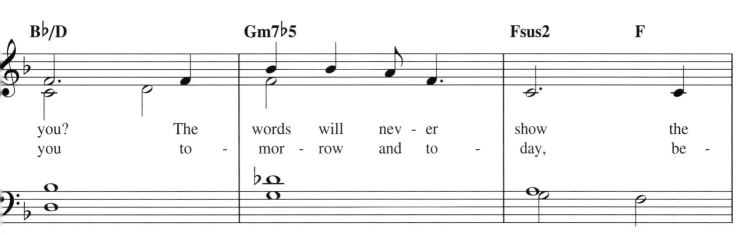

you? The words will nev - er show the
you to - mor - row and to - day, be -

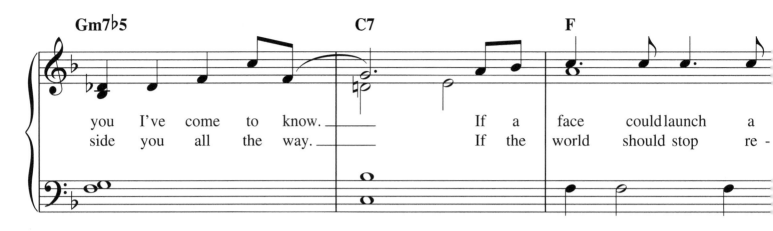

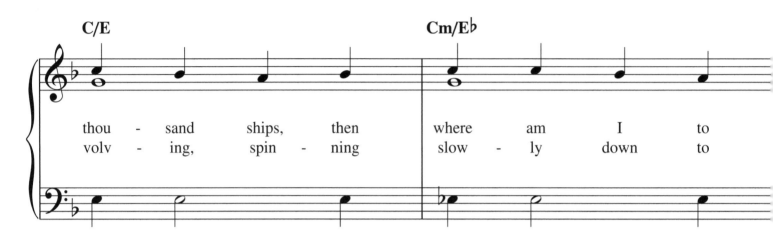

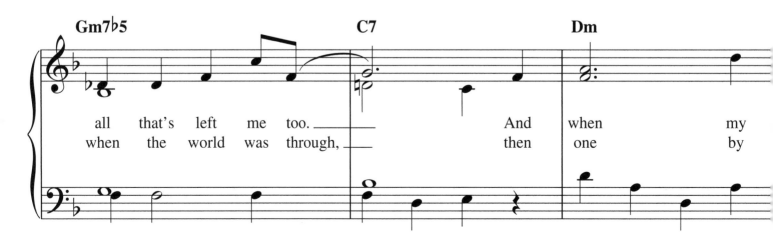

I WRITE THE SONGS

Words and Music
BRUCE JOHNSTC

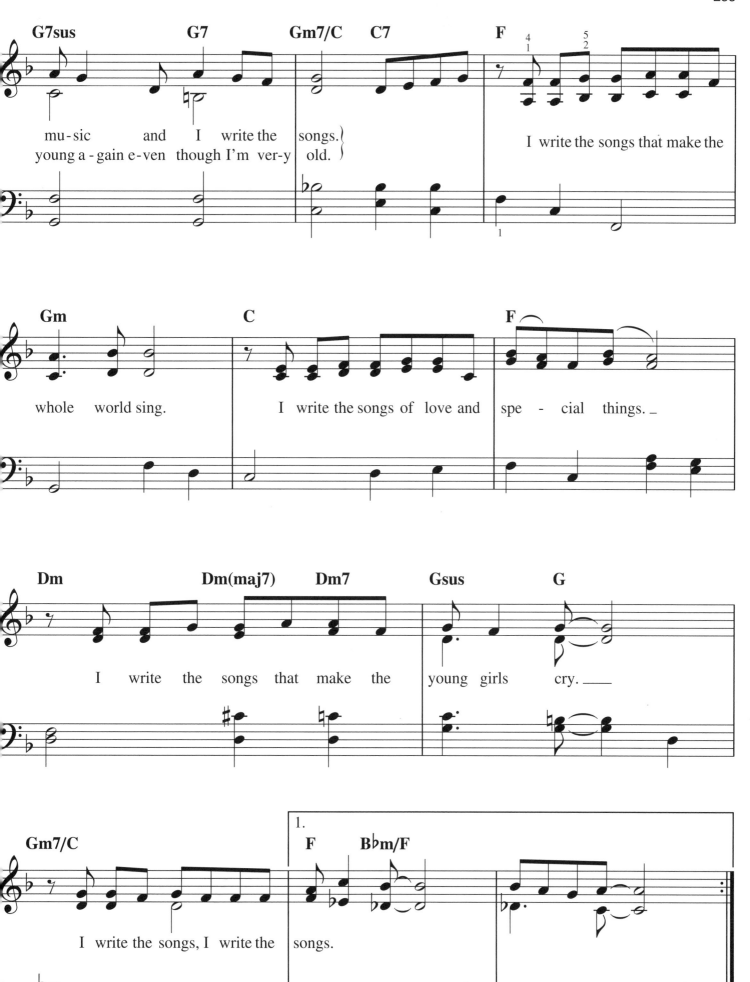

IF EVER I WOULD LEAVE YOU

from CAMELOT

Words by ALAN JAY LERNER
Music by FREDERICK LOEWE

Moderately fast

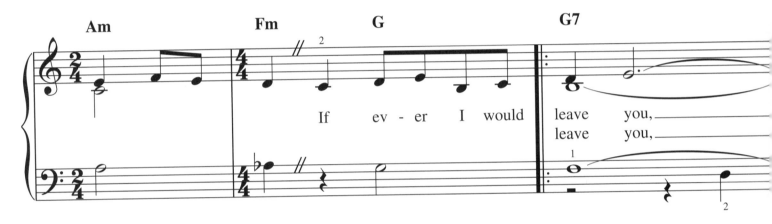

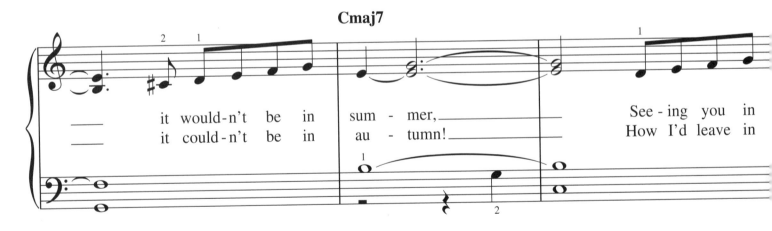

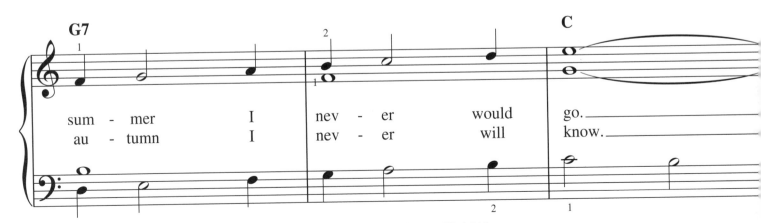

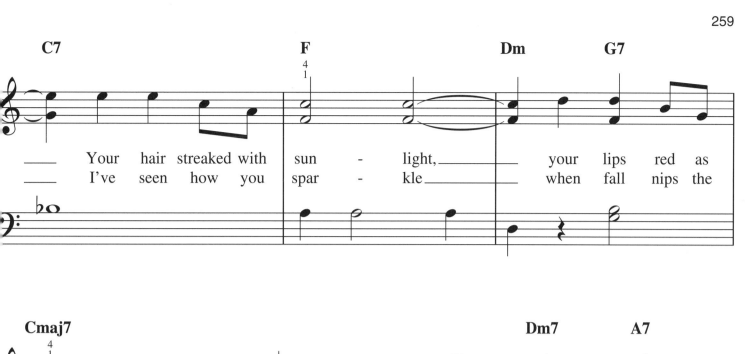

Your hair streaked with sun - light, _____ your lips red as
I've seen how you spar - kle _____ when fall nips the

flame, _____ your face with a lus - ter _____
air, _____ I know you in au - tumn _____

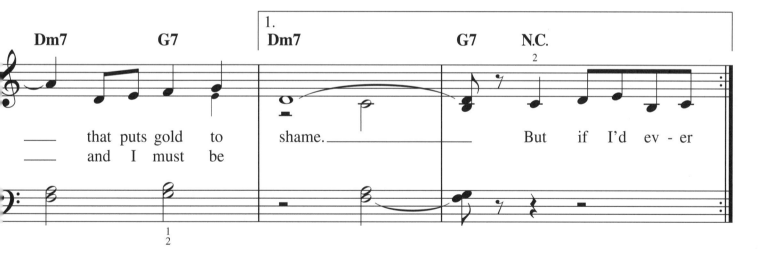

_____ that puts gold to shame. _____ But if I'd ev - er
_____ and I must be

there. _____ And could I leave you run - ning

Again in strict tempo

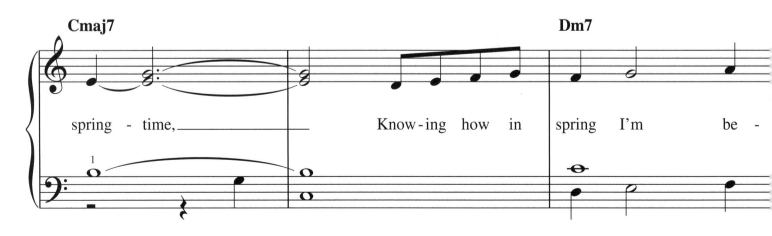

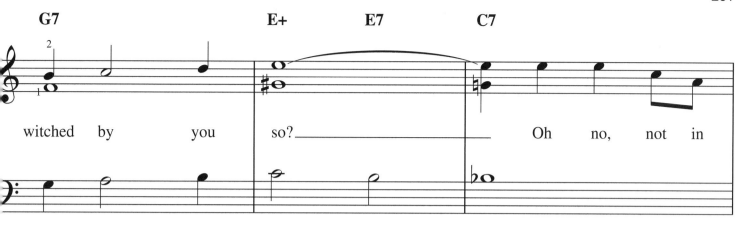

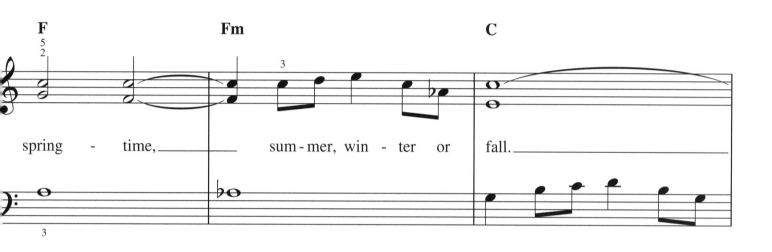

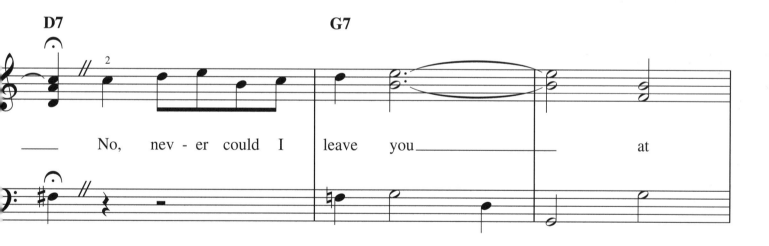

IF I LOVED YOU
from CAROUSEL

Lyrics by OSCAR HAMMERSTEIN
Music by RICHARD RODGERS

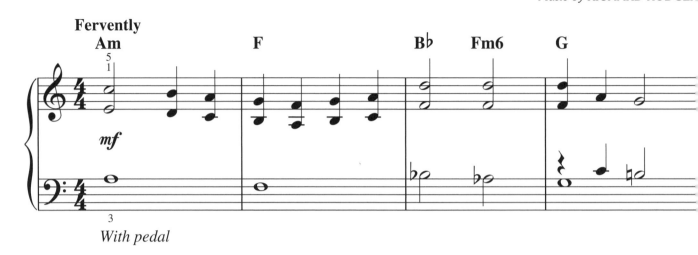

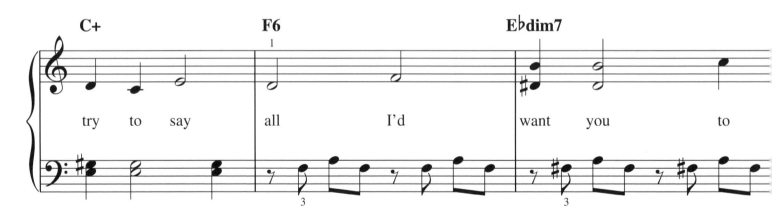

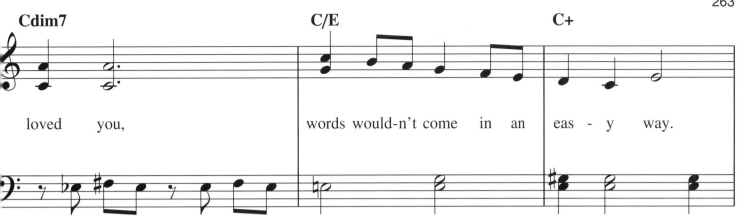

loved you,   words would-n't come in an eas - y way.

'Round in   cir - cles I'd go.

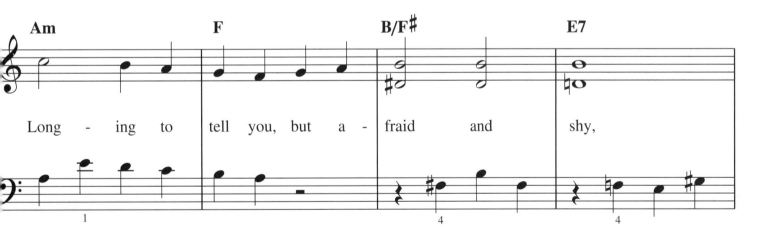

Long - ing to tell you, but a - fraid and shy,

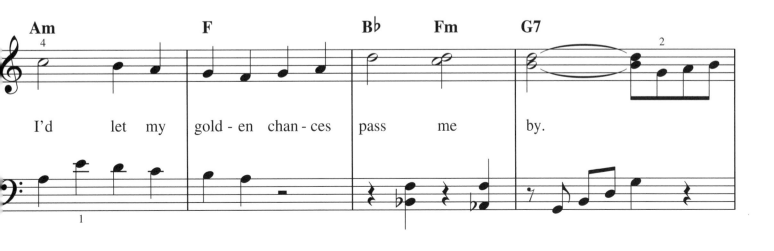

I'd let my gold - en chan - ces pass me by.

Soon you'd leave me. Off you would go in the

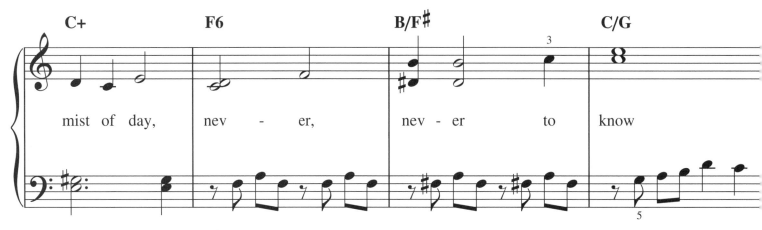

mist of day, nev - er, nev - er to know

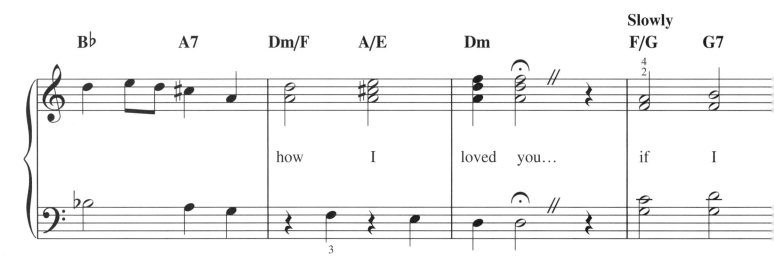

how I loved you... if I

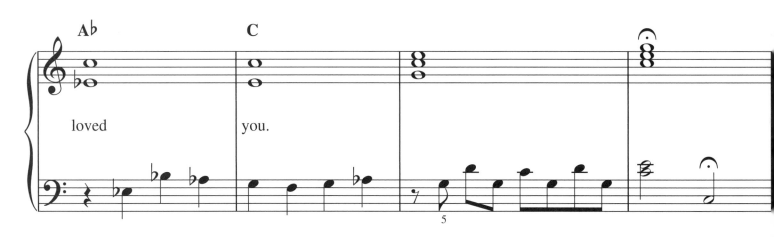

loved you.

IF I WERE A BELL

from GUYS AND DOLLS

By FRANK LOESSER

Bb — Bbm — C7 — F — Bb7

have, Boy, if I were a lamp I'd light, Or if
looked, Boy, if I were a duck I'd quack, Or if

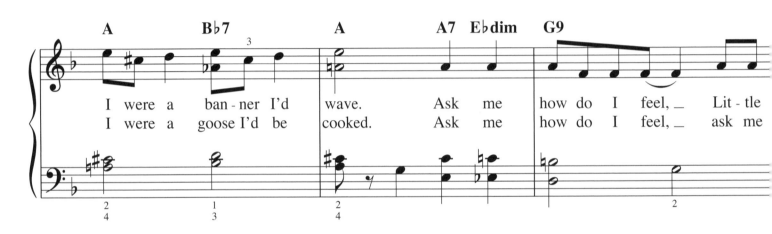

A — Bb7 — A — A7 — Ebdim — G9

I were a ban-ner I'd wave. Ask me how do I feel, __ Lit-tle
I were a goose I'd be cooked. Ask me how do I feel, __ ask me

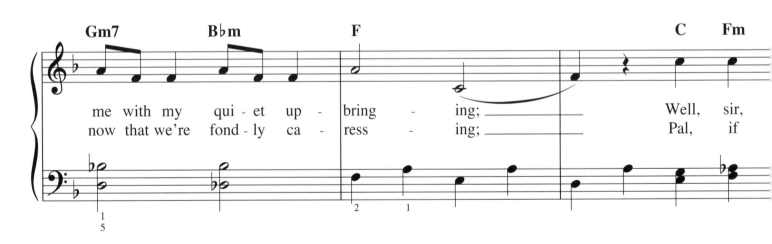

Gm7 — Bbm — F — C — Fm

me with my qui-et up-bring - ing; ___ Well, sir,
now that we're fond-ly ca - ress - ing; ___ Pal, if

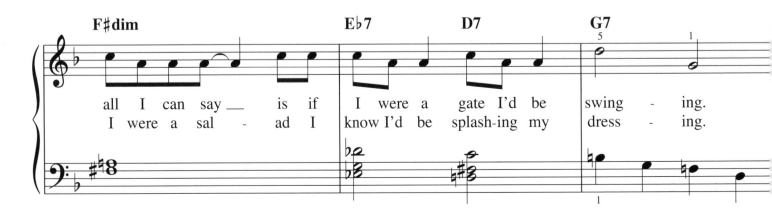

F#dim — Eb7 — D7 — G7

all I can say __ is if I were a gate I'd be swing - ing.
I were a sal - ad I know I'd be splash-ing my dress - ing.

IF I WERE A RICH MAN

from the Musical FIDDLER ON THE ROOF

Words by SHELDON HARNIC
Music by JERRY BOC

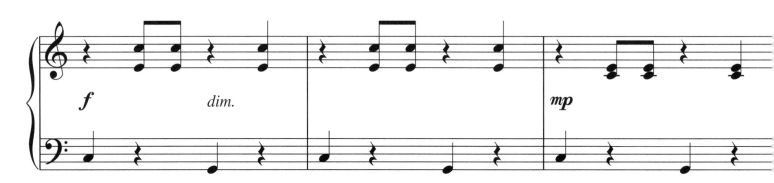

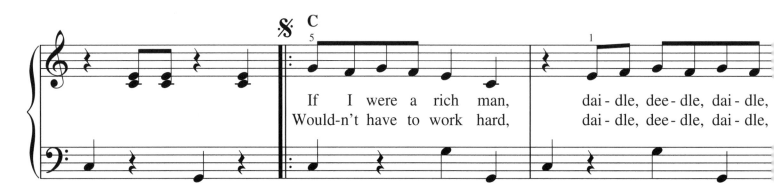

If I were a rich man,
Would-n't have to work hard,

dai - dle, dee - dle, dai - dle,
dai - dle, dee - dle, dai - dle,

dig - guh, dig - guh, dee - dle, dai - dle, dum,
dig - guh, dig - guh, dee - dle, dai - dle, dum,

all day long I'd
if I were a

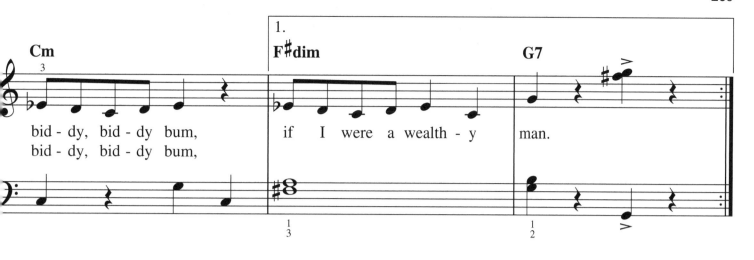

bid - dy, bid - dy bum,   if I were a wealth - y   man.
bid - dy, bid - dy bum,

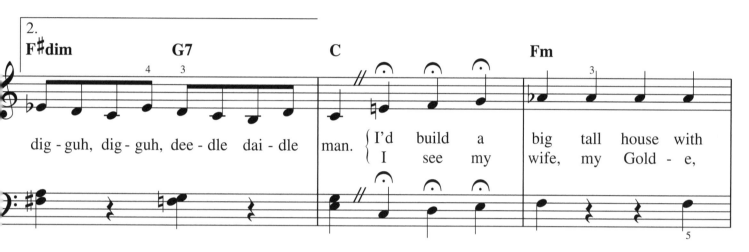

dig - guh, dig - guh, dee - dle dai - dle   man. { I'd build a   big tall house with
                                     { I see my   wife, my Gold - e,

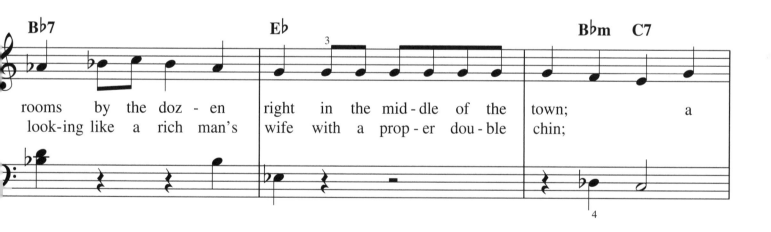

rooms by the doz - en   right in the mid - dle of the   town;   a
look - ing like a rich man's   wife with a prop - er dou - ble   chin;

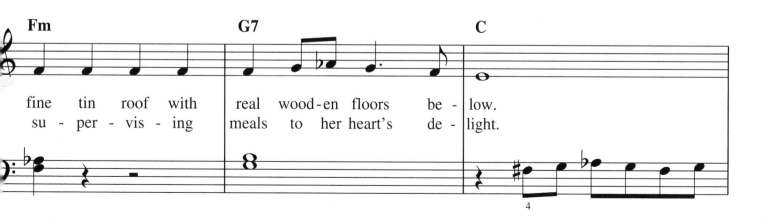

fine tin roof with   real wood - en floors be - low.
su - per - vis - ing   meals to her heart's de - light.

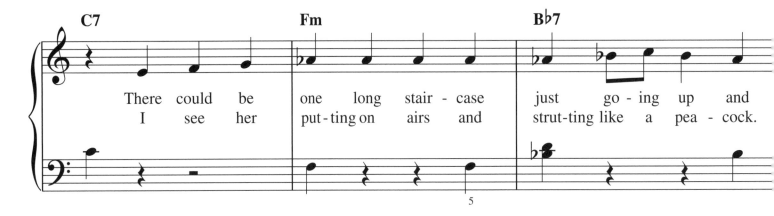

C7　　　　　　　　　　　**Fm**　　　　　　　　　　**B♭7**

There could be | one long stair - case | just go - ing up and
I see her | put - ting on airs and | strut-ting like a pea - cock.

E♭　　　　　　　　　　**B♭m6**　**C7**　　　　**Fm**

one e - ven long - er com - ing | down,　　　　　and | one more lead - ing
Oy! what a hap - py mood she's | in,　　　　　　　 | scream - ing at the

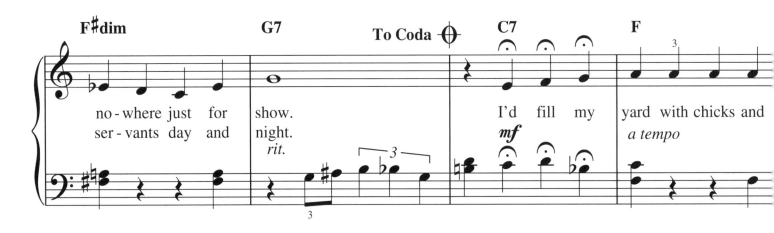

F♯dim　　　　　　　**G7**　　**To Coda**　　　**C7**　　　　**F**

no - where just for | show. | I'd fill my | yard with chicks and
ser - vants day and | night. | | *a tempo*

rit.

mf

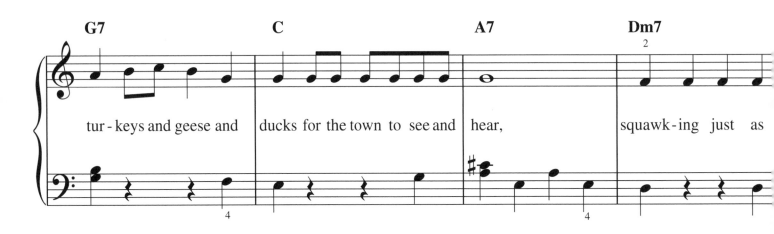

G7　　　　　　　　　**C**　　　　　　　　**A7**　　　　　**Dm7**

tur - keys and geese and | ducks for the town to see and | hear, | squawk-ing just as

no:s - i - ly as they can. And each loud quack and cluck and

gob - ble and honk will land like a trum-pet on the ear, as

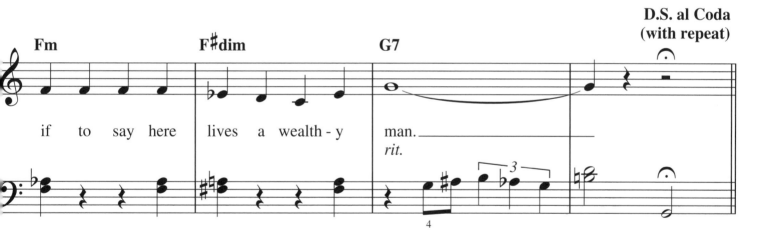

if to say here lives a wealth - y man.

rit.

D.S. al Coda
(with repeat)

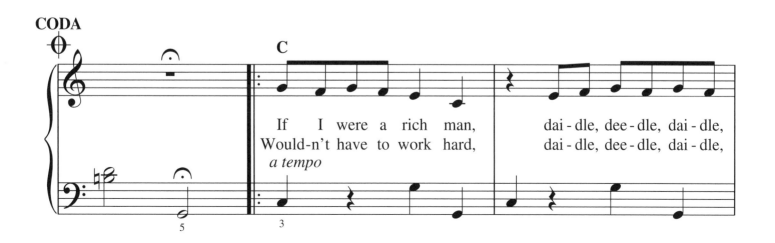

If I were a rich man, dai - dle, dee - dle, dai - dle,
Would-n't have to work hard, dai - dle, dee - dle, dai - dle,

a tempo

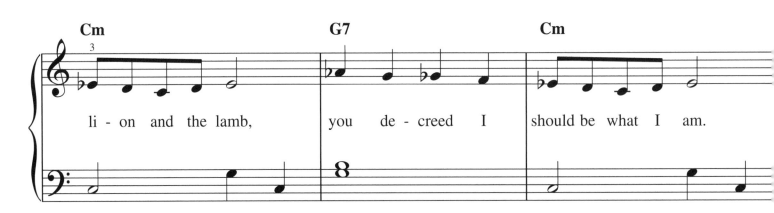

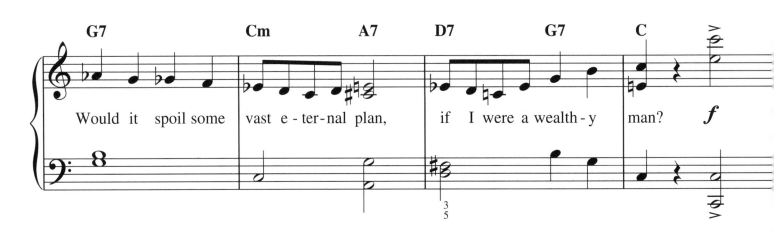

IT COULD HAPPEN TO YOU

from the Paramount Picture AND THE ANGELS SING

Words by JOHNNY BURKE
Music by JAMES VAN HEUSEN

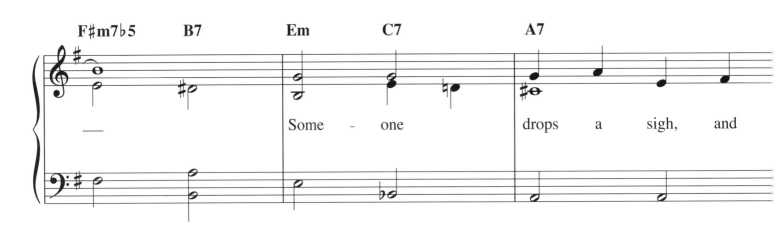

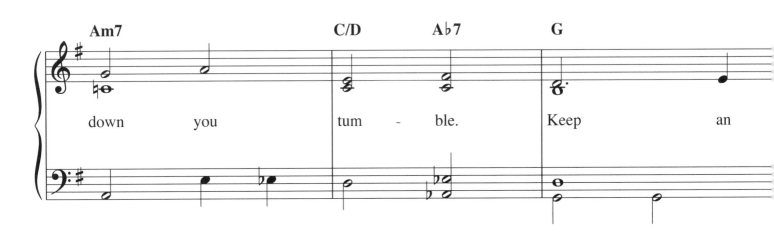

275

THE IMPOSSIBLE DREAM

(The Quest)
from MAN OF LA MANCHA

Lyric by JOE DARION
Music by MITCH LEIGH

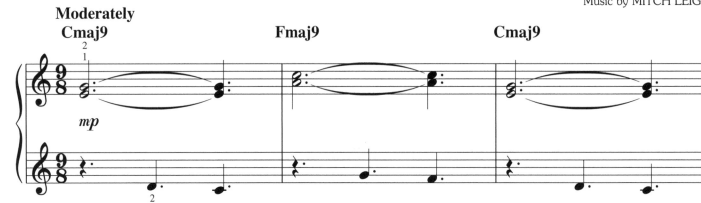

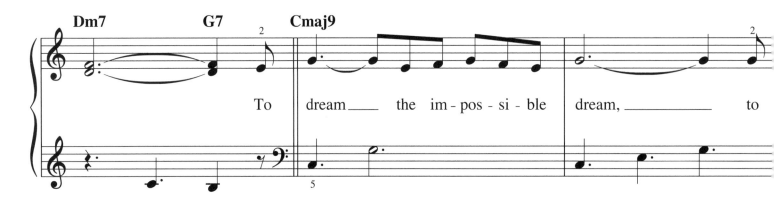

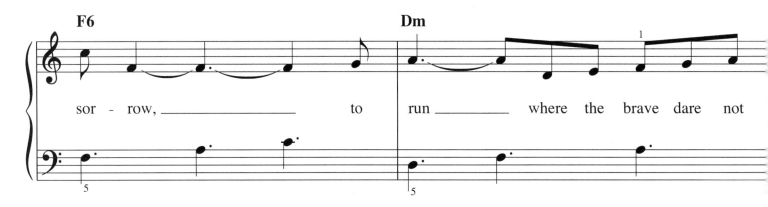

go. _____ To right _____ the un-right-a-ble wrong, _____ to

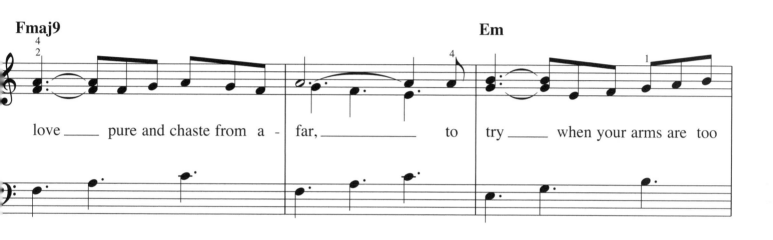

love _____ pure and chaste from a - far, _____ to try _____ when your arms are too

wea-ry, _____ to reach _____ the un-reach-a-ble star! This is my

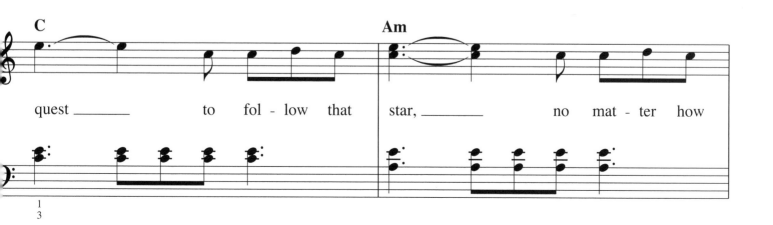

quest _____ to fol-low that star, _____ no mat-ter how

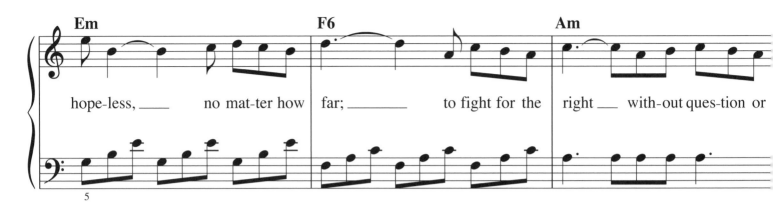

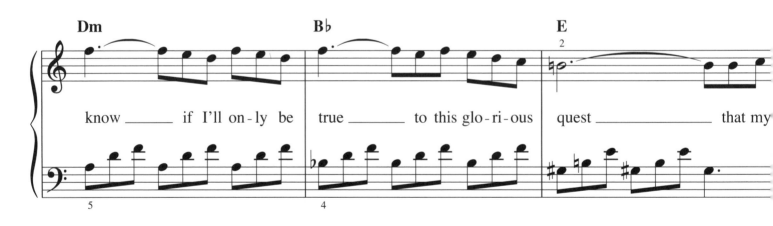

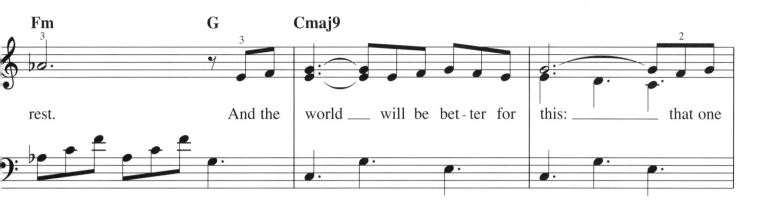

rest.   And the   world ___ will be bet-ter for   this: _____ that one

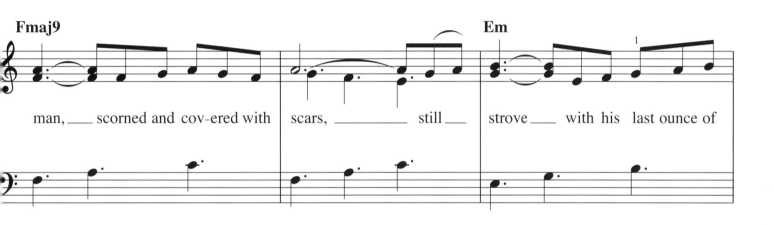

man, ___ scorned and cov-ered with   scars, _____ still ___   strove ___ with his last ounce of

cour - age _____   to   reach ___ the un-reach-a - ble   stars. _____

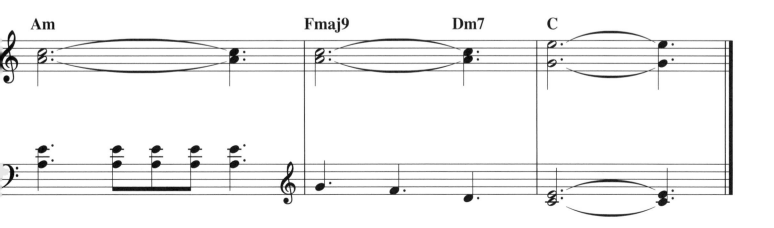

IN THE MOOD

By JOE GARLAND

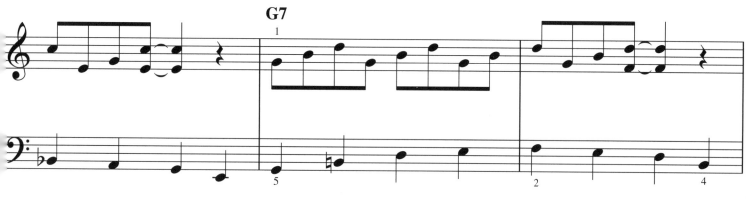

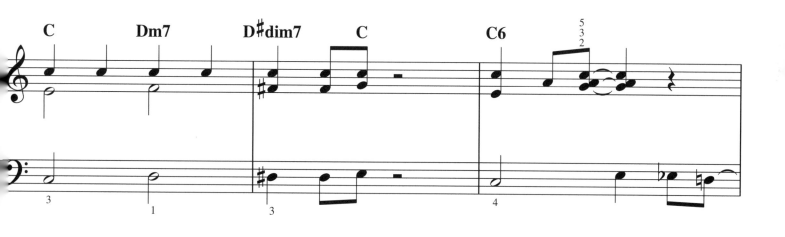

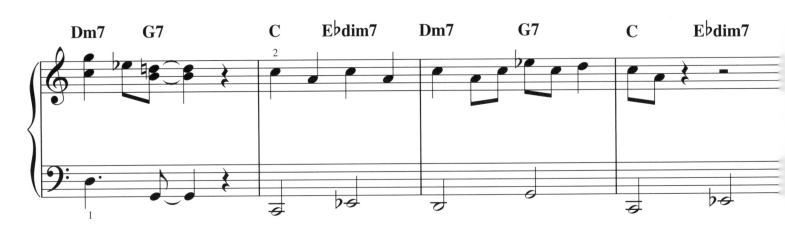

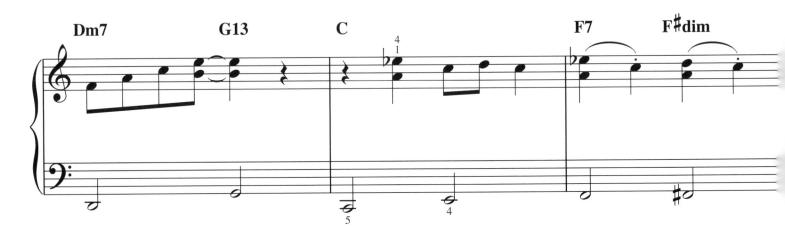

IT NEVER ENTERED MY MIND
from HIGHER AND HIGHER

Words by LORENZ HART
Music by RICHARD RODGERS

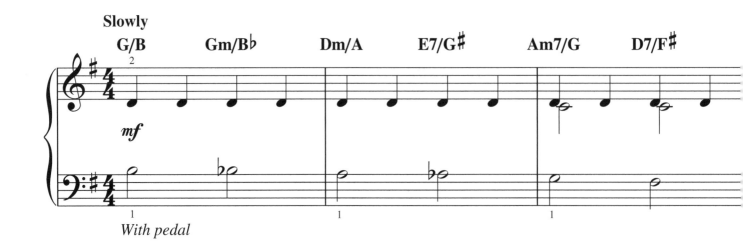

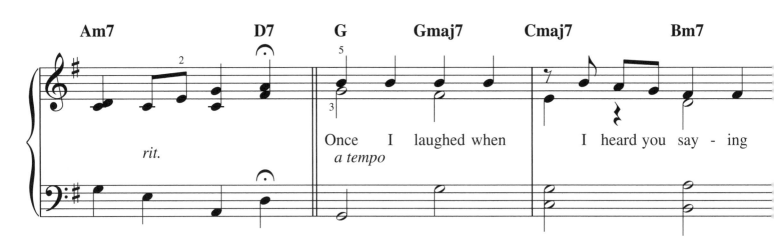

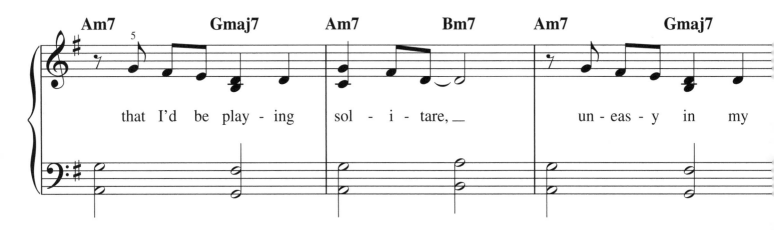

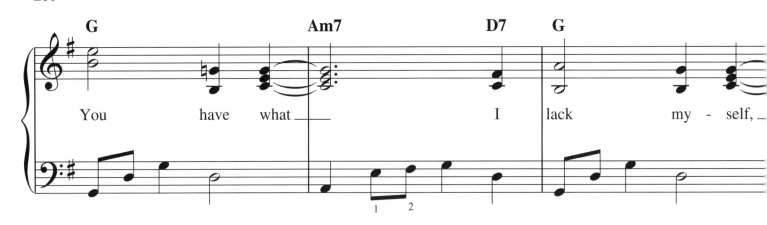

You have what ____ I lack my - self, ____

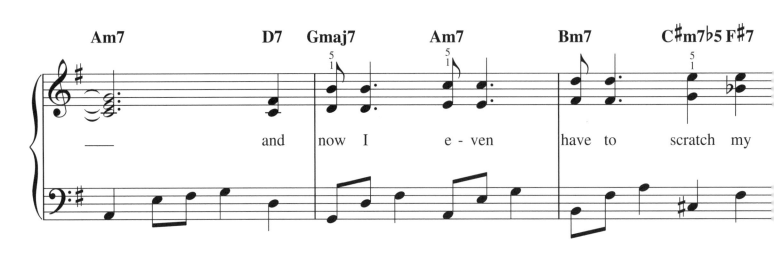

____ and now I e - ven have to scratch my

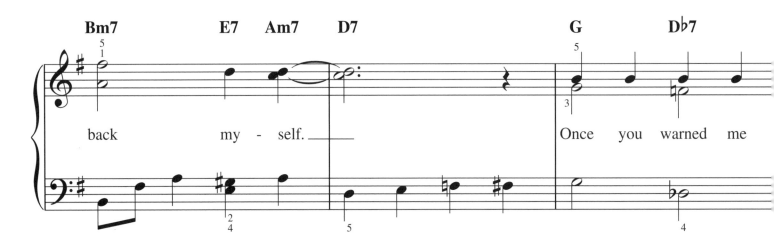

back my - self. ____ Once you warned me

that if you scorned me, I'd sing the maid - en's

IT'S A BIG WIDE WONDERFUL WORLD

from ALL IN FUN

Lyric and Music
JOHN RO[...]

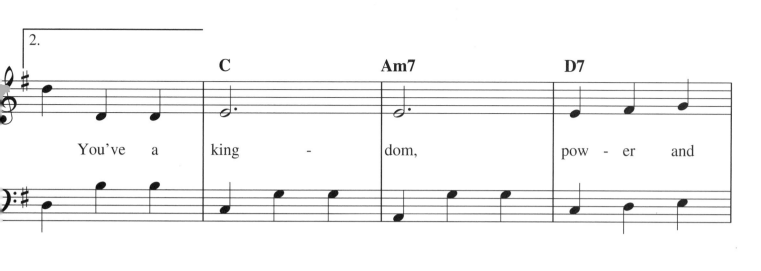

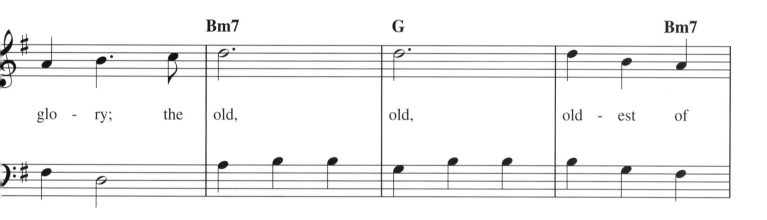

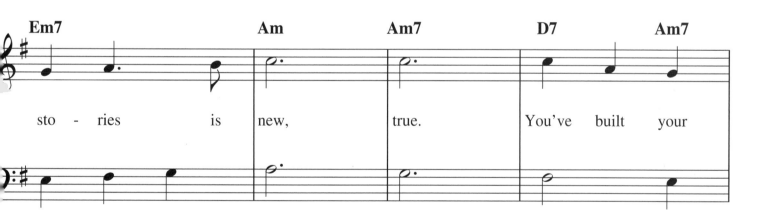

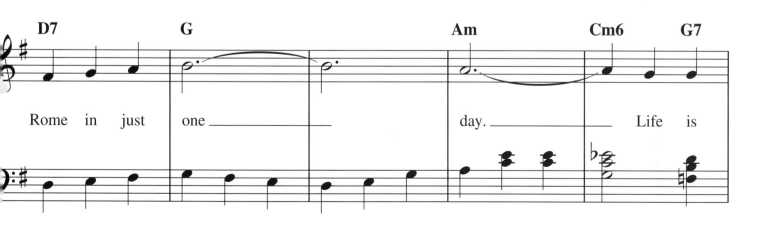

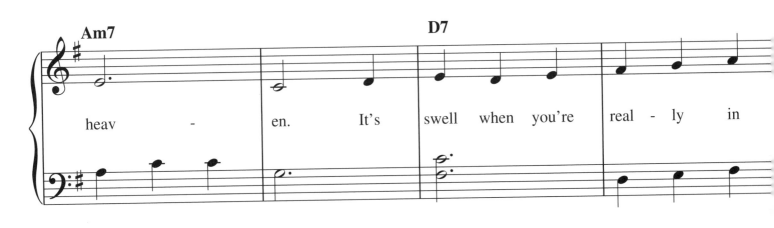

JUNE IN JANUARY
from the Paramount Picture HERE IS MY HEART

Words and Music by LEO ROBIN
and RALPH RAINGER

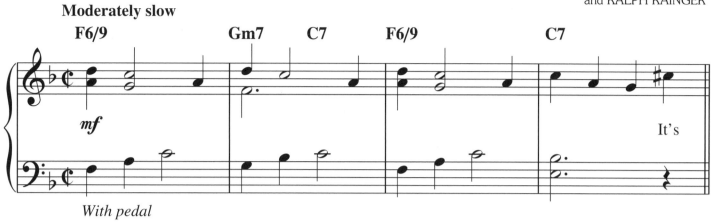

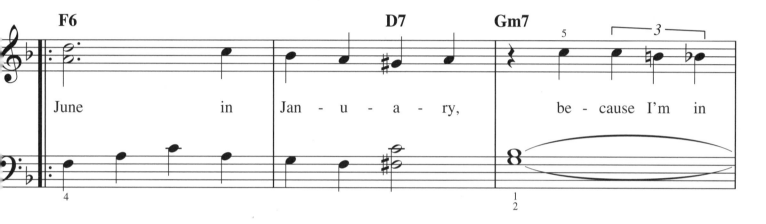

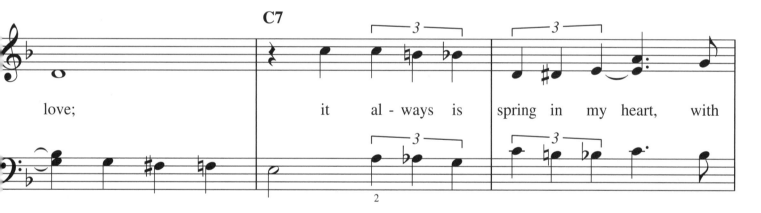

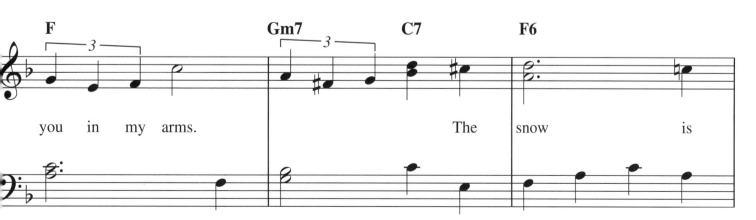

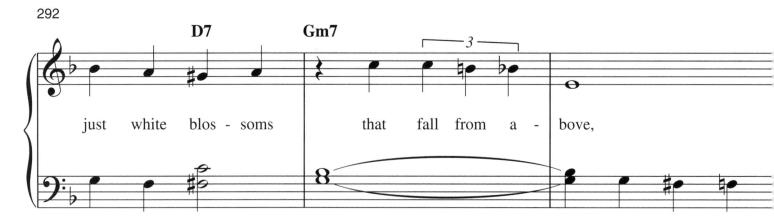

just white blos - soms   that fall from a - bove,

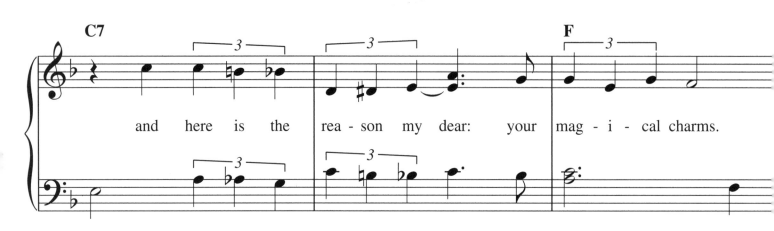

and here is the   rea - son my dear: your   mag - i - cal charms.

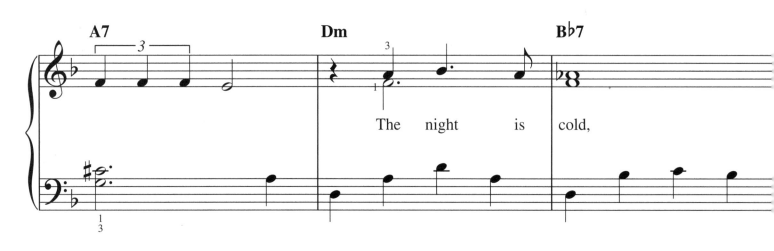

The night is cold,

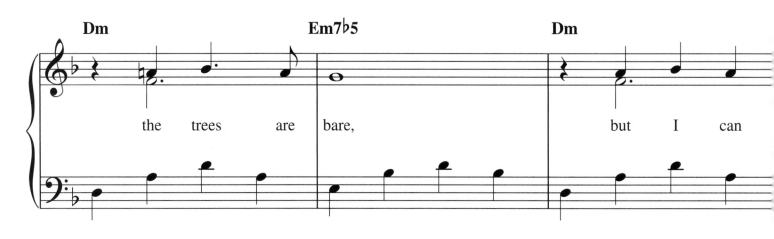

the trees are bare,   but I can

feel the scent of ros - es in the air. It's

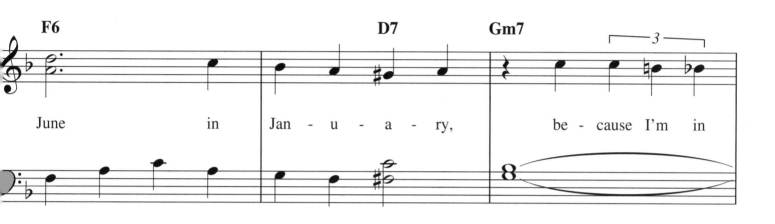

June in Jan - u - a - ry, be - cause I'm in

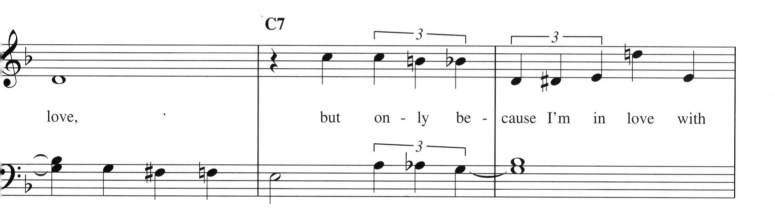

love, but on - ly be - cause I'm in love with

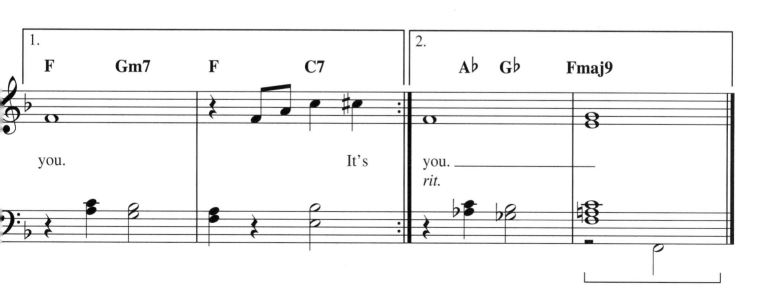

you. It's

you.
rit.

IT'S IMPOSSIBLE
(Somos novios)

English Lyric by SID WAYNE
Spanish Words and Music by ARMANDO MANZANERO

Somos no - vios ___ pues los
It's im - pos - si - ble, tell the

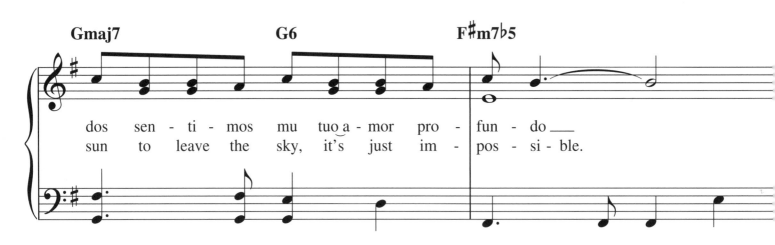

dos sen - ti - mos mu tuo a - mor pro - fun - do ___
sun to leave the sky, it's just im - pos - si - ble.

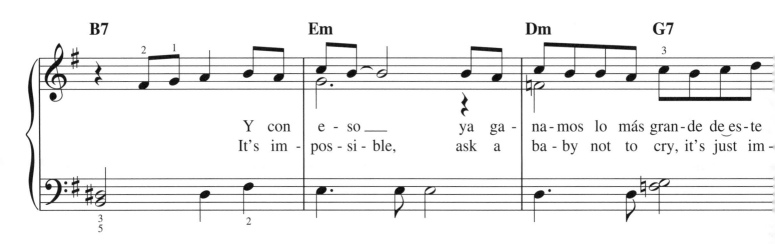

Y con e - so ___ ya ga - na - mos lo más gran - de de es - te
It's im - pos - si - ble, ask a ba - by not to cry, it's just im-

ne - mos un ca - ri - ño lim - pio y | pu - ro.___
rush - ing to the shore? It's just im - | pos - si - ble.

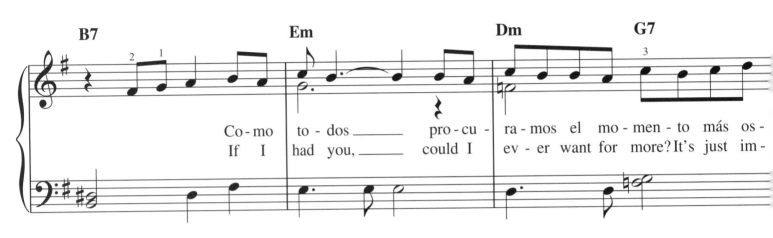

Co - mo | to - dos _____ pro - cu - | ra - mos el mo - men - to más os -
If I | had you, _____ could I | ev - er want for more? It's just im -

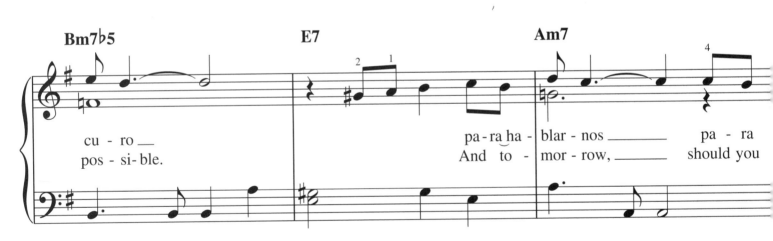

cu - ro ___ | pa - ra ha - blar - nos _____ pa - ra
pos - si - ble. | And to - mor - row, _____ should you

dar - nos el más dul - ce de los | be - sos _____ re - cor -
ask me for the world, some - how I'd | get it. _____ I would

IT'S SO NICE TO HAVE A MAN AROUND THE HOUSE

Lyric by JACK ELLIOT
Music by HAROLD SPINA

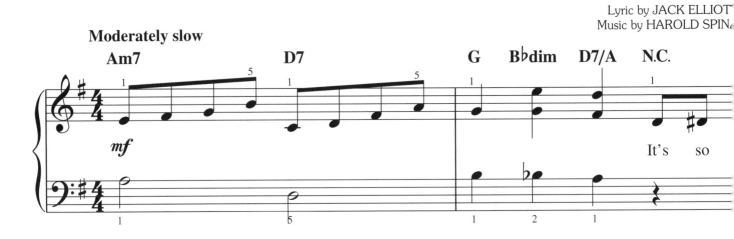

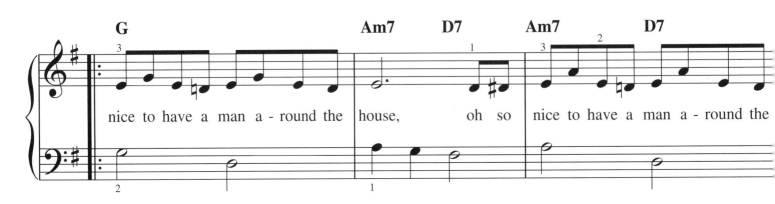

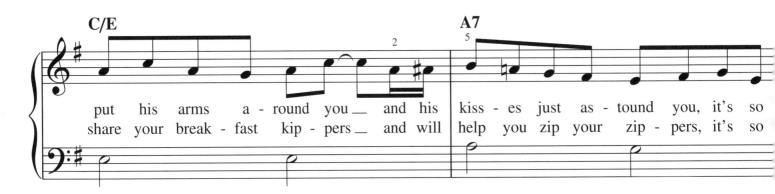

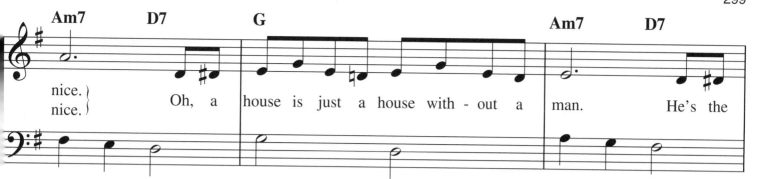

Am7   **D7**   **G**   **Am7**   **D7**

nice. }
nice. }   Oh, a   house is just a house with-out a   man.   He's the

Am7   **D7**   **G**   **G7**   **G7/F**

nec-es-sar-y e-vil in your plan.

{There are   man-y things a-bout him, you just
{Some-one   kind who knows you treas-ure an-y

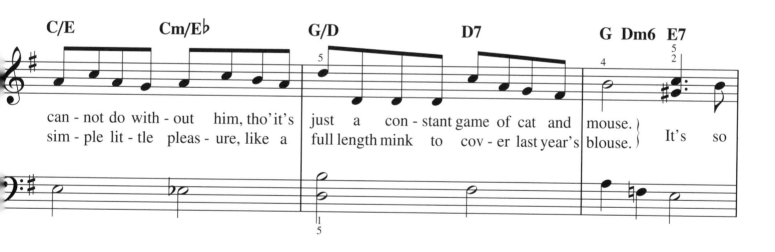

C/E   **Cm/E♭**   **G/D**   **D7**   **G Dm6 E7**

can-not do with-out   him, tho' it's   just a   con-stant game of cat and   mouse. }
sim-ple lit-tle pleas-ure, like a   full length mink to cov-er last year's blouse. }   It's so

Am7   **D7**   **1. G B♭dim D7/A N.C.**   **2. G D7 G**

nice to have a man a-round the   house.   It's so   house.

JUST ONE MORE CHANCE

Words by SAM COSLOW
Music by ARTHUR JOHNSTON

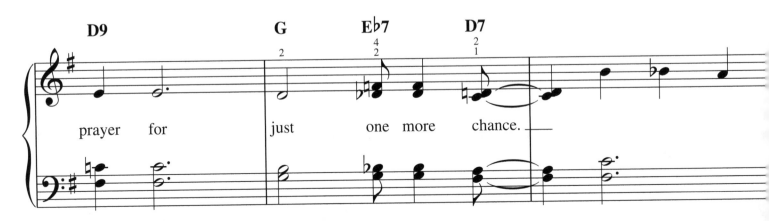

Just one more night ____ to taste the kiss - es that en -

chant me. I'd want no oth - ers if you'd grant me

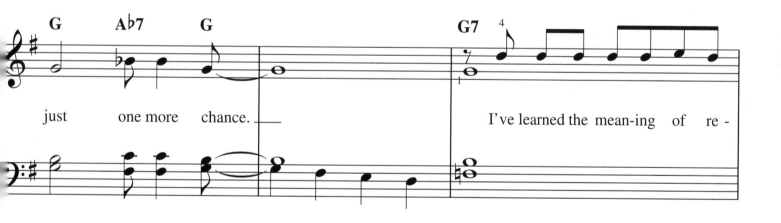

just one more chance. ____ I've learned the mean-ing of re -

pen - tance, now you're the ju - ry at my trial.

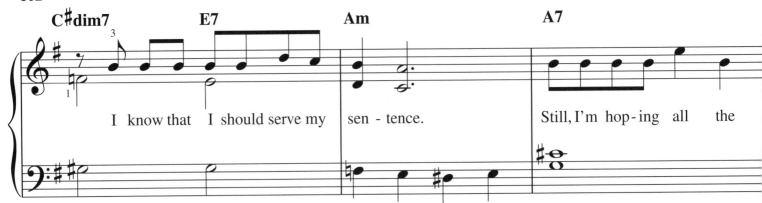

I know that I should serve my sen - tence. Still, I'm hop-ing all the

while you'll give me just one more word.

I said that I was glad to start out, but now I'm back to cry my

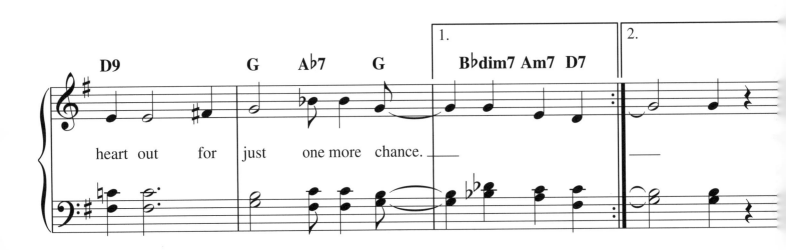

heart out for just one more chance.

LAZYBONES

Words and Music by HOAGY CARMICHAEL
and JOHNNY MERCER

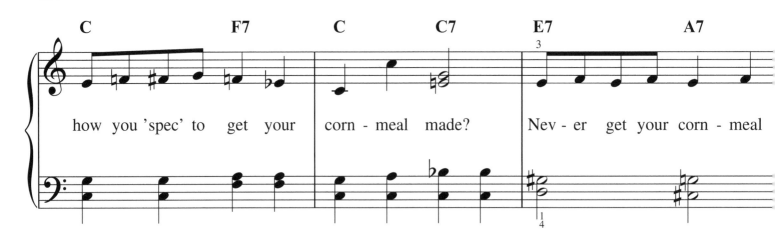

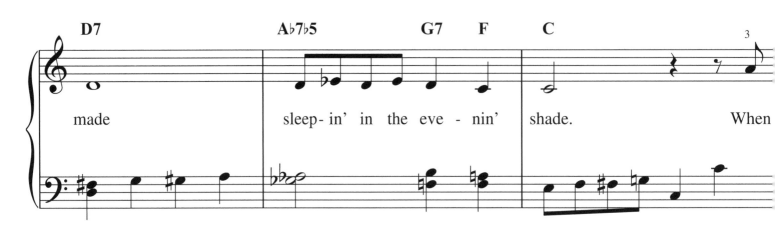

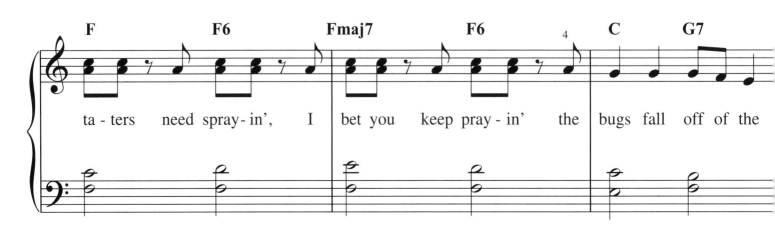

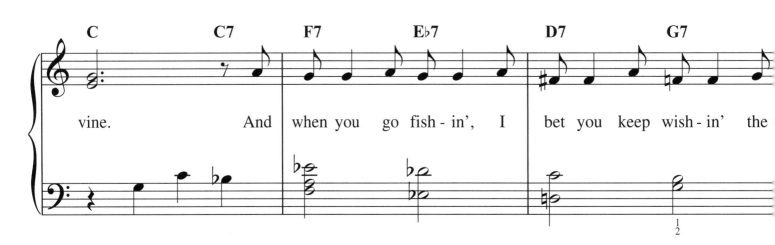

LAZY RIVER

from THE BEST YEARS OF OUR LIVES

Words and Music by HOAGY CARMICHAEL
and SIDNEY ARODIN

LITTLE GIRL BLUE
from JUMBO

Words by LORENZ HART
Music by RICHARD RODGERS

When I was ver-y young the world was ev'ry
strung the with

young-er than I, as mer-ry as a car-ou-
star in the sky a-bove the ring I loved so

1.
sel. The cir-cus tent was

2.
well. _____

2. F   E♭   D♭   F   C7

blue.   No use, old   girl,   you   may as well sur-

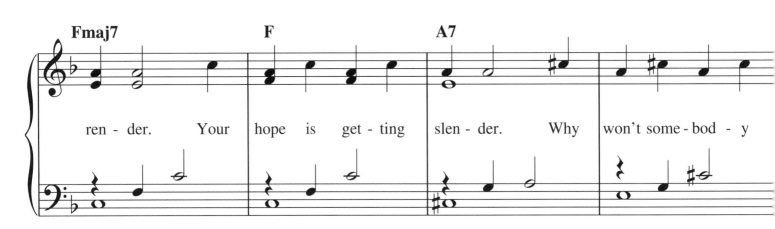

Fmaj7   F   A7

ren - der.   Your   hope   is   get - ting   slen - der.   Why   won't some-bod-y

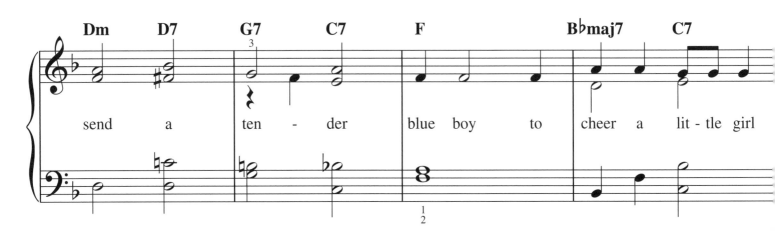

Dm   D7   G7   C7   F   B♭maj7   C7

send   a   ten - der   blue boy   to   cheer a   lit-tle girl

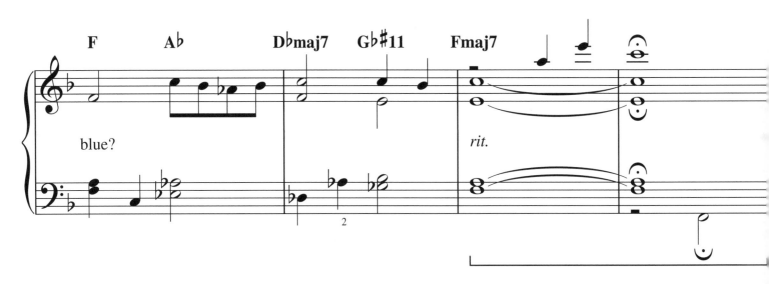

F   A♭   D♭maj7   G♭#11   Fmaj7

blue?   *rit.*

LONG AGO
(And Far Away)
from COVER GIRL

Words by IRA GERSHWIN
Music by JEROME KERN

LOVE IS JUST AROUND THE CORNER

from the Paramount Picture HERE IS MY HEART

Words and Music by LEO ROBIN
and LEWIS E. GENSLER

Lyrics: Love is just a-round the cor-ner, an-y co-zy lit-tle cor-ner. Love is just a-round the cor-ner when I'm a-round you. I'm a sen-ti-men-tal

mourn - er   and   I could - n't be   for - lorn - er,

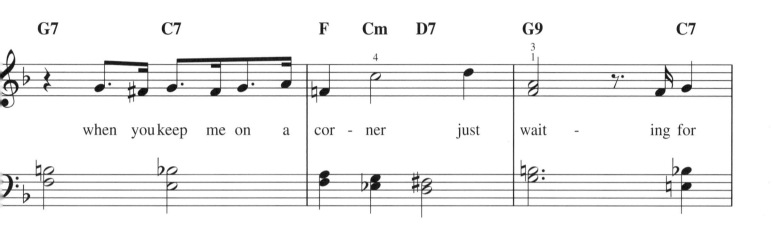

when you keep me on   a   cor - ner   just   wait -   ing for

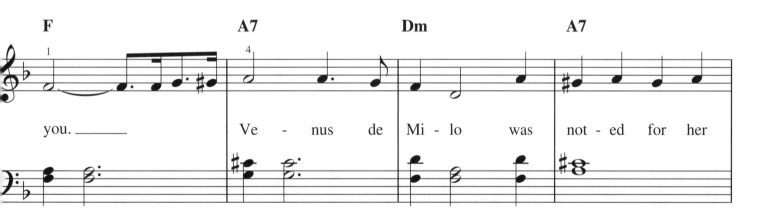

you. _____   Ve - nus de   Mi - lo   was   not - ed for her

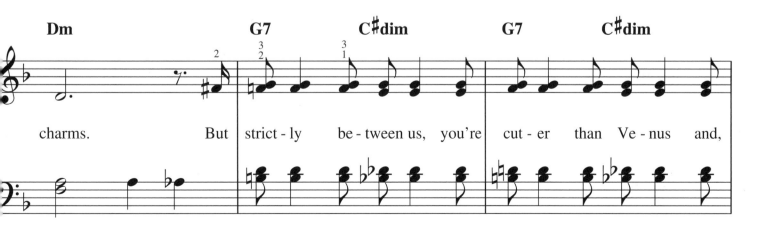

charms.   But strict - ly   be - tween us, you're   cut - er   than Ve - nus and,

whats's more, you got arms. So let's go cud-dle in a cor-ner,

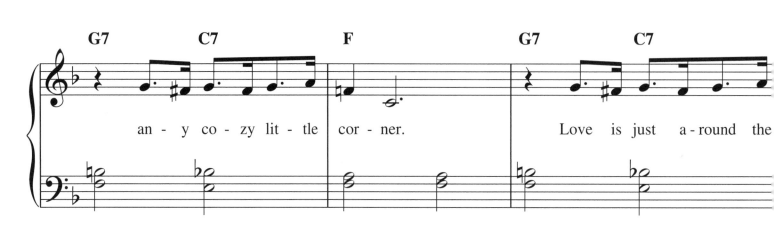

an - y co - zy lit - tle cor - ner. Love is just a - round the

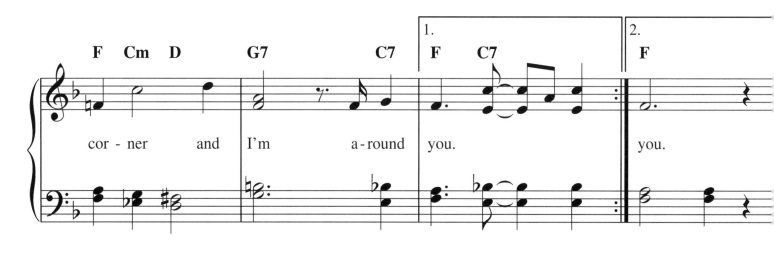

cor - ner and I'm a - round you. you.

Oo. _____

LULLABY OF BIRDLAND

Words by GEORGE DAVID WEISS
Music by GEORGE SHEARING

LOVER
from the Paramount Picture LOVE ME TONIGHT

Words by LORENZ HART
Music by RICHARD RODGERS

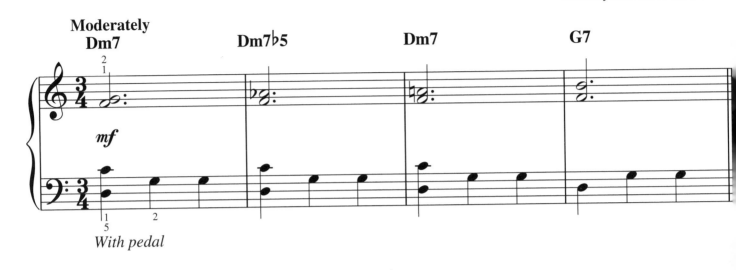

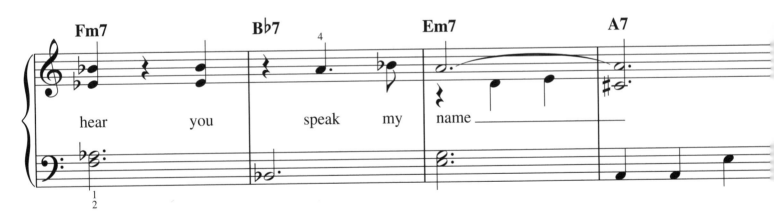

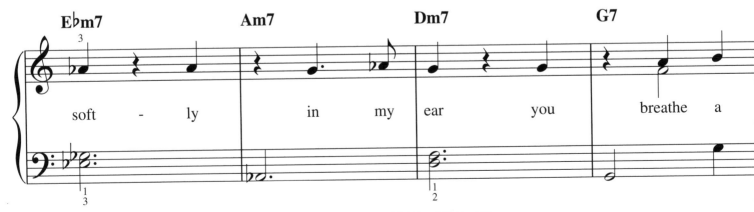

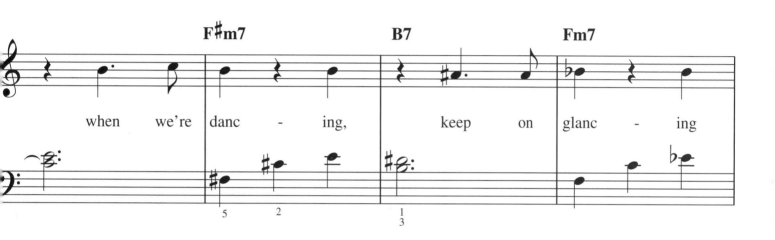

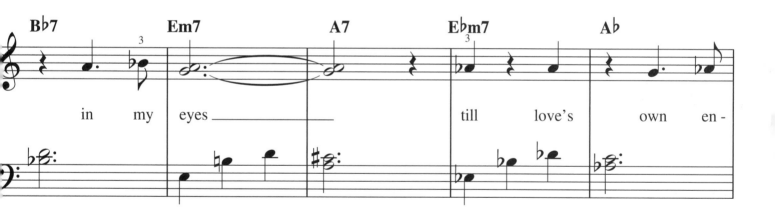

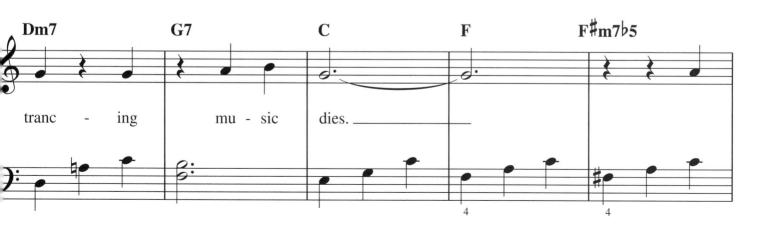

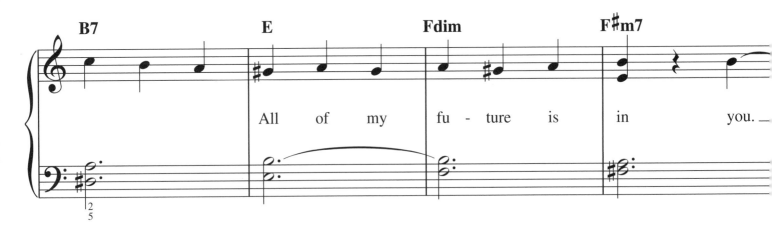

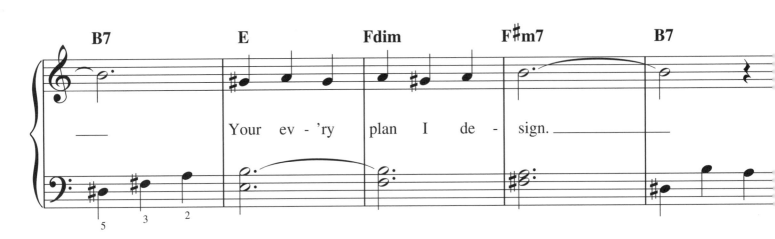

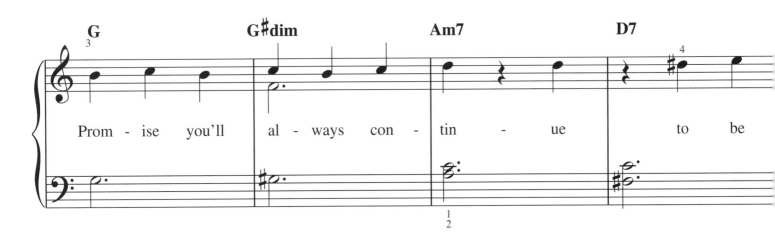

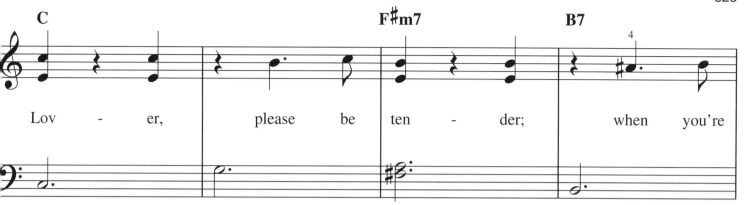

Lov - er, please be ten - der; when you're

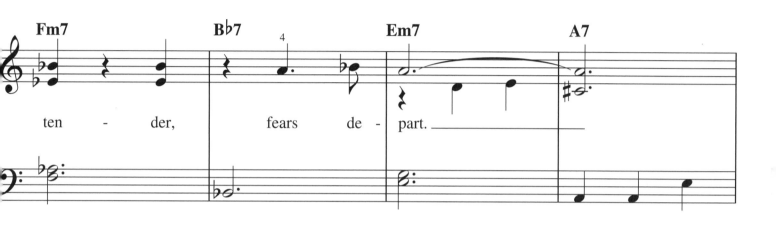

ten - der, fears de - part.

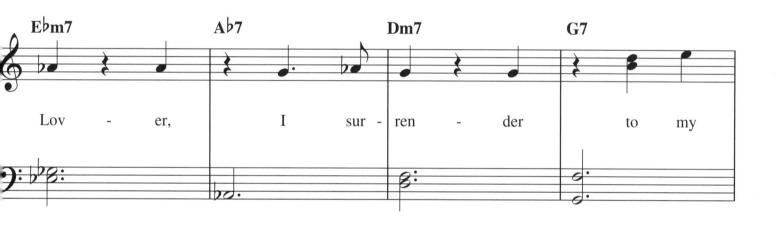

Lov - er, I sur - ren - der to my

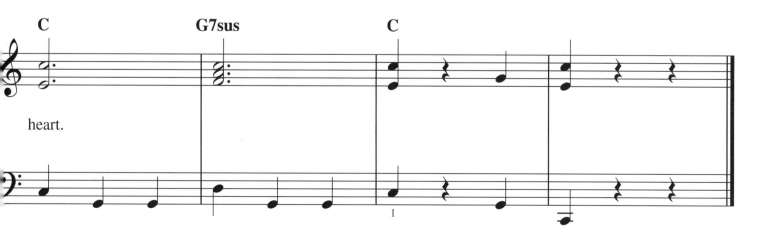

heart.

MAKE BELIEVE

from SHOW BOAT

Lyrics by OSCAR HAMMERSTEIN II
Music by JEROME KERN

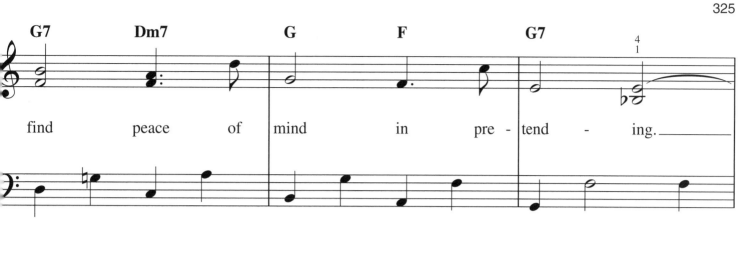

find   peace   of   mind   in   pre - tend   -   ing.___

___   Could - n't   you?   Could - n't   I?   Could - n't

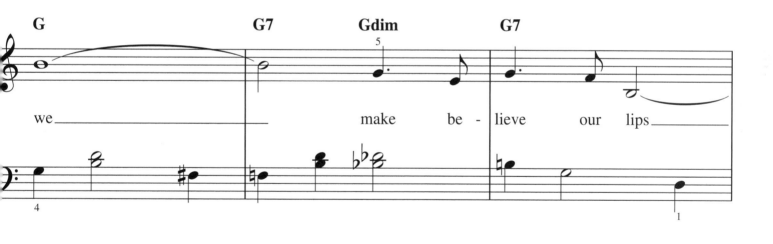

we___   make   be - lieve   our   lips___

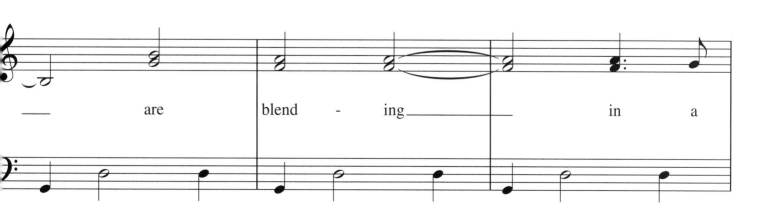

___   are   blend   -   ing___   in   a

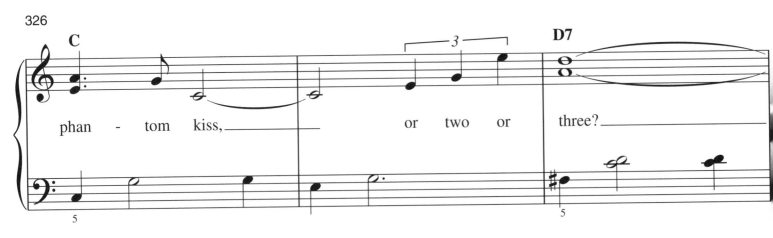

phan - tom kiss, _____ or two or three? _____

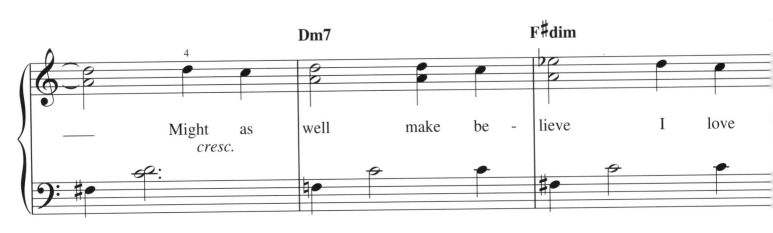

Might as well make be - lieve I love

cresc.

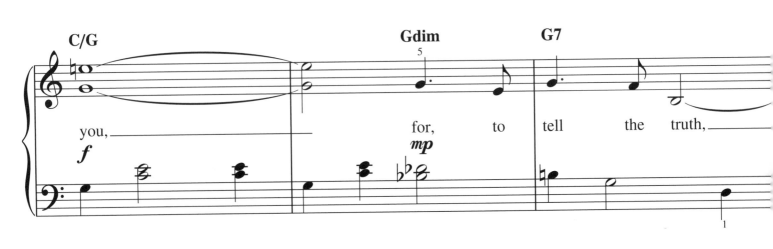

you, _____ for, to tell the truth, _____

f

mp

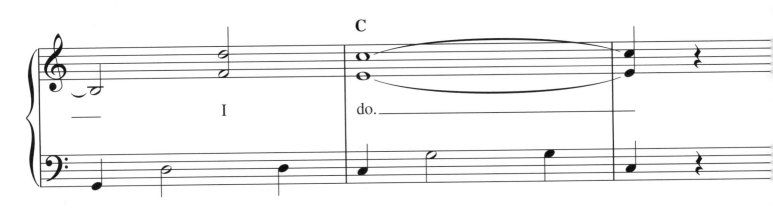

I do. _____

MISTER SANDMAN

Lyric and Music by
PAT BALLARD

A7

peach - es and cream. ___
I've ev - er seen. ___

D7

Give her two
Give him the

G7

lips   like   ros - es   in   clo - ver, }
word   that   I'm   not   a   ro - ver, }

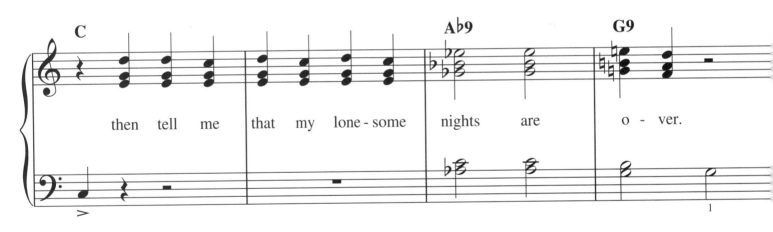

C

then tell me   that my lone-some   nights are   o - ver.

Ab9   **G9**

C

Sand - man,

B7

I'm so a - lone, ___

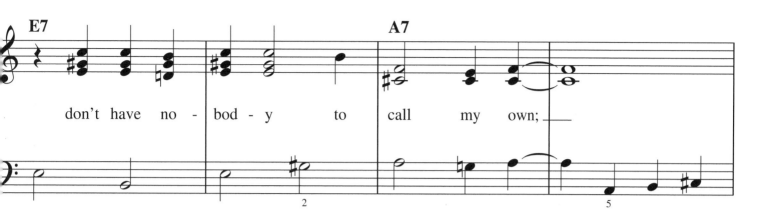

don't have no - bod - y to call my own; ___

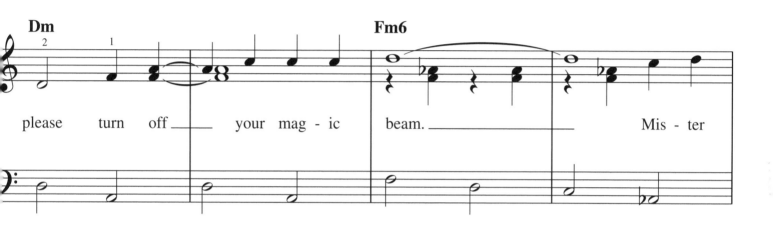

please turn off ___ your mag - ic beam. ___ Mis - ter

Sand - man, bring me a dream. Mis - ter

dream.

MANHATTAN
from the Broadway Musical THE GARRICK GAIETIES

Words by LORENZ HART
Music by RICHARD RODGERS

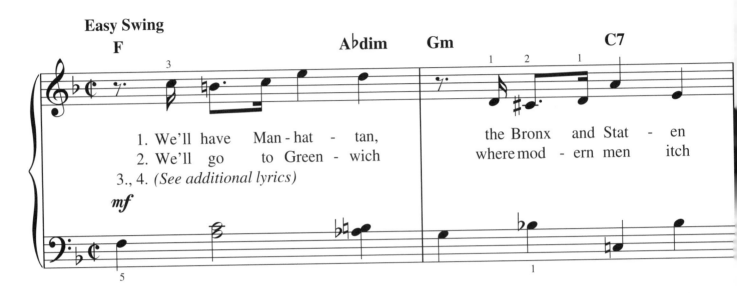

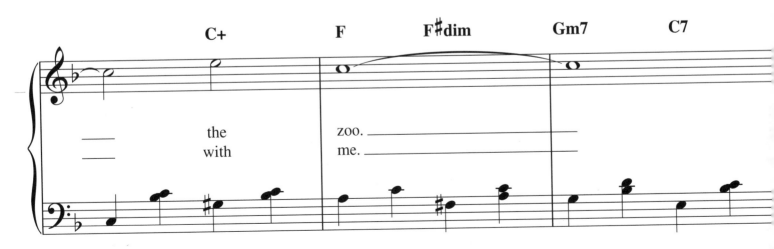

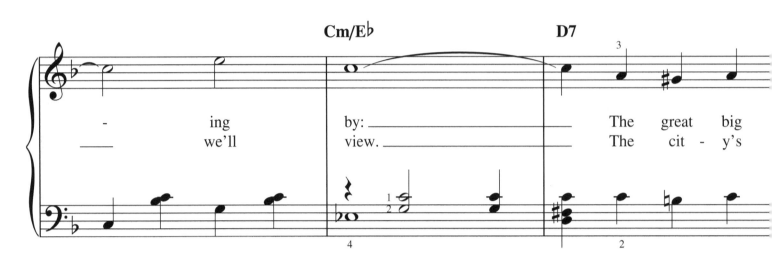

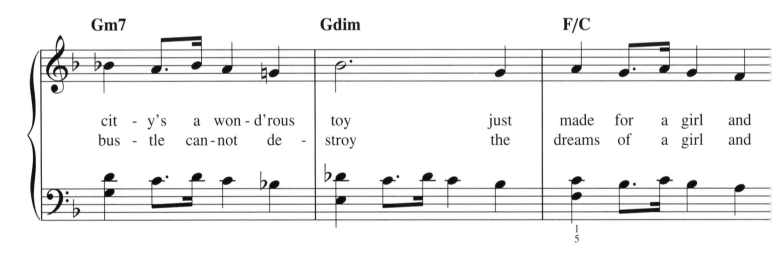

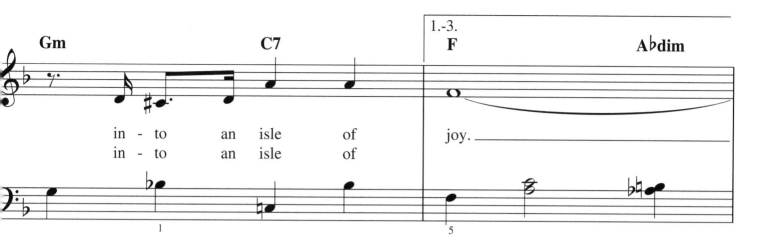

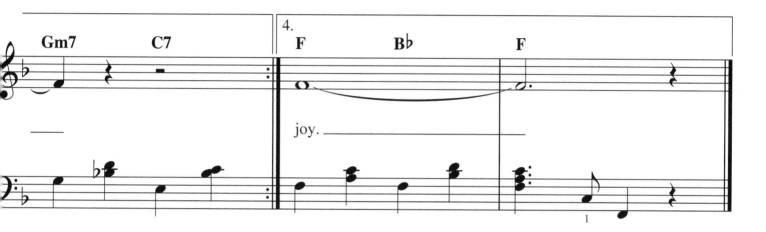

Additional Lyrics

3. We'll go to Yonkers where true love conquers in the wilds;
   And starve together, dear, in Childs'.
   We'll go to Coney and eat bologny on a roll;
   In Central Park we'll stroll, where our first kiss we stole, soul to soul.
   And for some high fare, we'll go to "My Fair Lady," say,
   We'll hope to see it close some day.
   The city's clamor can never spoil
   The dreams of a boy and goil.
   We'll turn Manhattan into an isle of joy.

4. We'll have Manhattan, the Bronx and Staten Island, too;
   We'll try to cross Fifth Avenue.
   As black as onyx we'll find the Bronix Park Express;
   Our Flatbush flat, I guess, will be a big success, more or less.
   A short vacation on Inspiration Point we'll spend,
   And in the station house we'll end.
   But civic virtue cannot destroy
   The dreams of a girl and boy.
   We'll turn Manhattan into an isle of joy.

MOON RIVER
from the Paramount Picture BREAKFAST AT TIFFANY'S

Words by JOHNNY MERCE
Music by HENRY MANCI

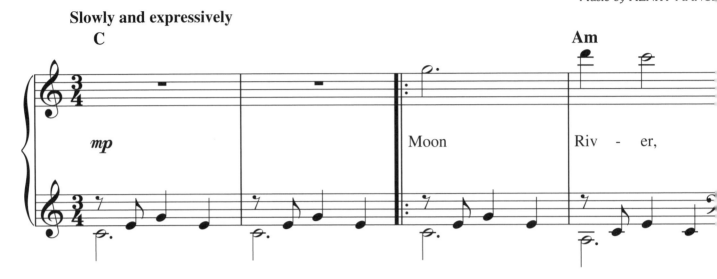

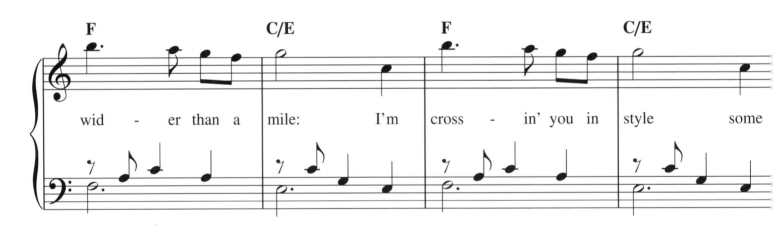

MOONLIGHT BECOMES YOU

from the Paramount Picture ROAD TO MOROCCO

Words by JOHNNY BURKE
Music by JAMES VAN HEUSEN

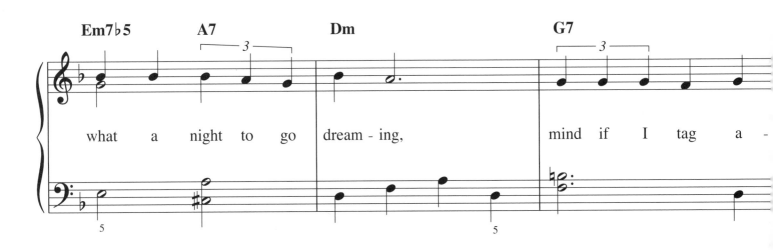

MORE THAN YOU KNOW

Words by WILLIAM ROSE and EDWARD ELISCU
Music by VINCENT YOUMANS

MY FOOLISH HEART
from MY FOOLISH HEART

Words by NED WASHINGTON
Music by VICTOR YOUNG

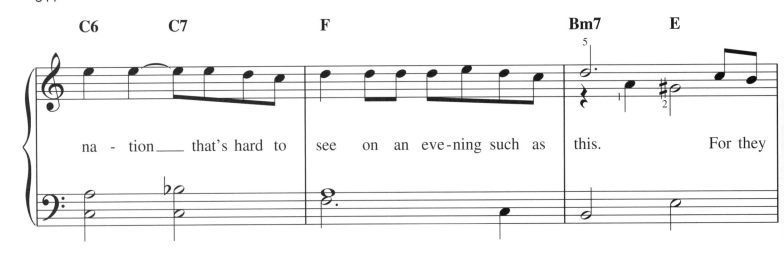

na - tion___ that's hard to see on an eve-ning such as this. For they

both give the ver - y same sen - sa - tion when you're lost in the mag-ic of a

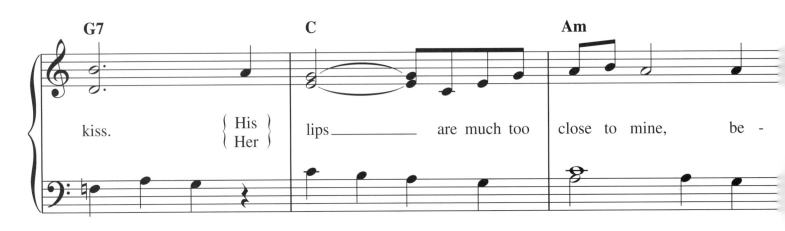

kiss. { His / Her } lips___ are much too close to mine, be -

ware___ my fool-ish heart. But should___ our ea - ger

lips com-bine then let_____ the fire__ start. For

this time it is-n't fas-ci - na - tion or a dream that will fade and fall a-

part. It's love this time, it's love, my fool - ish

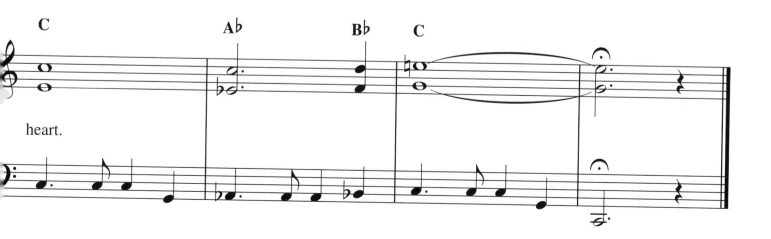

heart.

MY HEART WILL GO ON
(Love Theme from 'Titanic')
from the Paramount and Twentieth Century Fox Motion Picture TITANIC

Music by JAMES HORNE
Lyric by WILL JENNING

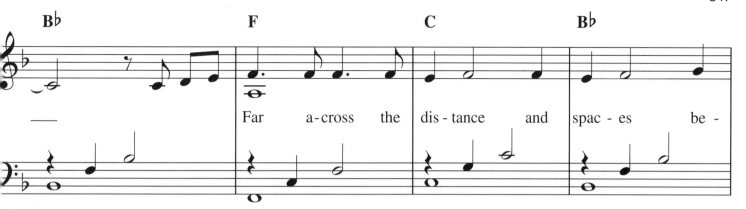

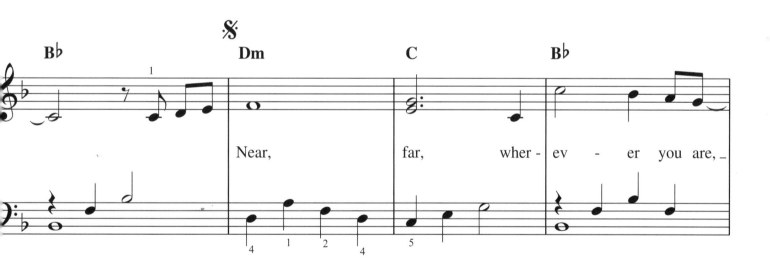

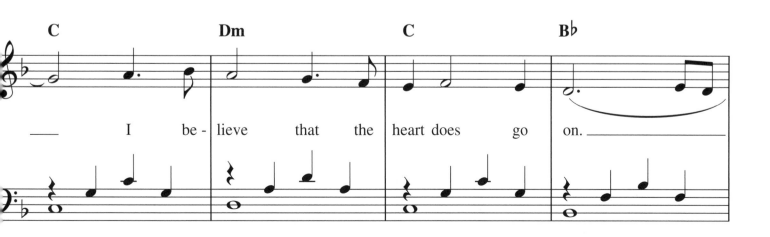

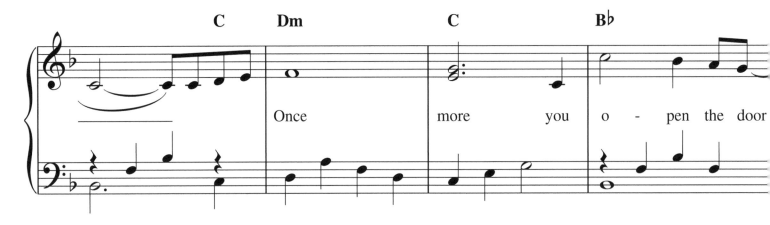

C   **Dm**   **C**   **B♭**

Once   more   you   o - pen the door

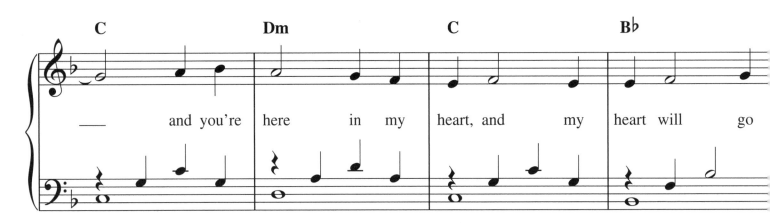

C   **Dm**   **C**   **B♭**

and you're   here   in   my   heart, and   my   heart will   go

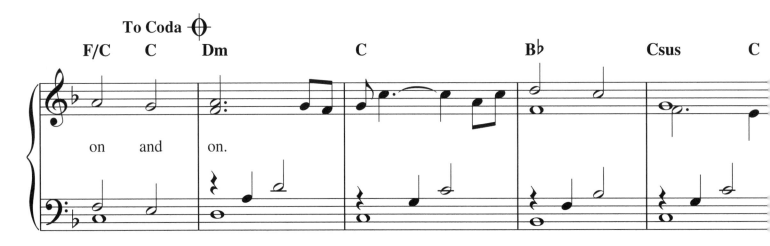

To Coda ⊕

F/C   **C**   **Dm**   **C**   **B♭**   **Csus**   **C**

on   and   on.

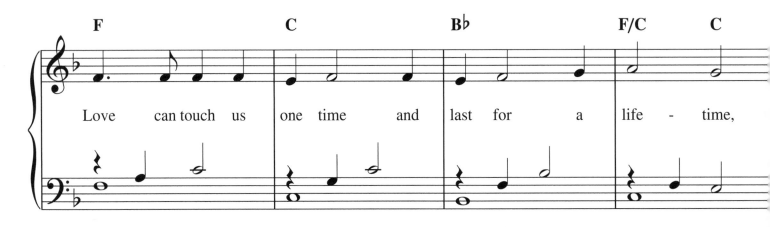

F   **C**   **B♭**   **F/C**   **C**

Love   can touch us   one time   and   last for   a   life - time,

349

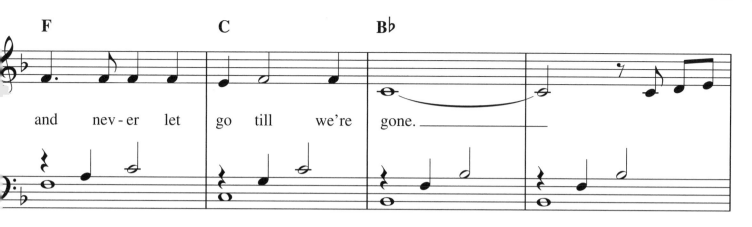

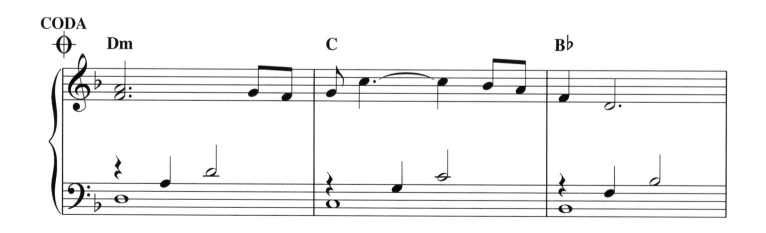

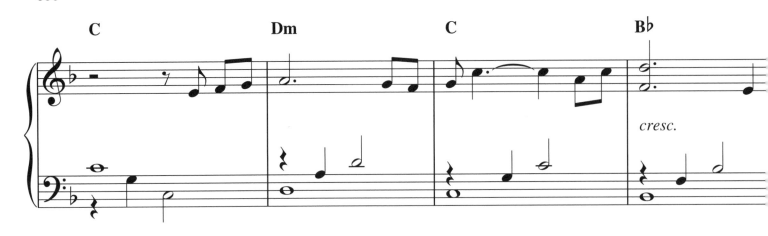

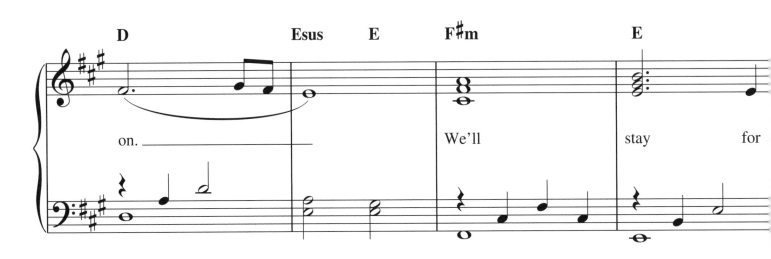

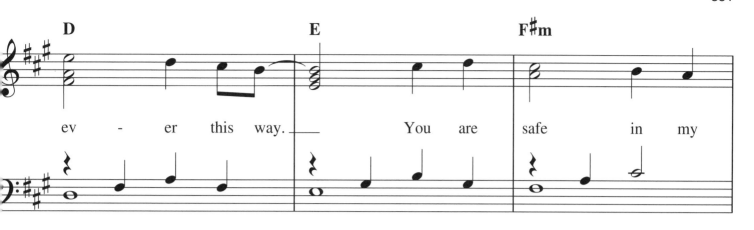

ev - er this way. You are safe in my

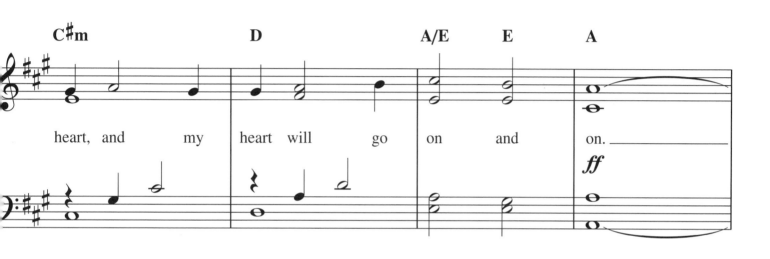

heart, and my heart will go on and on.

ff

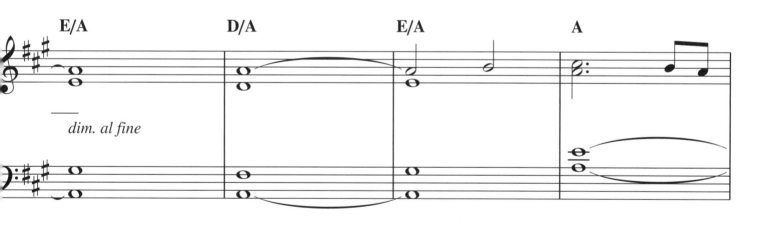

dim. al fine

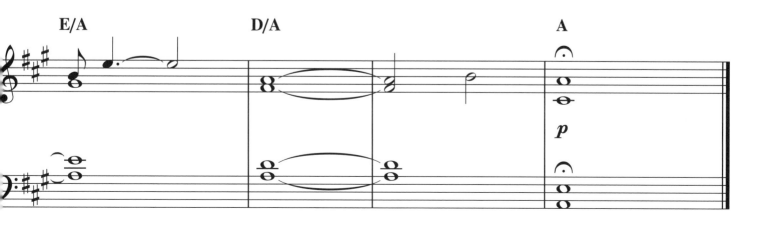

p

MY OLD FLAME

from the Paramount Picture BELLE OF THE NINETIES

Words and Music by ARTHUR JOHNSTO
and SAM COSLO

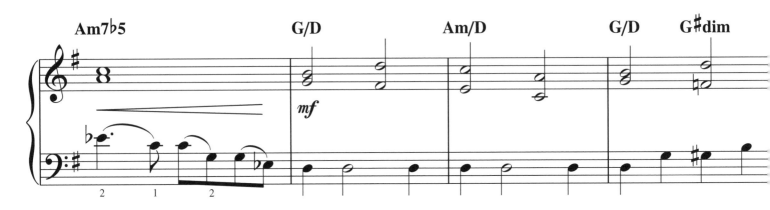

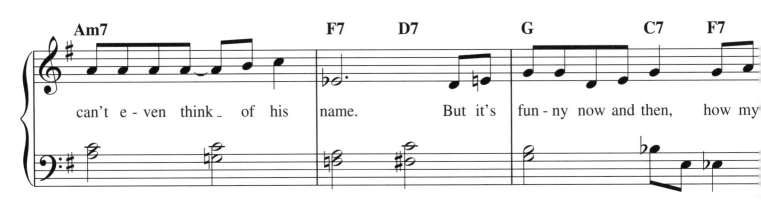

flame. I've met so man - y who had fas - ci - nat - in' ways, a

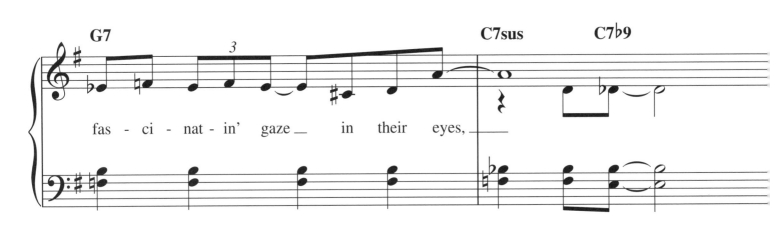

fas - ci - nat - in' gaze in their eyes,

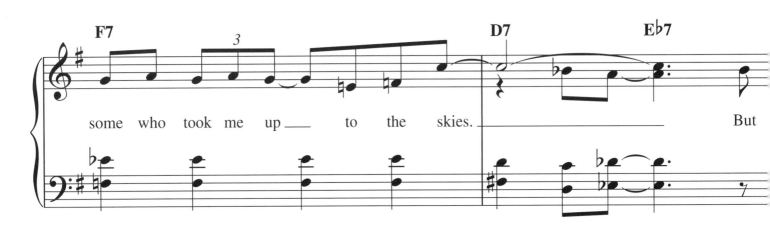

some who took me up to the skies. But

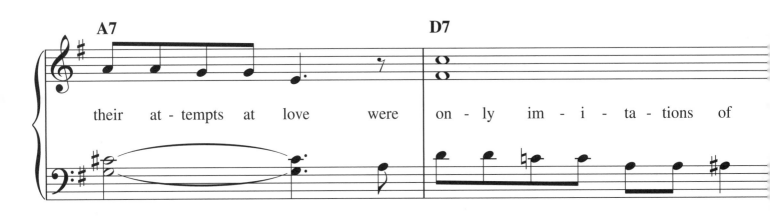

their at - tempts at love were on - ly im - i - ta - tions of

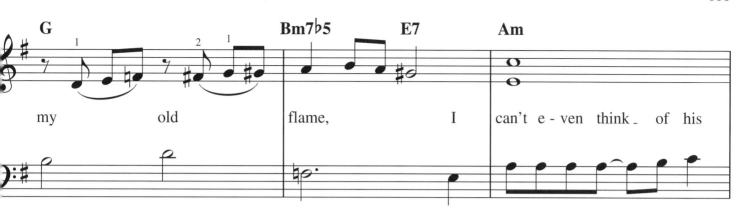

my old flame, I can't e - ven think of his

name. But I'll nev - er be the same, un - til

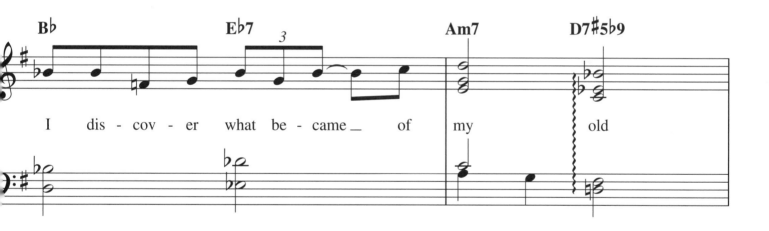

I dis - cov - er what be - came of my old

Very slowly

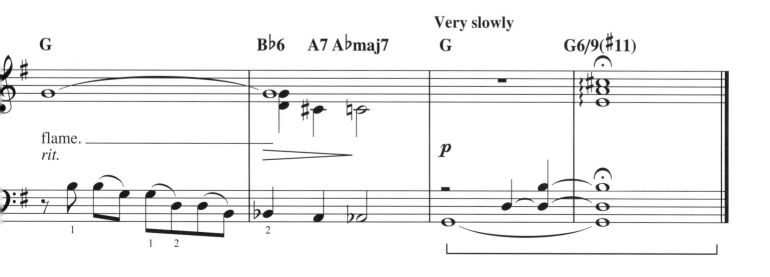

flame.
rit.

MY ONE AND ONLY LOVE

Words by ROBERT MELL
Music by GUY WOO

my one and on - ly love. The

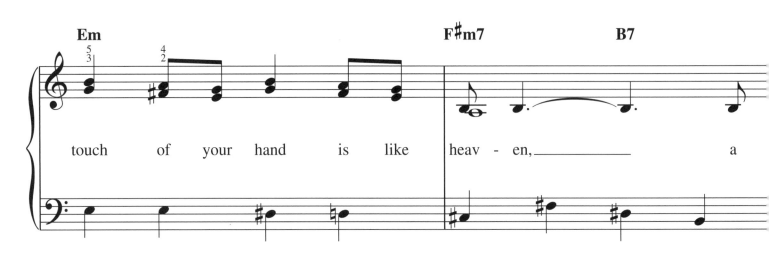

touch of your hand is like heav - en, _____ a

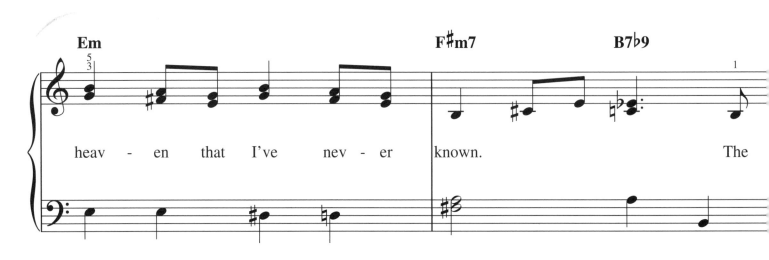

heav - en that I've nev - er known. The

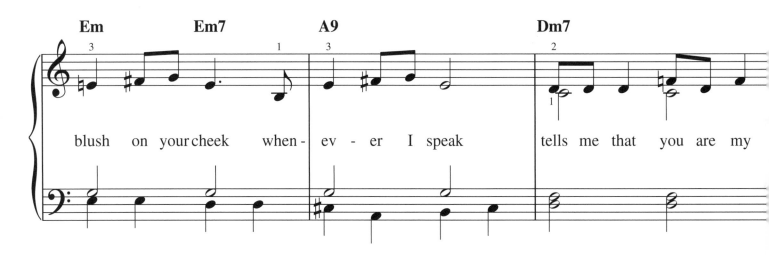

blush on your cheek when - ev - er I speak tells me that you are my

MY SHIP
from the Musical Production LADY IN THE DARK

Words by IRA GERSHWIN
Music by KURT WEILL

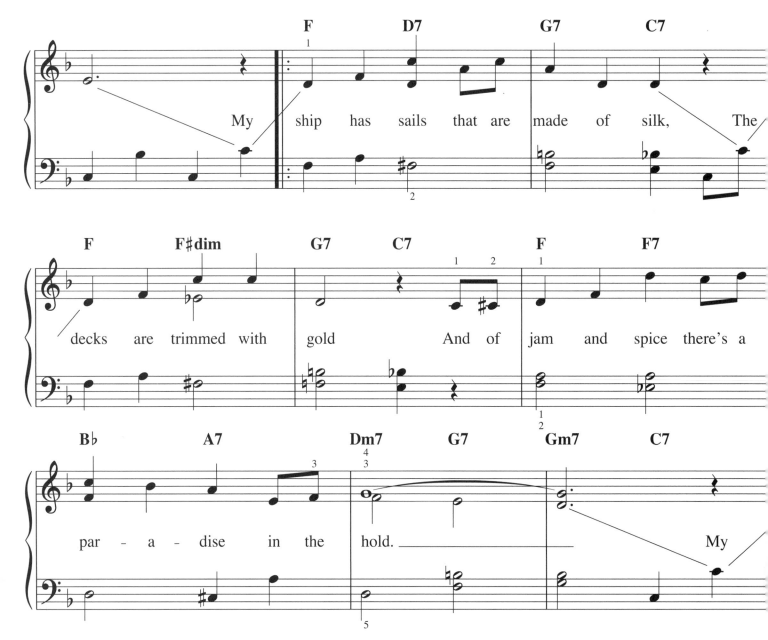

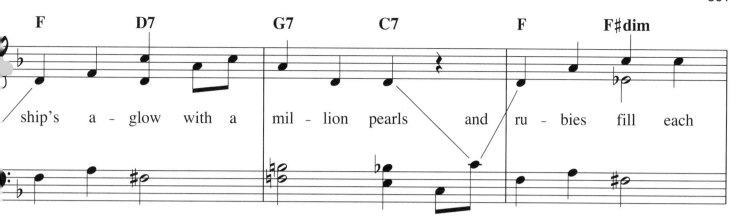

ship's a - glow with a mil - lion pearls and ru - bies fill each

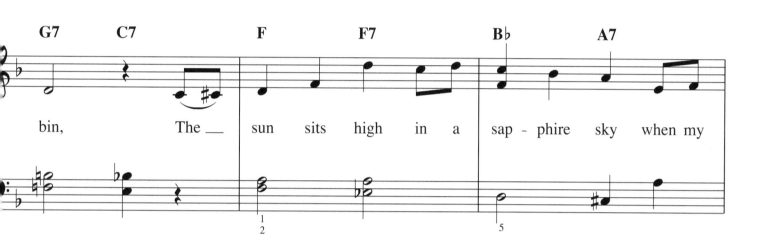

bin, The __ sun sits high in a sap - phire sky when my

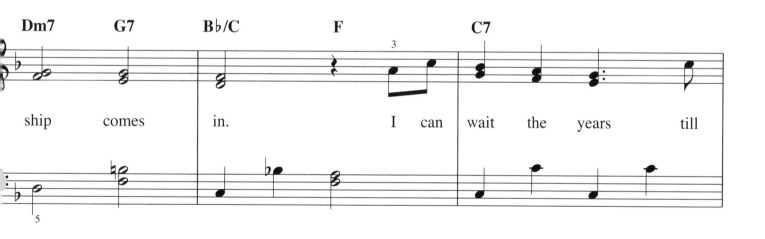

ship comes in. I can wait the years till

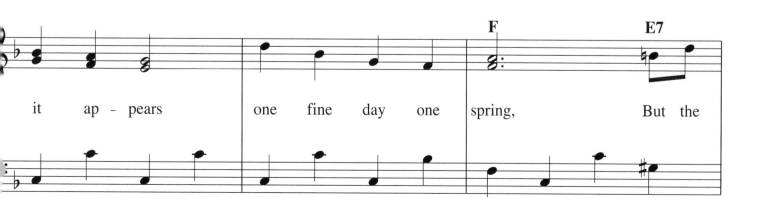

it ap - pears one fine day one spring, But the

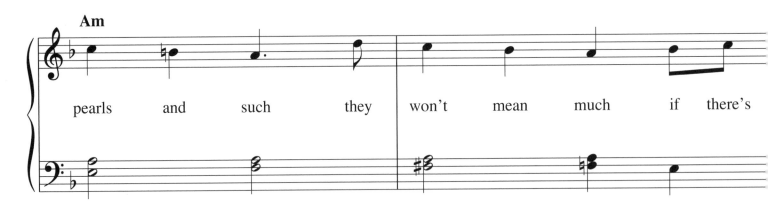

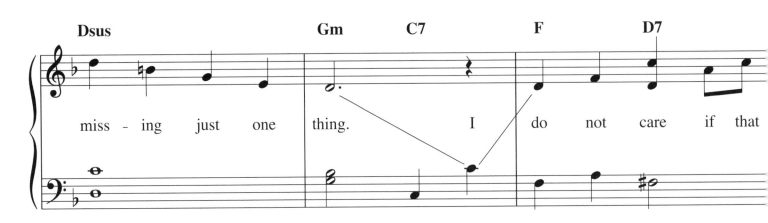

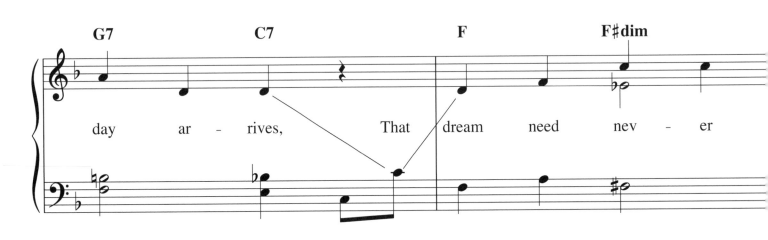

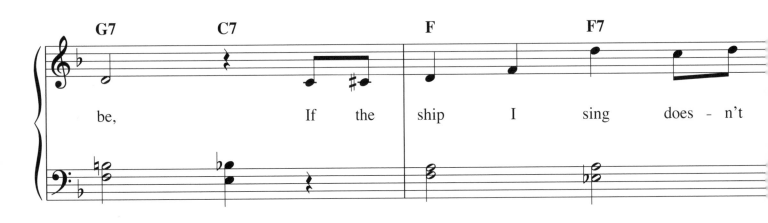

MY SILENT LOVE

Words by EDWARD HEYMAN
Music by DANA SUESSE

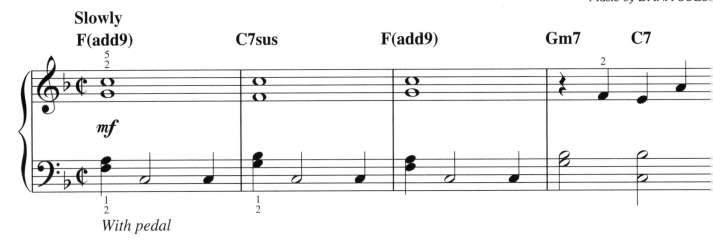

I reach for you like I'd reach for a star,

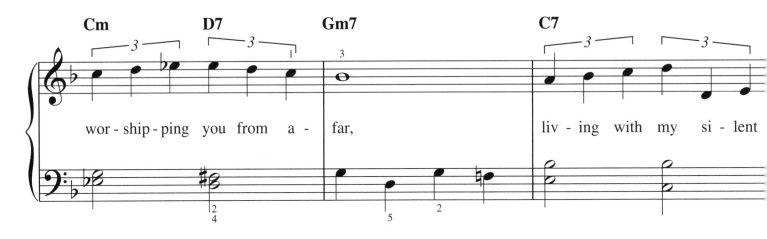

wor-ship-ping you from a-far, liv-ing with my si-lent

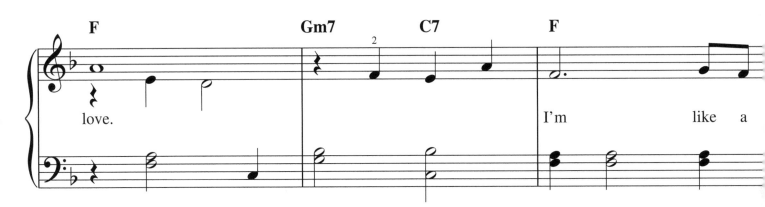

love. I'm like a

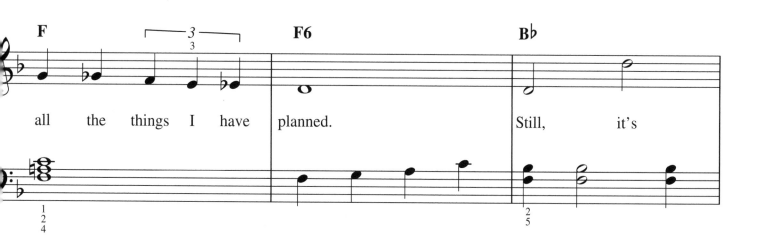

wrong to tell; you would not un - der - stand.

You'll go a - long nev - er dream - ing I care,

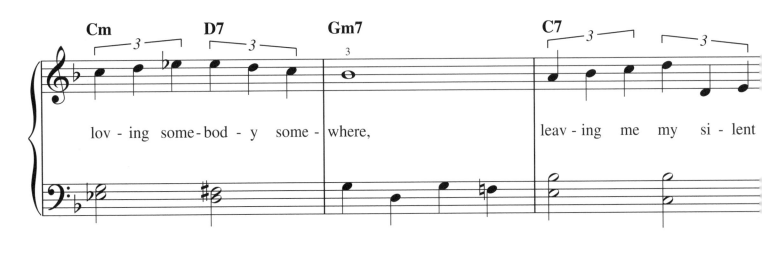

lov - ing some-bod - y some - where, leav - ing me my si - lent

1. love.

2. love.
molto rit.

NADIA'S THEME
from THE YOUNG AND THE RESTLESS

By BARRY DeVORZON
and PERRY BOTKIN, JR.

Moderately, with expression

NEVER NEVER LAND

from PETER PAN

Lyric by BETTY COMDEN and ADOLPH GRE
Music by JULE STY

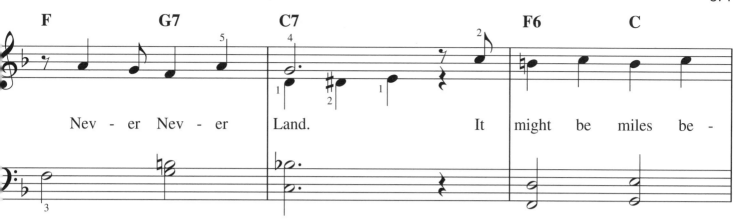

Nev - er Nev - er Land. It might be miles be -

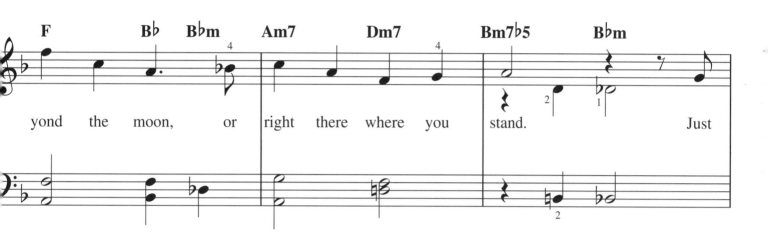

yond the moon, or right there where you stand. Just

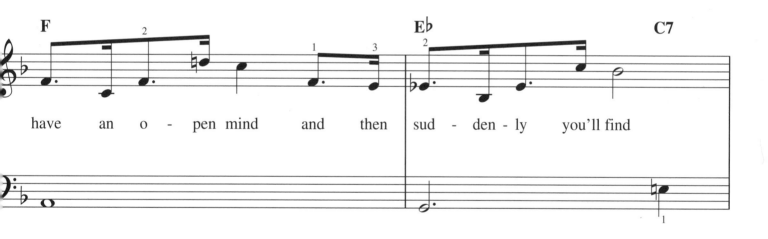

have an o - pen mind and then sud - den - ly you'll find

Nev - er Nev - er Land. You'll have a treas - ure if you

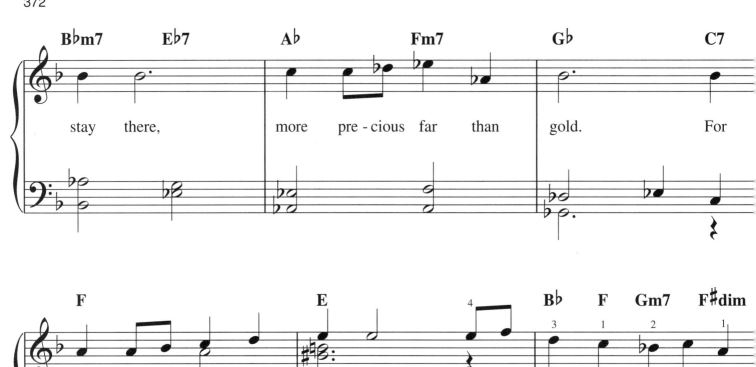

stay there, more pre - cious far than gold. For

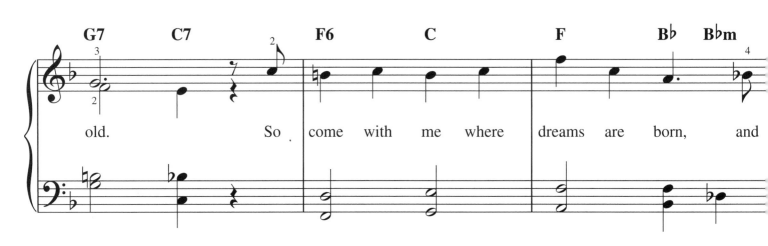

once you have found your way there you can nev - er, nev - er grow

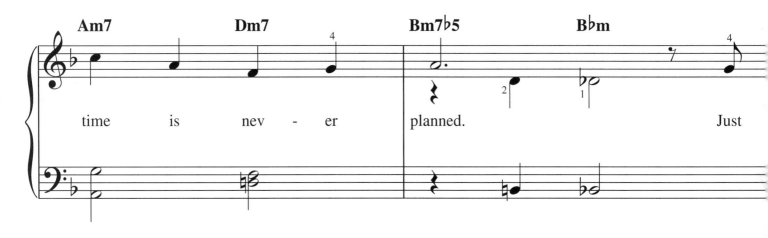

old. So come with me where dreams are born, and

time is nev - er planned. Just

think of love - ly things and your heart will fly on wings, for -

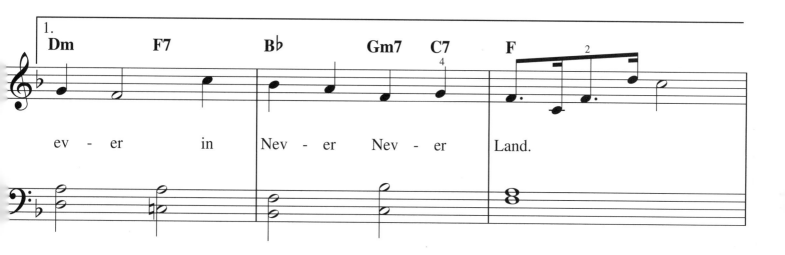

ev - er in Nev - er Nev - er Land.

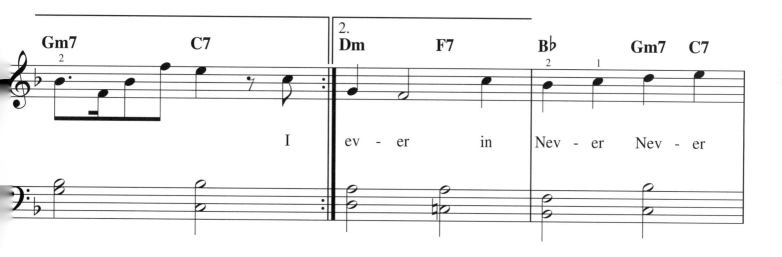

I ev - er in Nev - er Nev - er

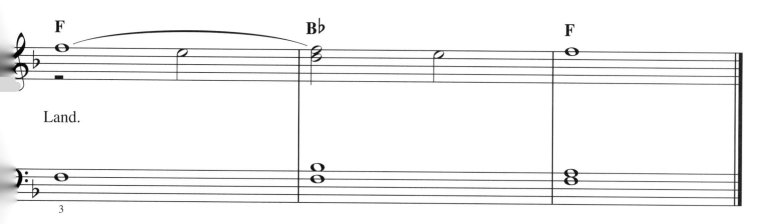

Land.

NEVER ON SUNDAY

from Jules Dassin's Motion Picture NEVER ON SUNDAY

Words by BILLY TOWNE
Music by MANOS HADJIDAKIS

Moderately, with a Latin feel

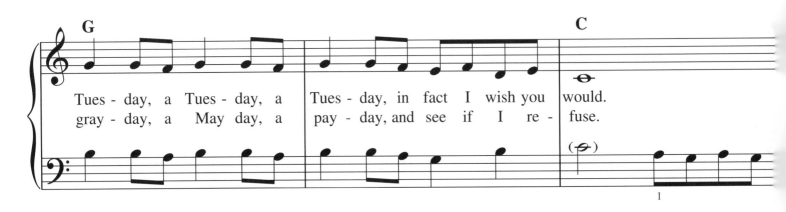

best.
guest.
But nev - er, nev - er on a Sun - day, a Sun - day, a
But nev - er, nev - er on a Sun - day, a Sun - day, the

To Coda

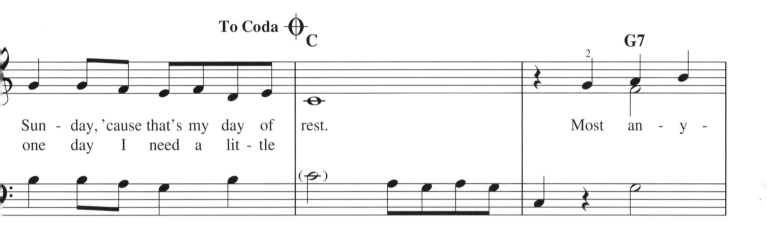

Sun - day, 'cause that's my day of rest.
one day I need a lit - tle

Most an - y -

day

you can be my guest.

An - y day you say,

but my day of

rest.

Just name the day

that you like the best,

on-ly stay a-

way

on my day of rest.

D.S. al Coda

Oh, you can kiss me on a

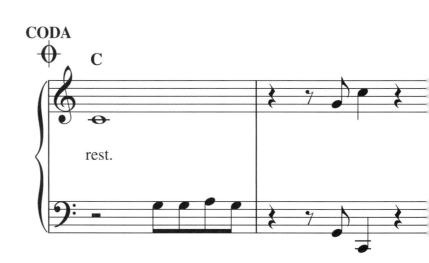

CODA

C

rest.

ONCE IN LOVE WITH AMY

from WHERE'S CHARLEY?

By FRANK LOESSER

Slow and easy Soft Shoe tempo

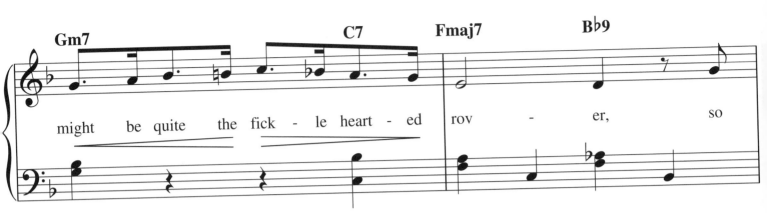

Gm7 · C7 · Fmaj7 · B♭9

might be quite the fick - le heart - ed rov - er, so

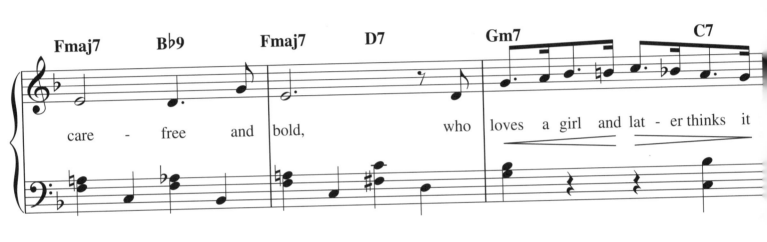

Fmaj7 · B♭9 · Fmaj7 · D7 · Gm7 · C7

care - free and bold, who loves a girl and lat - er thinks it

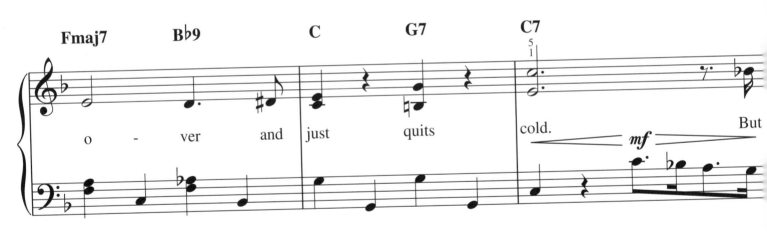

Fmaj7 · B♭9 · C · G7 · C7

o - ver and just quits cold. But

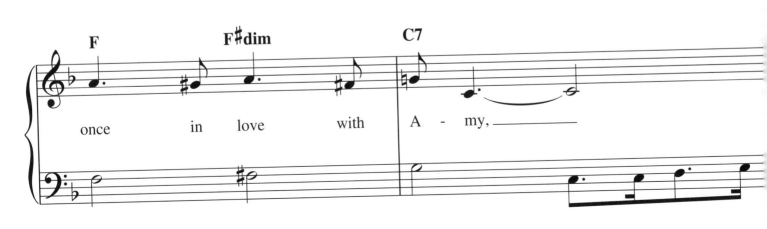

F · F♯dim · C7

once in love with A - my,

al - ways in love with A - my. _____ Ev - er and ev - er

sweet - ly you'll ro-mance 'er. Trou - ble is, the an - swer will

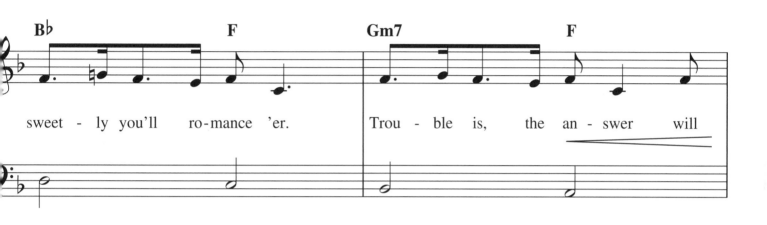

be That A - my'd rath - er stay in

love with me.

A NIGHTINGALE SANG IN BERKELEY SQUARE

Lyric by ERIC MASCHW[...]
Music by MANNING SHERW[...]

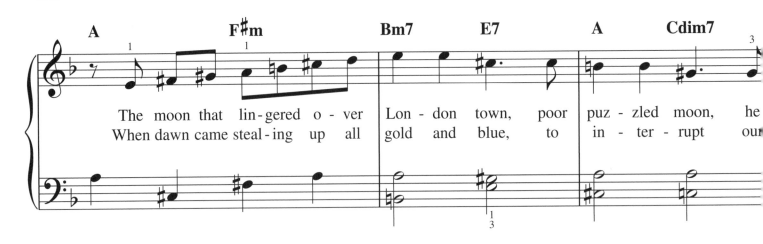

The moon that lin-gered o - ver London town, poor puz-zled moon, he
When dawn came steal-ing up all gold and blue, to in - ter - rupt our

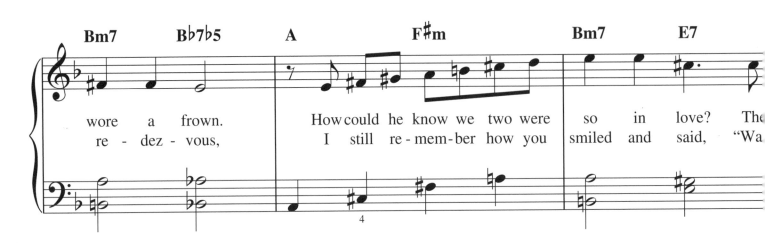

wore a frown. How could he know we two were so in love? The
re - dez - vous, I still re-mem-ber how you smiled and said, "Wa

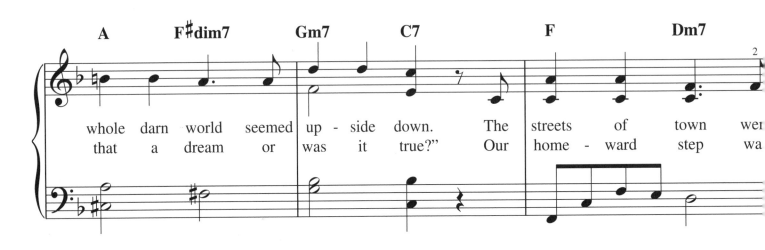

whole darn world seemed up - side down. The streets of town wer
that a dream or was it true?" Our home - ward step wa

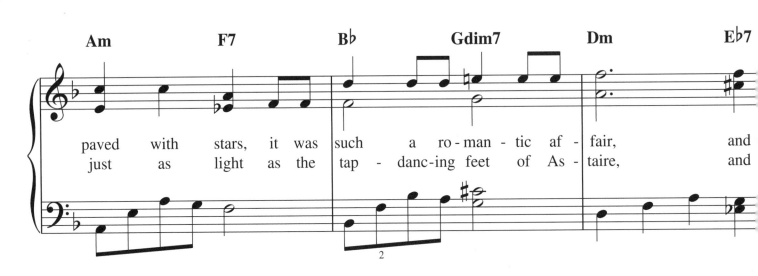

paved with stars, it was such a ro-man-tic af - fair, and
just as light as the tap - danc-ing feet of As - taire, and

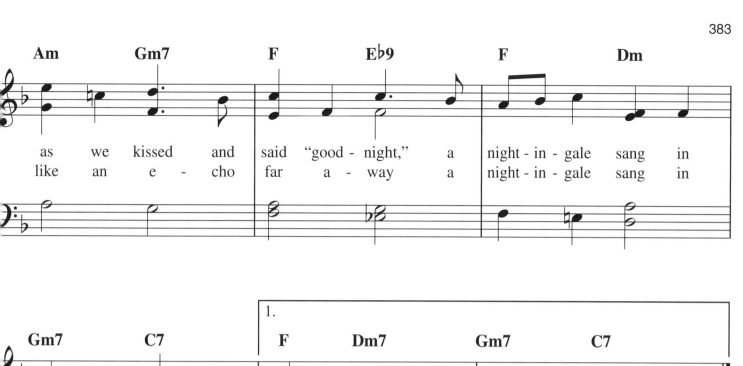

Am   Gm7   F   E♭9   F   Dm

as   we   kissed   and   said   "good - night,"   a   night - in - gale   sang   in

like   an   e - cho   far   a - way   a   night - in - gale   sang   in

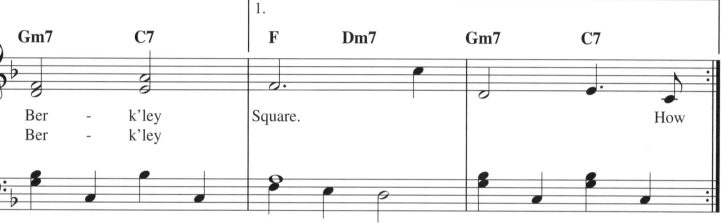

Gm7   C7   **1.**   F   Dm7   Gm7   C7

Ber - k'ley   Square.   How

Ber - k'ley

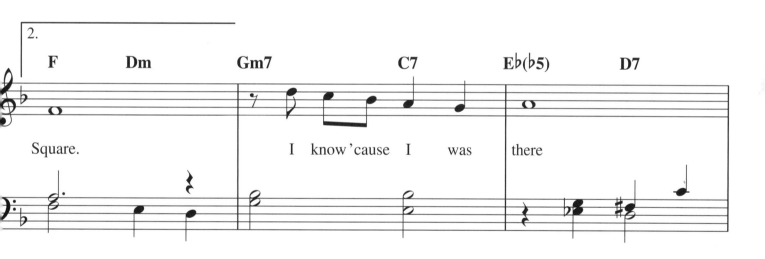

2.   F   Dm   Gm7   C7   E♭(♭5)   D7

Square.   I   know 'cause   I   was   there

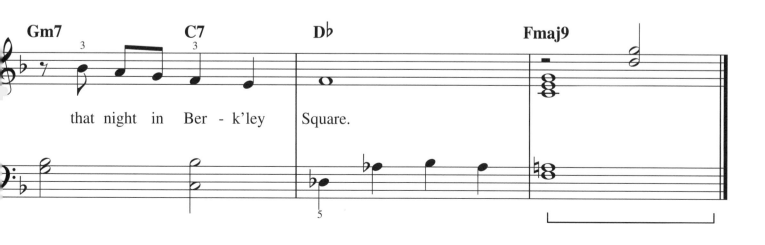

Gm7   C7   D♭   Fmaj9

that   night   in   Ber - k'ley   Square.

ON THE STREET WHERE YOU LIVE

from MY FAIR LADY

Words by ALAN JAY LERNER
Music by FREDERICK LOEWE

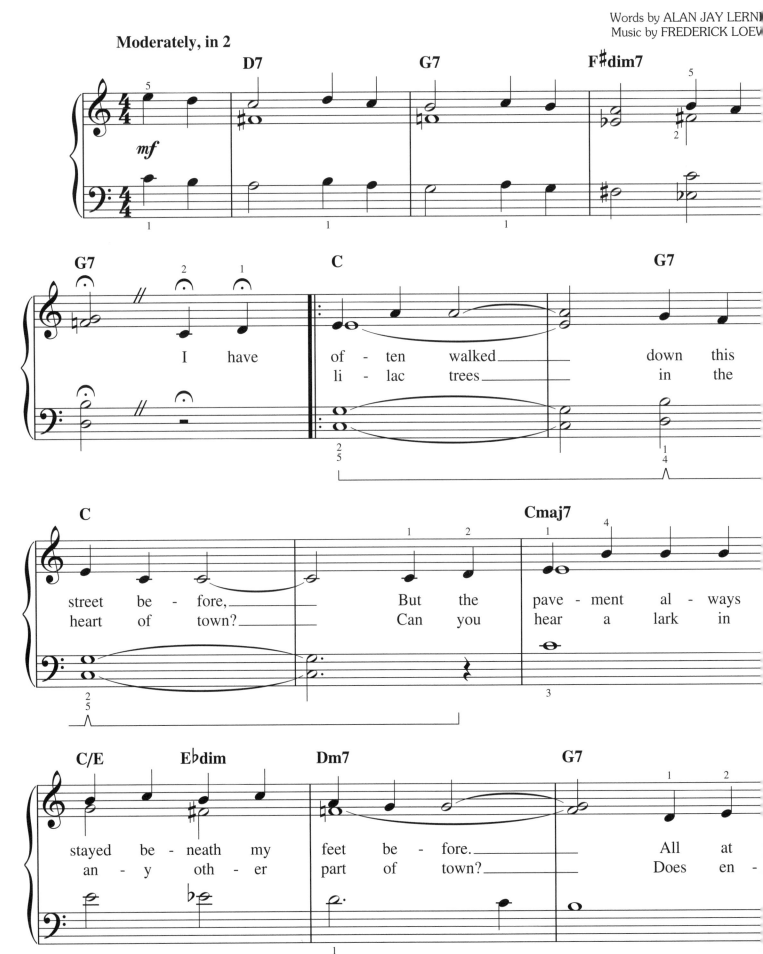

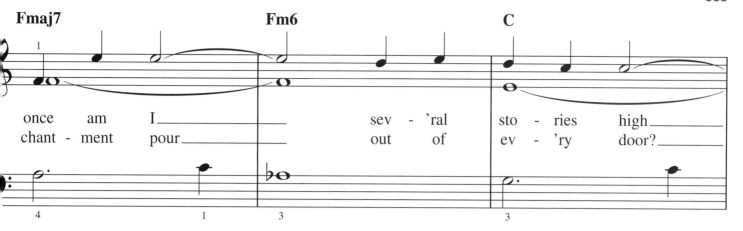

once am I_____ sev - 'ral sto - ries high_____
chant - ment pour_____ out of ev - 'ry door?_____

_____ Know - ing I'm on the street where you
_____ No, it's

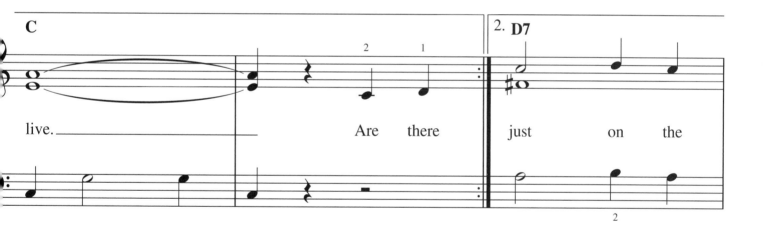

live._____ Are there just on the

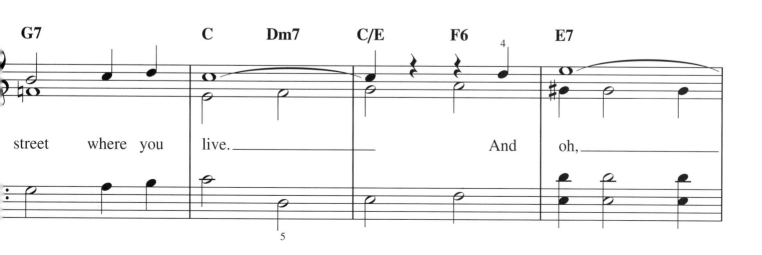

street where you live._____ And oh,_____

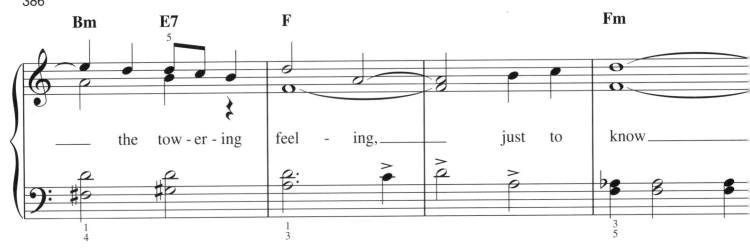

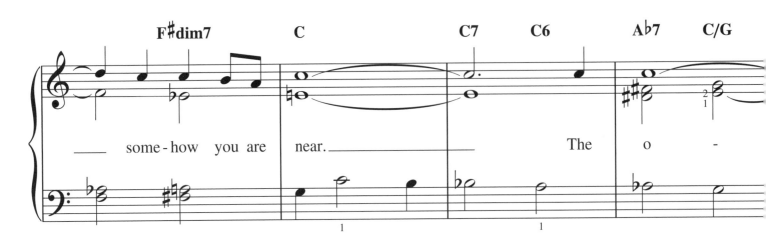

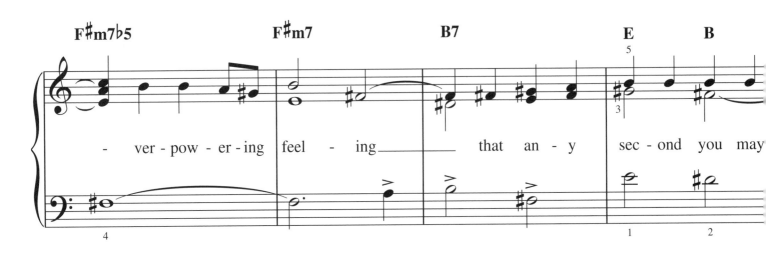

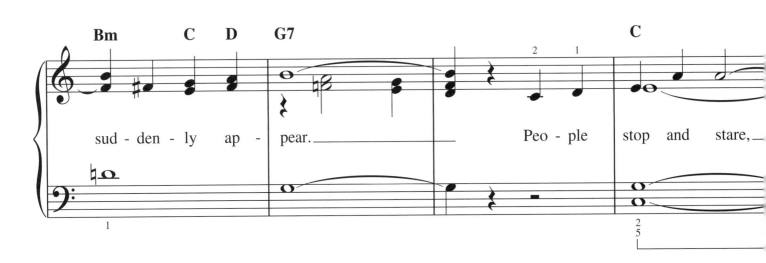

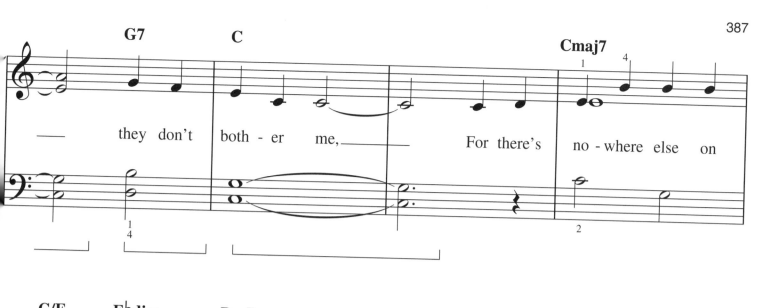

they don't both-er me,_____ For there's no-where else on

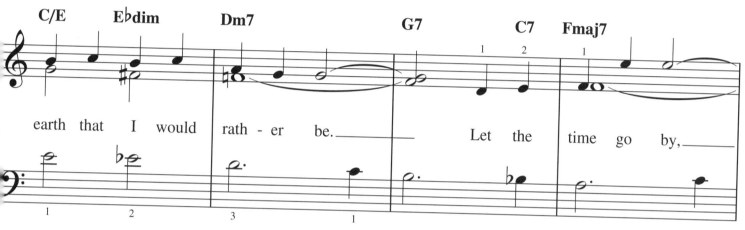

earth that I would rath-er be._____ Let the time go by,_____

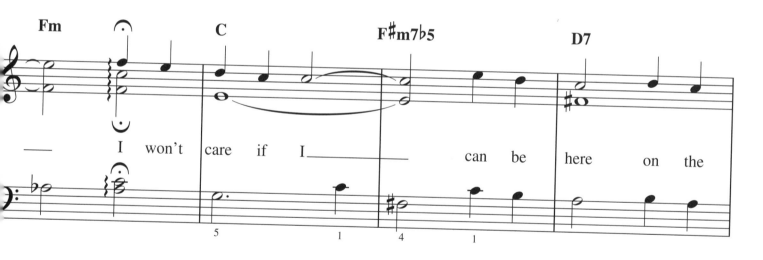

___ I won't care if I_____ can be here on the

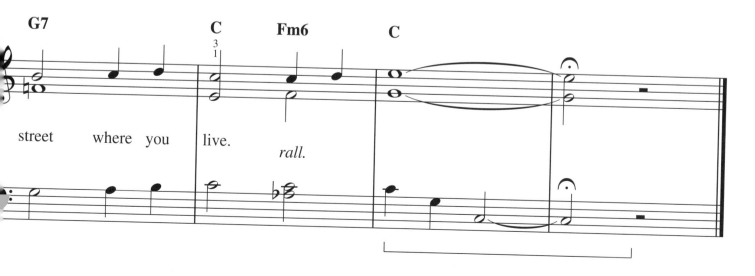

street where you live. *rall.*

ONCE UPON A TIME
from the Broadway Musical ALL AMERICAN

Lyric by LEE ADAMS
Music by CHARLES STROUSE

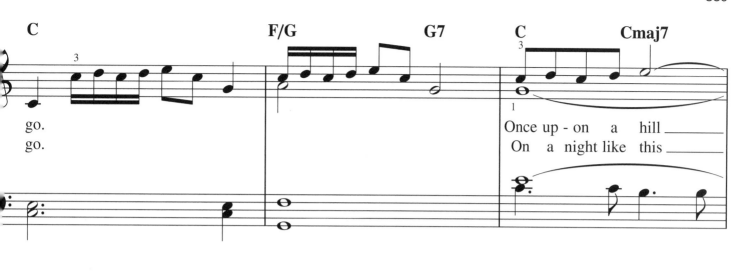

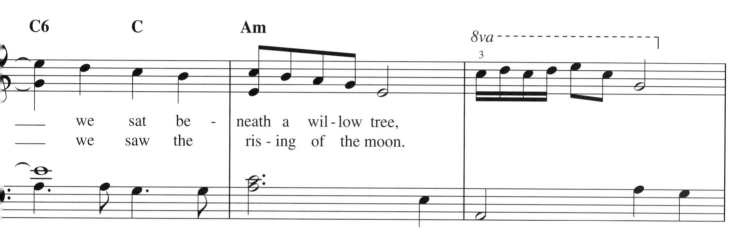

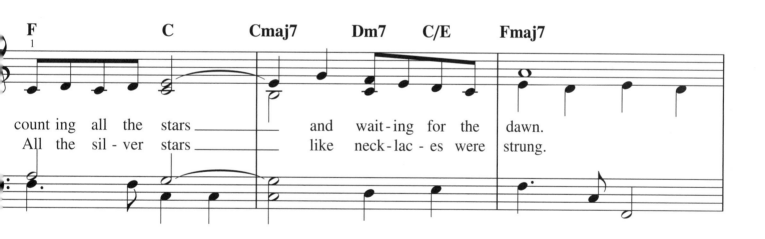

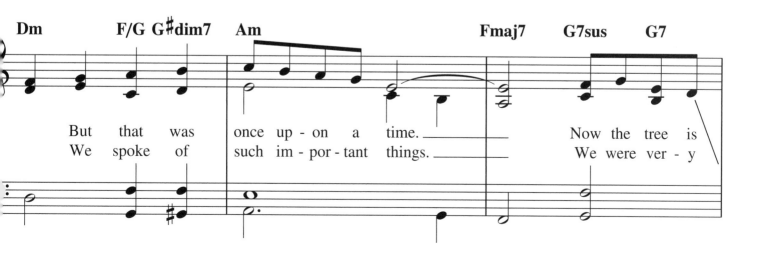

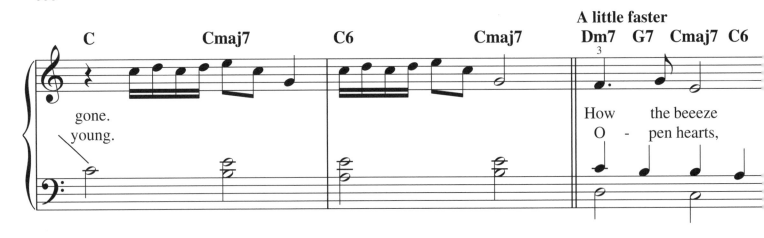

C — Cmaj7 — C6 — Cmaj7 — **A little faster** — Dm7 — G7 — Cmaj7 — C6

gone.
young.

How the beeeze
O - pen hearts,

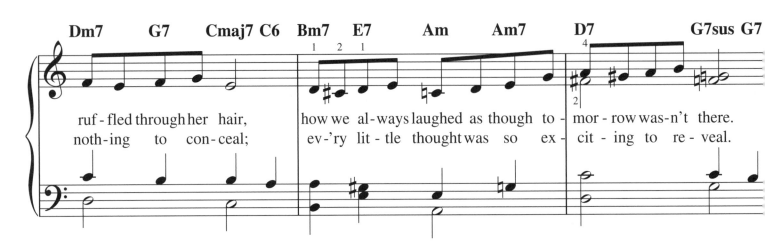

Dm7 — G7 — Cmaj7 C6 — Bm7 — E7 — Am — Am7 — D7 — G7sus G7

ruf - fled through her hair,
noth-ing to con-ceal;

how we al-ways laughed as though to - mor - row was-n't there.
ev-'ry lit - tle thought was so ex - cit - ing to re - veal.

G7/F — C/E — G7/F — C/E — Am7 — D9

We were young and
All our dreams we

did - n't have a care.
knew would soon be real.

Where did it
Where did they

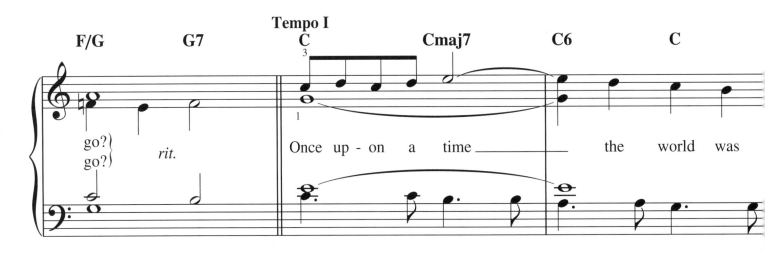

F/G — G7 — **Tempo I** — C — Cmaj7 — C6 — C

go?
go?

rit.

Once up-on a time _____ the world was

ONE NOTE SAMBA
(Samba de uma nota so)

Original Lyrics by NEWTON MENDONÇ
English Lyrics by ANTONIO CARLOS JOB
Music by ANTONIO CARLOS JOB

Lightly, with movement

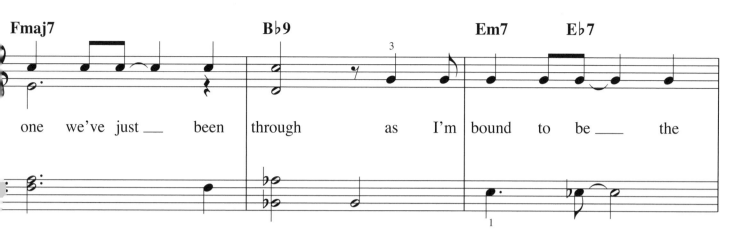

one we've just ___ been through as I'm bound to be ___ the

un - a - void - a - ble con - se - quence ___ of you.

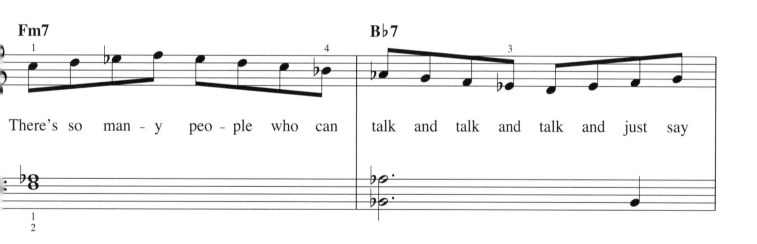

There's so man - y peo - ple who can talk and talk and talk and just say

noth - ing, ___ or near - ly noth - ing. ___

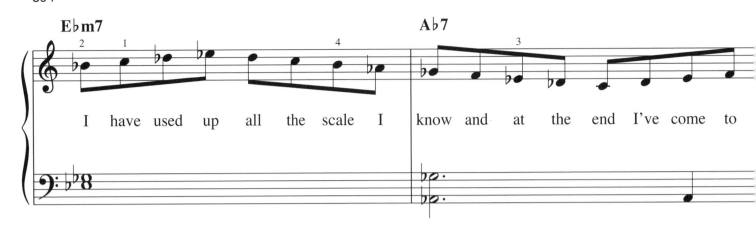

I have used up all the scale I know and at the end I've come to

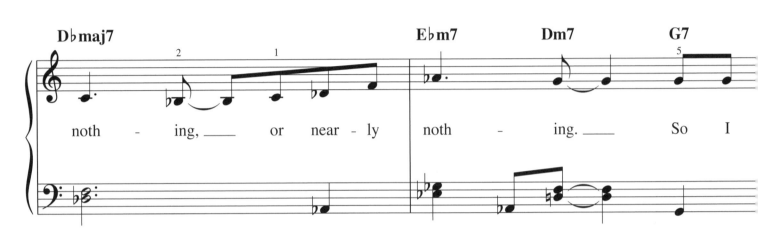

noth - ing, ____ or near - ly noth - ing. ____ So I

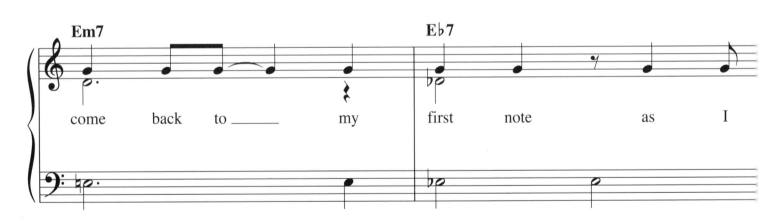

come back to ____ my first note as I

must come back __ to you. I will pour in - to ____ that

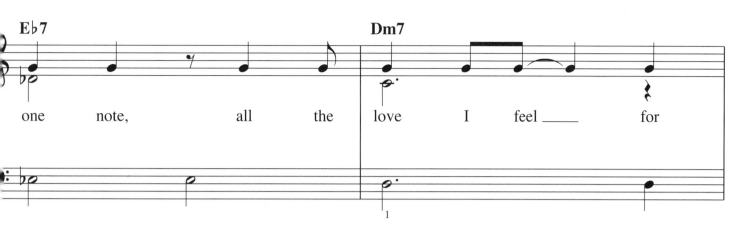

one note, all the love I feel _____ for

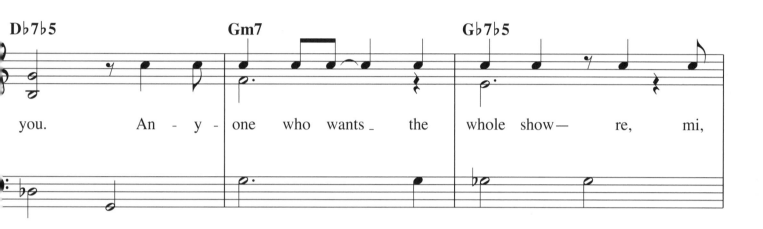

you. An - y - one who wants _ the whole show— re, mi,

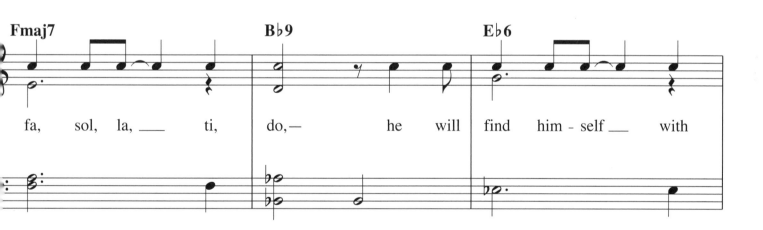

fa, sol, la, _____ ti, do,— he will find him - self _ with

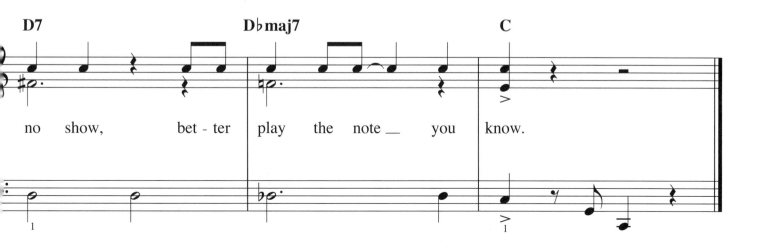

no show, bet - ter play the note _ you know.

ONLY TRUST YOUR HEART

Words by SAMMY CAHN
Music by BENNY CARTER

Never trust the stars____ when you're a-
Never trust the moon____ when you're a-

bout to fall in love.____
bout to taste his kiss.____

Look for hid-den
He knows all the

signs____ be-fore you start to sigh.
lines,____ and he knows how to lie.

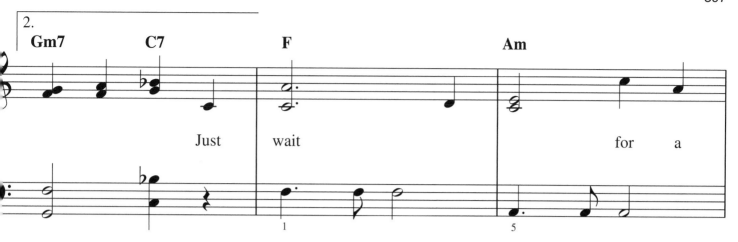

2.

Gm7   **C7**   **F**   **Am**

Just   wait   for   a

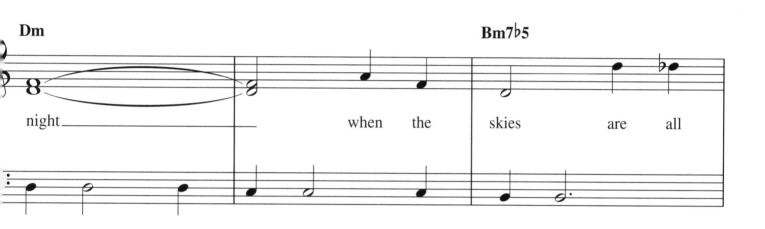

Dm   **Bm7♭5**

night   when   the   skies   are   all

E7♯5   **Am**   **Am7**   **A♭m7**   **Gm7**   **C7**

bare.   Then,   if   you   still   care,

F   **B7**   **Em7**

nev - er   trust   your   dream   when you're a - bout   to   fall   in

love,_____ for your dream will quick - ly fall a

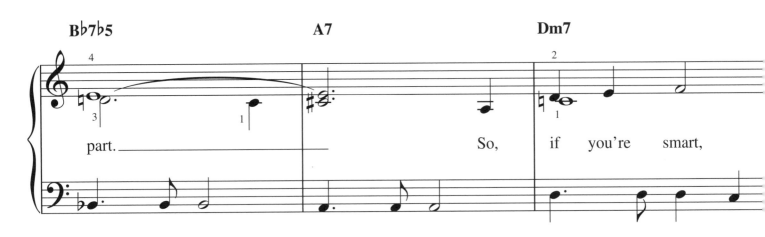

part._____ So, if you're smart,

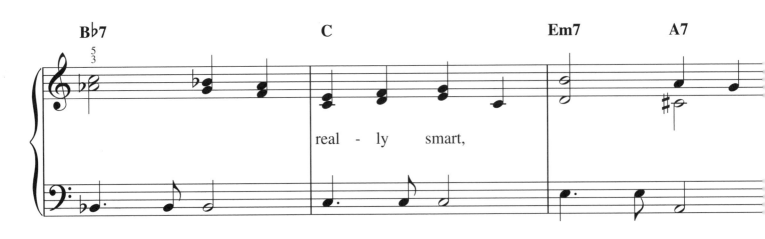

real - ly smart,

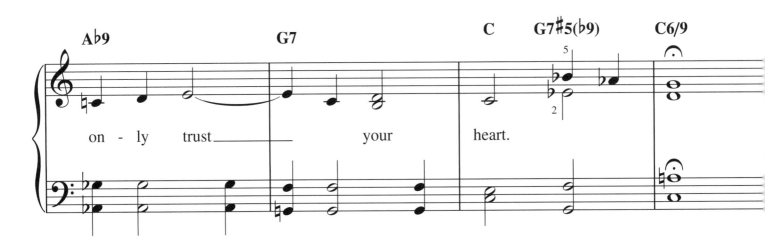

on - ly trust_____ your heart.

OUT OF NOWHERE

from the Paramount Picture DUDE RANCH

Words by EDWARD HEYMAN
Music by JOHNNY GREEN

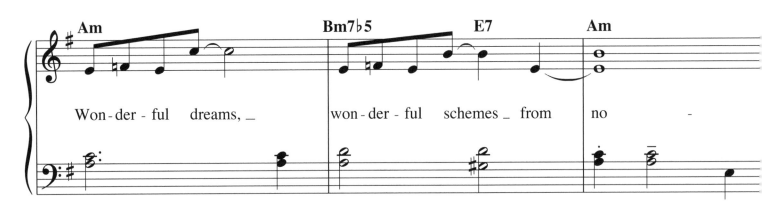

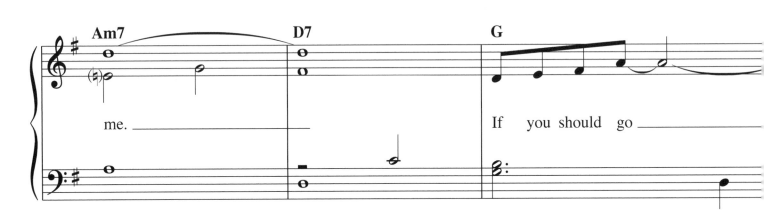

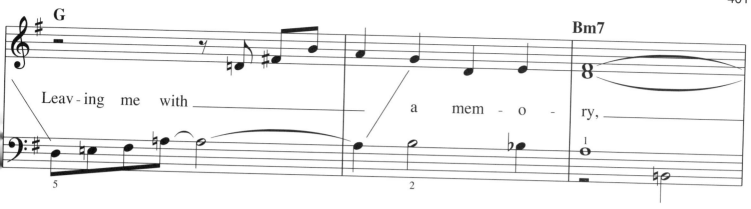

Leav - ing me with _____ a mem - o - ry, _____

_____ I'll al - ways wait __ for your re - turn out of

no - where; Hop - ing you'll bring your love to

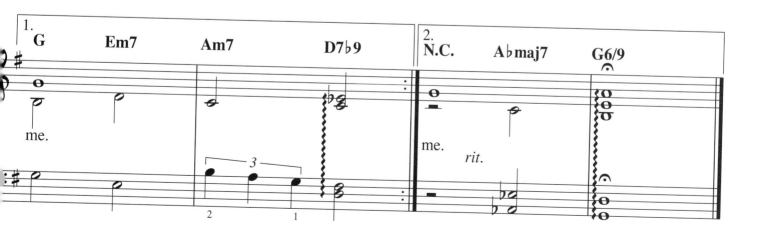

me. me. *rit.*

PENTHOUSE SERENADE

Words and Music by WILL JAS
and VAL BURT

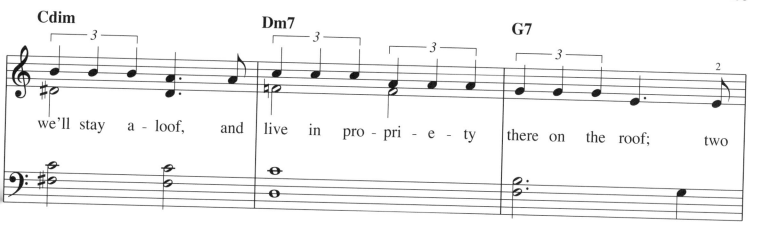

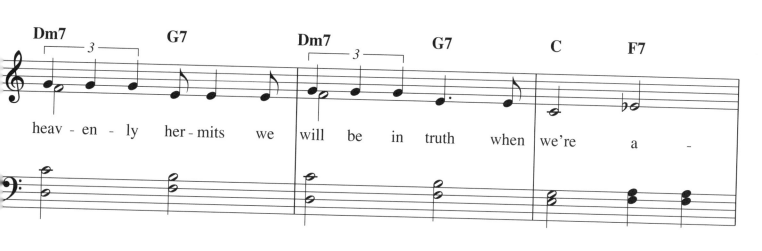

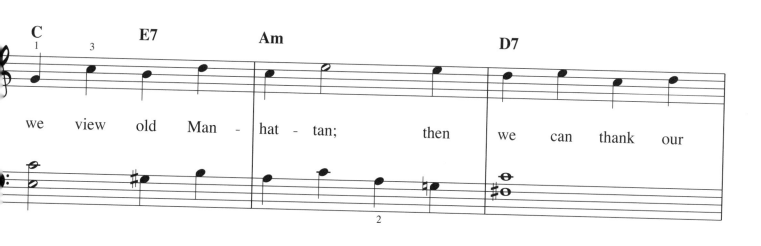

luck - y stars that we're liv - ing as we are. In

our lit - tle pent-house, we'll al - ways con - trive to keep love and ro - mance for -

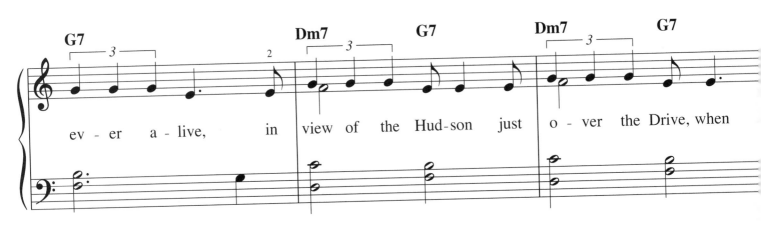

ev - er a - live, in view of the Hud-son just o - ver the Drive, when

we're a - lone. Just lone.

PUT ON A HAPPY FACE

from BYE BYE BIRDIE

Words by LEE ADAMS
Music by CHARLES STROUSE

Lightly, with a bounce

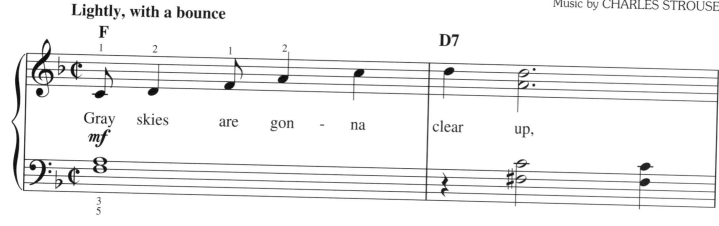

Gray skies are gon - na clear up,

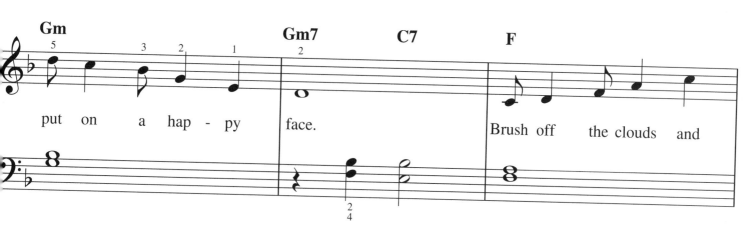

put on a hap - py face. Brush off the clouds and

cheer up, put on a hap - py face.

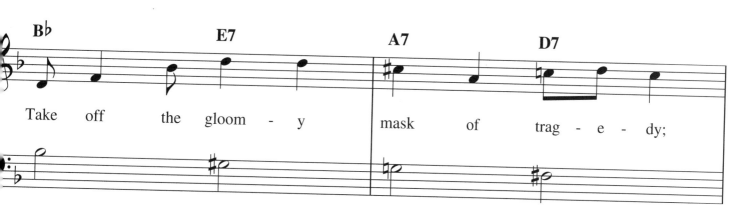

Take off the gloom - y mask of trag - e - dy;

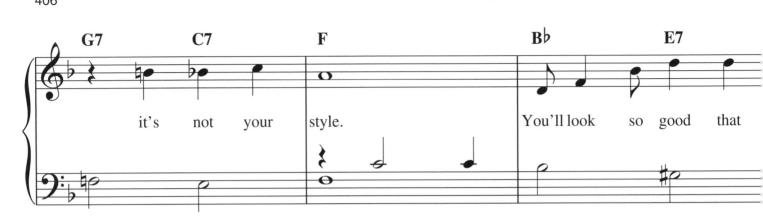

it's   not   your   style.   You'll look   so   good   that

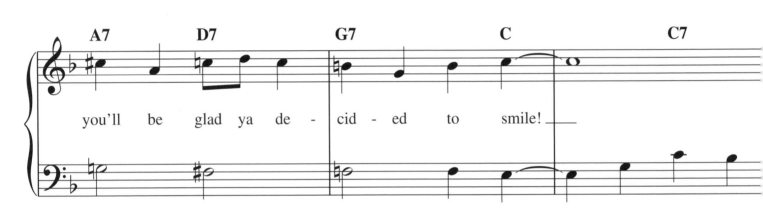

you'll   be   glad ya   de - cid - ed   to   smile!

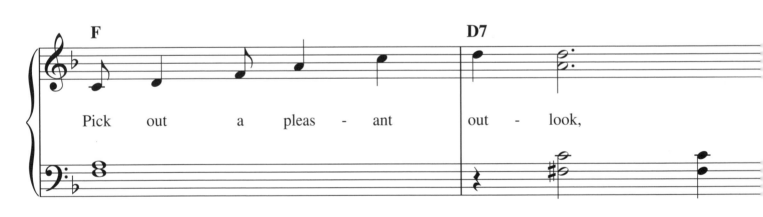

Pick   out   a   pleas - ant   out - look,

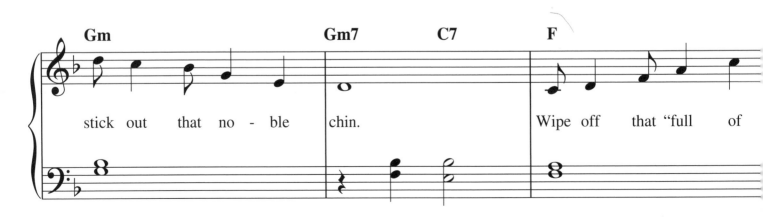

stick   out   that   no - ble   chin.   Wipe   off   that "full   of

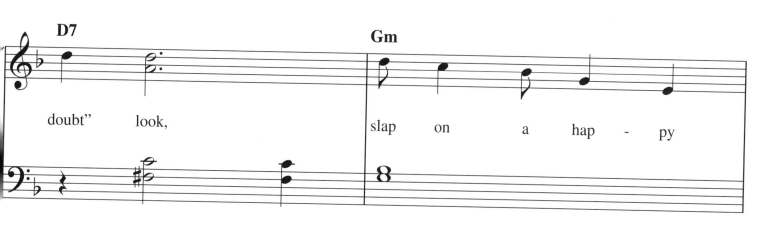

doubt"   look,   slap   on   a   hap - py

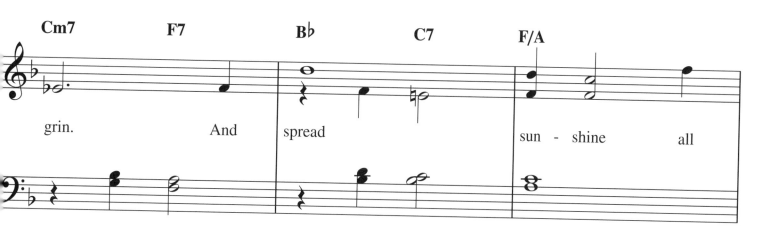

grin.   And   spread   sun - shine   all

o - ver   the   place;   just   put   on   a

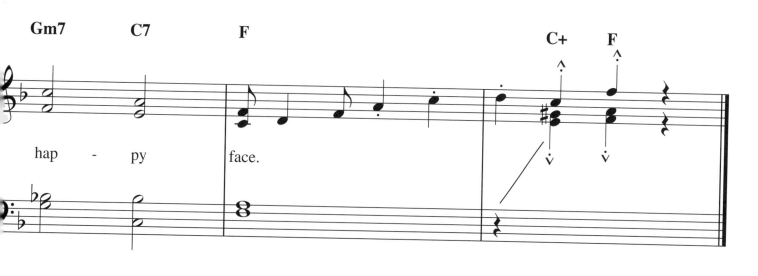

hap - py   face.

PUTTIN' ON THE RITZ

from the Motion Picture PUTTIN' ON THE RITZ

Words and Music by
IRVING BERLIN

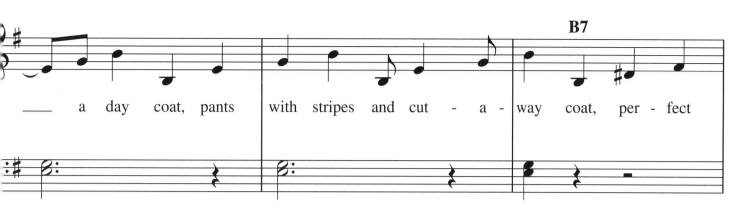

_____ a day coat, pants with stripes and cut - a - way coat, per - fect

fits, _____ put - tin' on the Ritz.

E7   **Am**   **E7**

Stroll - ing up the av - e - nue so
(Alt: Dressed up like a mil - lion dol - lar

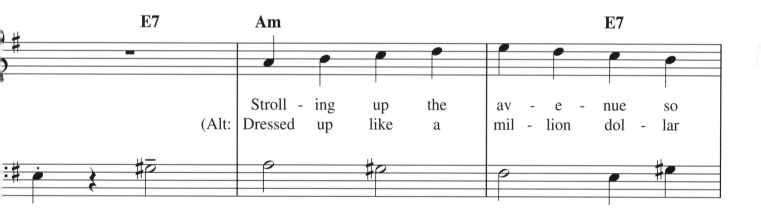

Am   **D7**   **G**

hap - py. ____   All dressed up just
troup - er. ____   Try - ing hard to

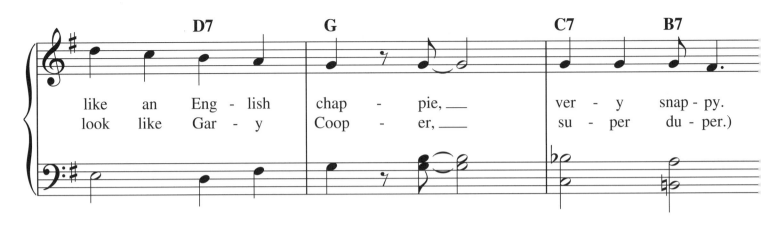

like an Eng - lish chap - pie, ___ ver - y snap - py.
look like Gar - y Coop - er, ___ su - per du - per.)

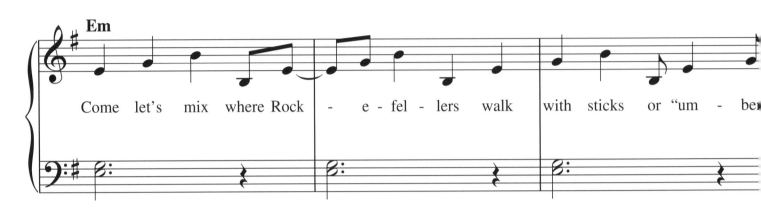

Come let's mix where Rock - e - fel - lers walk with sticks or "um - ber-

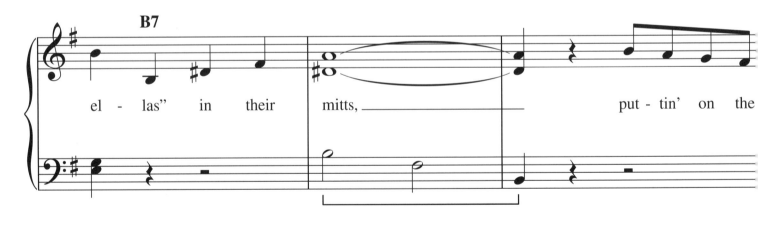

el - las" in their mitts, ___ put - tin' on the

1.
Ritz.

2.
Ritz.

QUE SERA, SERA
(Whatever Will Be, Will Be)
from THE MAN WHO KNEW TOO MUCH

Words and Music by JAY LIVINGSTON
and RAY EVANS

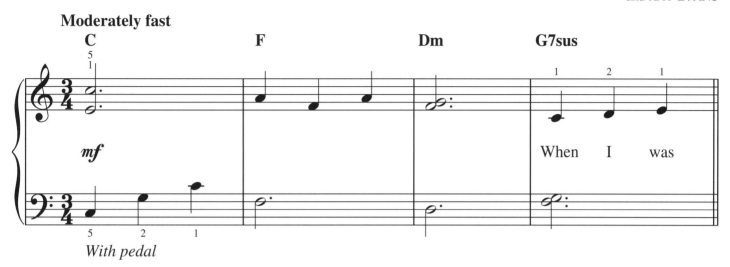

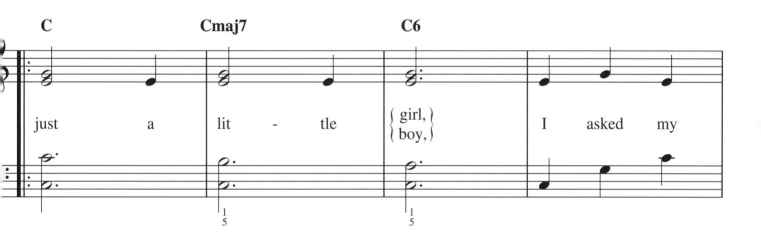

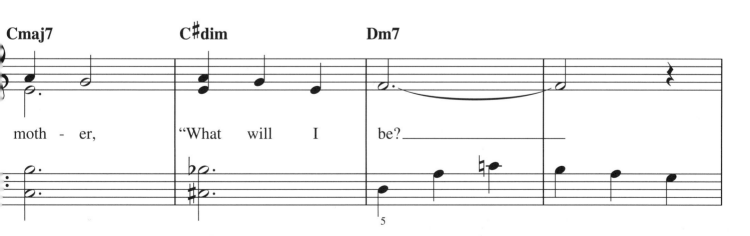

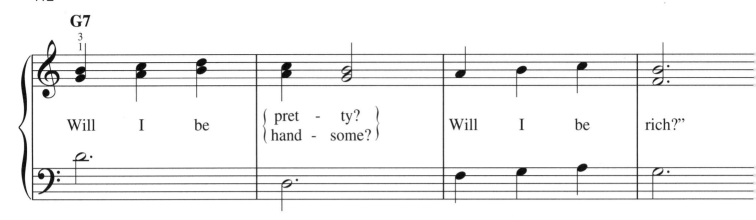

G7

Will I be { pret - ty? / hand - some? } Will I be rich?"

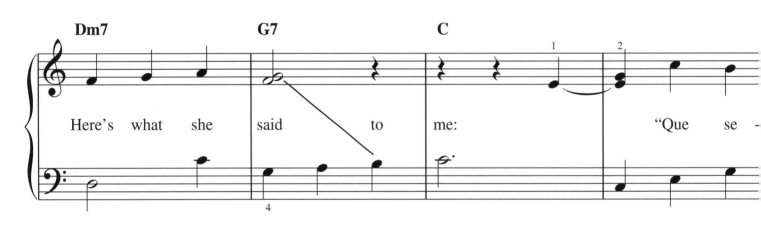

Dm7   **G7**   **C**

Here's what she said to me: "Que se -

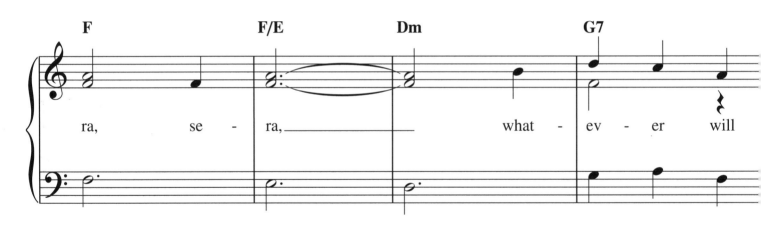

F   **F/E**   **Dm**   **G7**

ra, se - ra,___ what - ev - er will

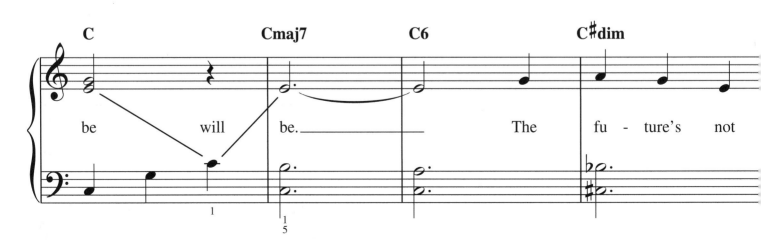

C   **Cmaj7**   **C6**   **C#dim**

be will be.___ The fu - ture's not

THE RAINBOW CONNECTION
from THE MUPPET MOVIE

Words and Music by PAUL WILLIA...
and KENNETH L. ASCH...

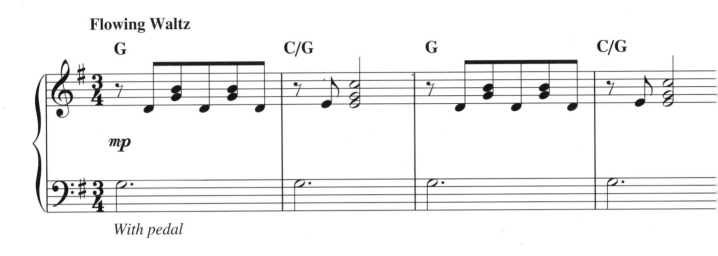

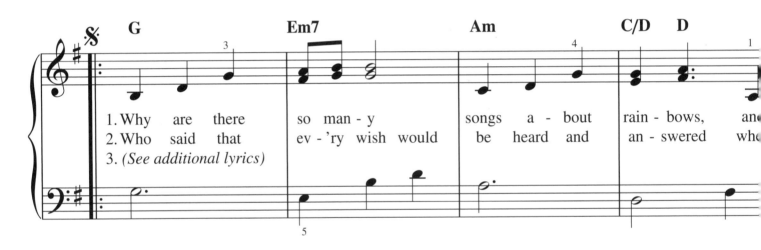

1. Why are there so man-y songs a-bout rain-bows, an...
2. Who said that ev-'ry wish would be heard and an-swered whe...
3. *(See additional lyrics)*

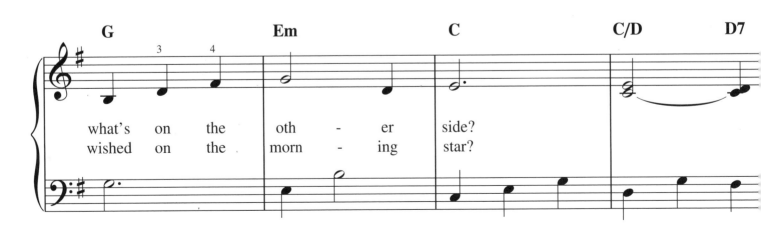

what's on the oth - er side?
wished on the morn - ing star?

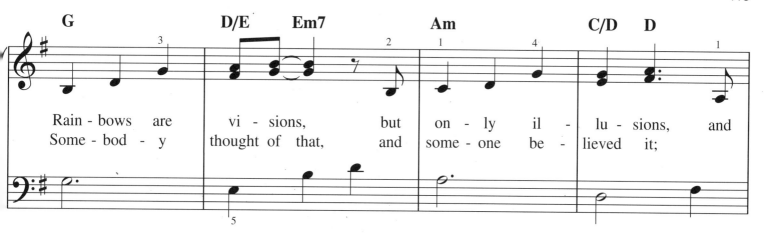

Rain - bows are | vi - sions, but | on - ly il - lu - sions, and
Some - bod - y | thought of that, and | some - one be - lieved it;

rain - bows have | noth - ing to | hide.
look what it's | done ___ so | far.

So we've been | told, and some | choose to be - lieve it;
What's so a - | maz - ing that | keeps us star - gaz - ing and

I know they're | wrong; wait and | see. _____
what do we | think we might | see? _____

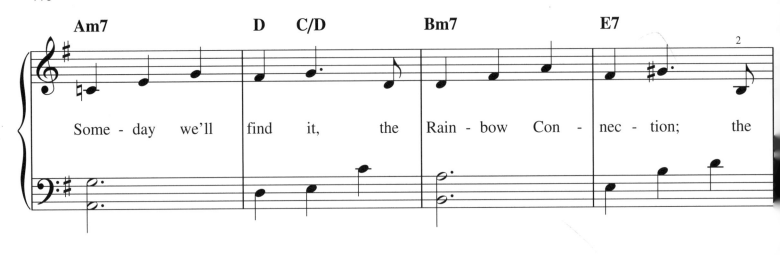

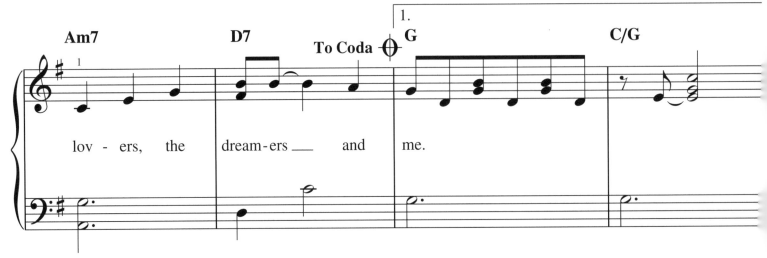

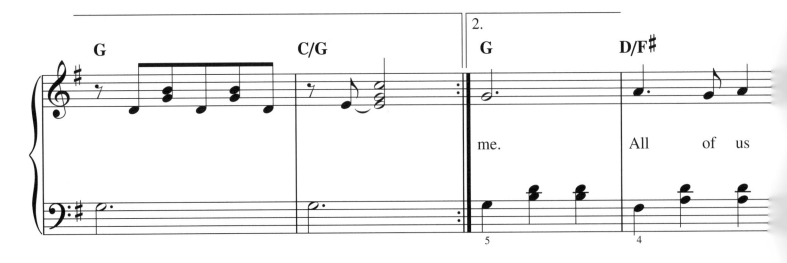

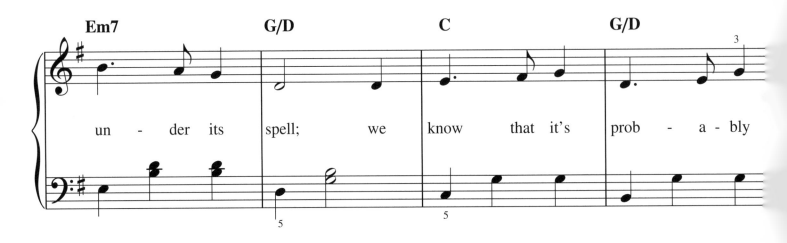

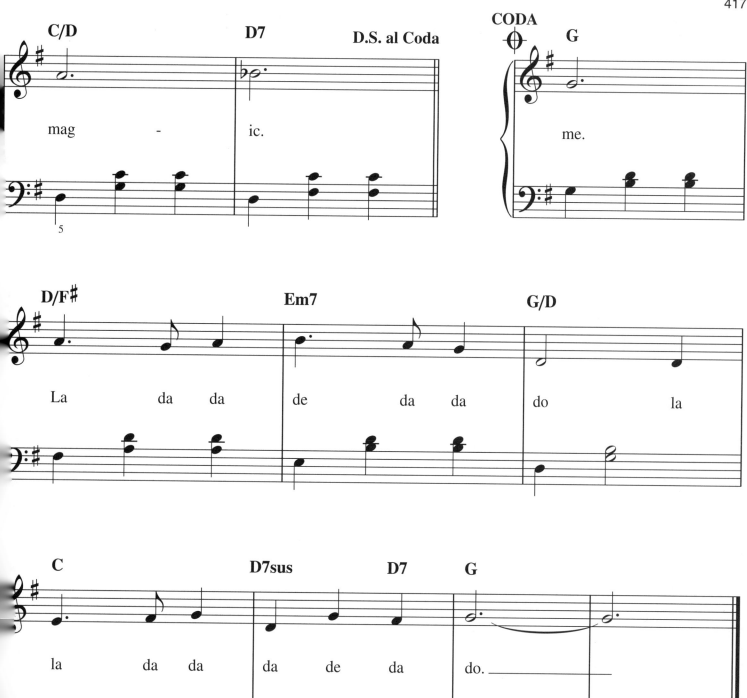

Additional Lyrics

3. Have you been half asleep and have you heard voices?
   I've heard them calling my name.
   Is this the sweet sound that calls the young sailors?
   The voice might be one and the same.
   I've heard it too many times to ignore it.
   It's something that I'm s'posed to be.
   Someday we'll find it,
   The Rainbow Connection;
   The lovers, the dreamers and me.

ROCKIN' CHAIR

Words and Music by
HOAGY CARMICHAEL

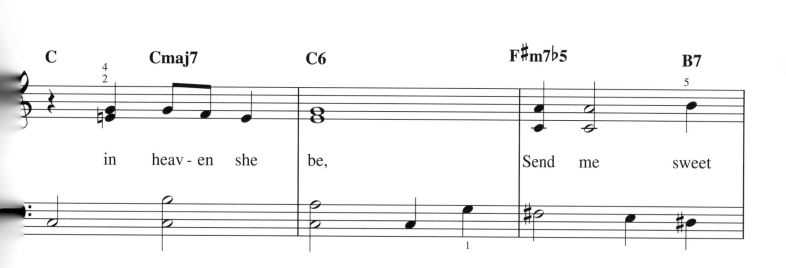

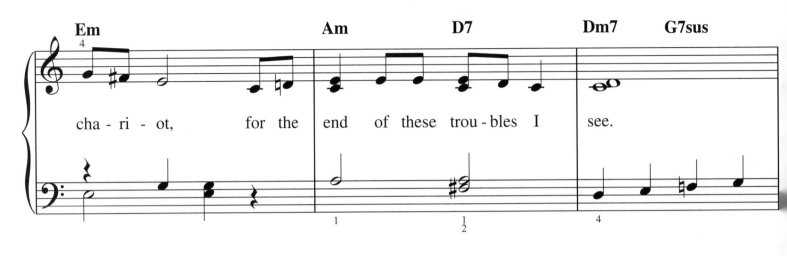

cha - ri - ot,   for the   end   of these trou - bles I   see.

Old   rock - in' chair   gits it, _____   Judg - ment   day   is

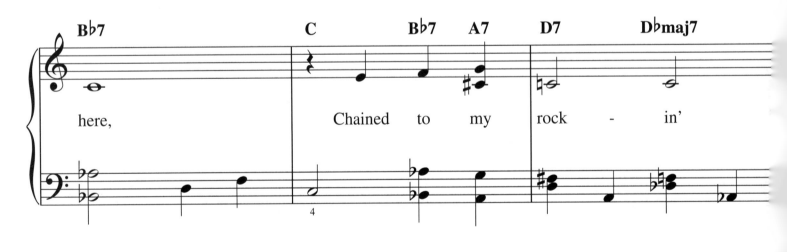

here,   Chained   to   my   rock -   in'

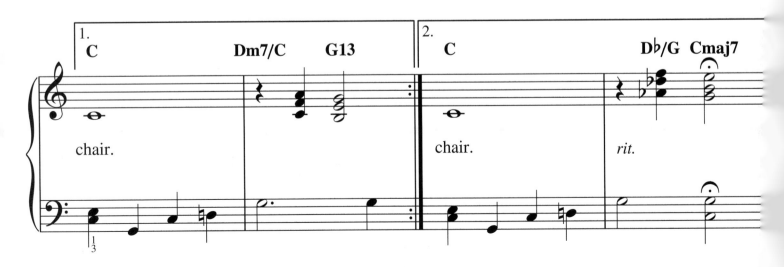

chair.   chair.   *rit.*

A SLEEPIN' BEE

from HOUSE OF FLOWERS

Lyric by TRUMAN CAPOTE and HAROLD ARLEN
Music by HAROLD ARLEN

Moderately slow

With pedal

When a bee lies sleep - in' _____ in the palm of your hand, _____

_____ you're be - witch'd and deep in _____ love's long

look'd af - ter land, _____ where you'll see a sun-up sky

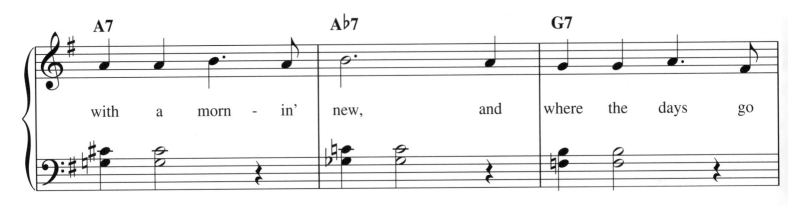

with a morn - in' new, and where the days go

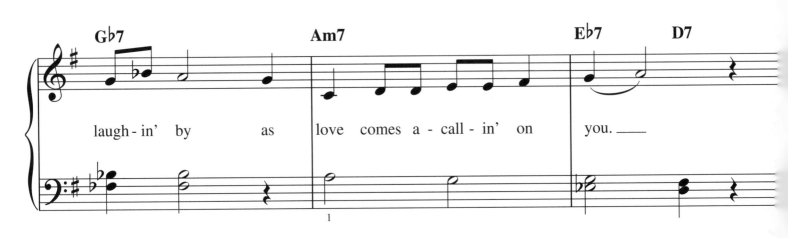

laugh - in' by as love comes a - call - in' on you.

Sleep on, bee, don't wak - en, __ can't be - lieve what just passed. __

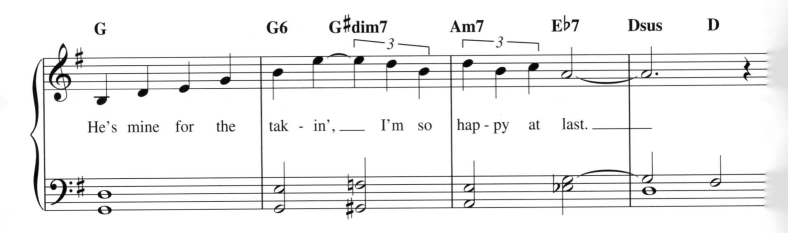

He's mine for the tak - in', __ I'm so hap - py at last. __

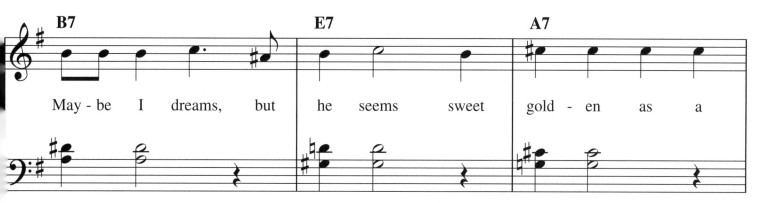

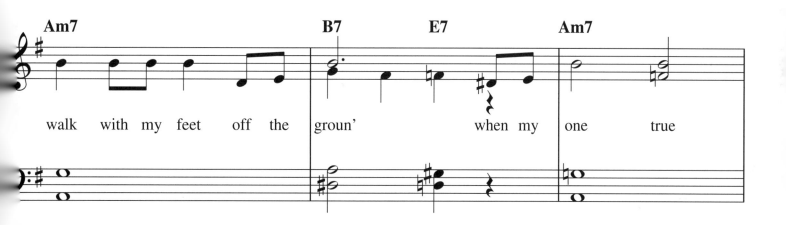

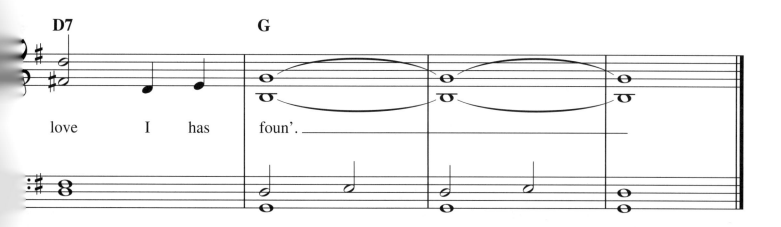

SMALL FRY

from the Paramount Picture SING, YOU SINNERS

Words by FRANK LOESSER
Music by HOAGY CARMICHAEL

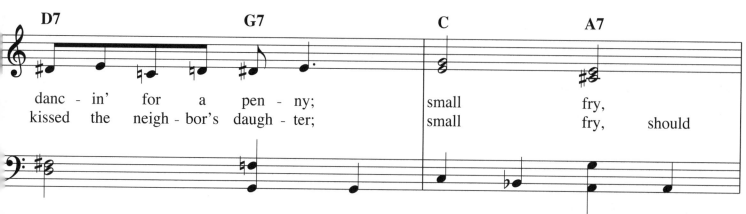

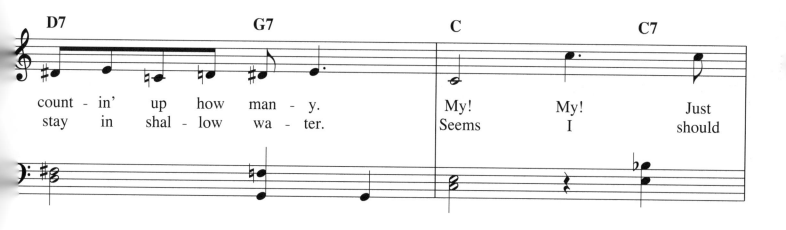

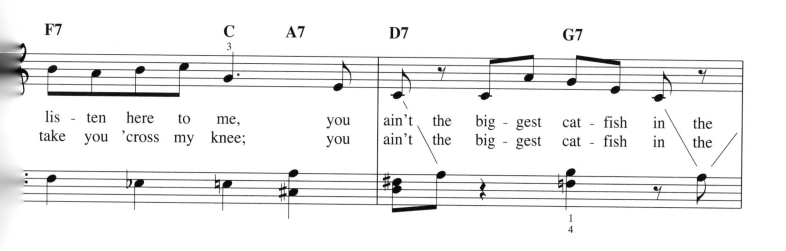

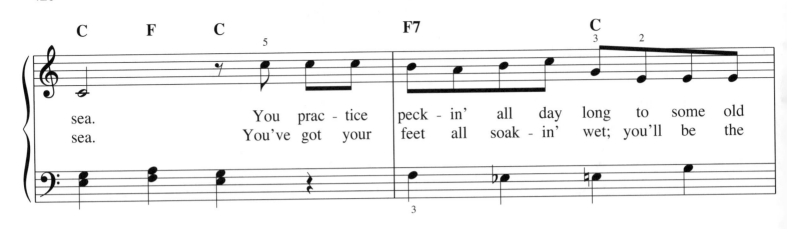

sea.   You prac - tice   peck - in' all day long to some old
sea.   You've got your   feet all soak - in' wet; you'll be the

ra - di - o song.__ Oh yes,__ oh yes,__ oh yes!__   You bet - ter
death of me yet.__ Oh me,__ oh my! __ Small fry!__

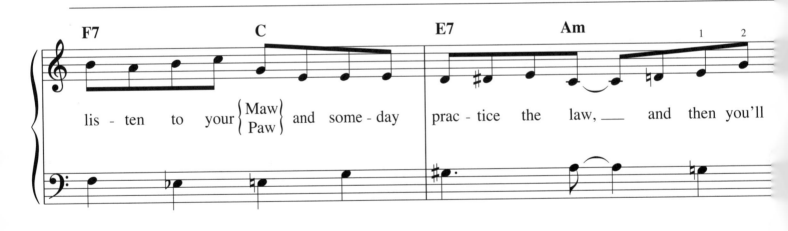

lis - ten to your {Maw} {Paw} and some - day   prac - tice the law, __ and then you'll

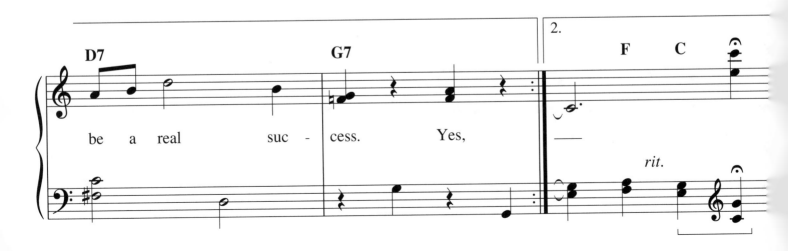

be a real suc - cess.   Yes, __

rit.

SMALL WORLD
from GYPSY

Words by STEPHEN SONDHEIM
Music by JULE STYNE

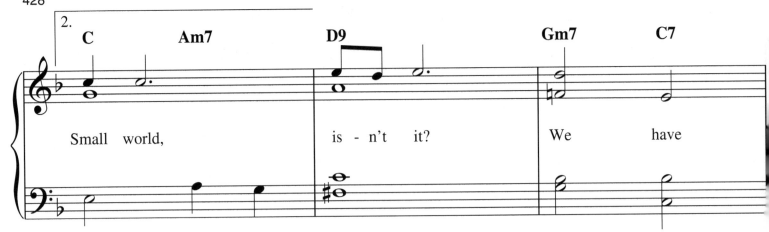

2.

C　　　　Am7　　　　　　D9　　　　　　　　Gm7　　　　C7

Small world,　　　　is - n't　it?　　　　We　have

F　　　　Am7　Abm7　Gm7　　　　Gb7　Fmaj7

so much in com - mon,　　　it's　a　phe-nom - e - non.

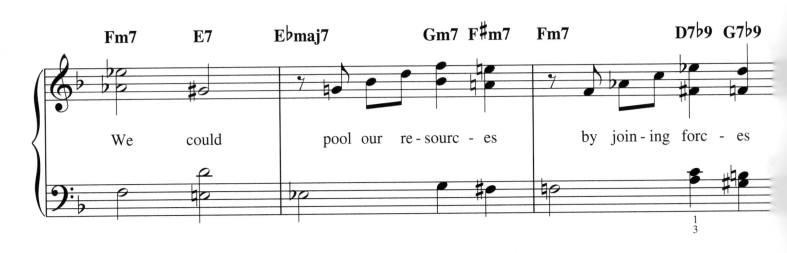

Fm7　　　　E7　　　　Ebmaj7　　　Gm7　F#m7　Fm7　　　　D7b9　G7b9

We　could　　　　pool our re - sourc - es　　　by join - ing forc - es

C7b9　　　　　　　　F　　　　　　　　Bb　　　F　Gm　F

from　now　on.　　　Luck - y ____　you're a　　girl who likes chil - dren,

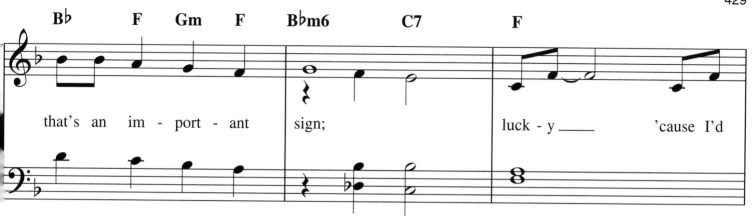

that's an im - port - ant sign; luck - y _____ 'cause I'd

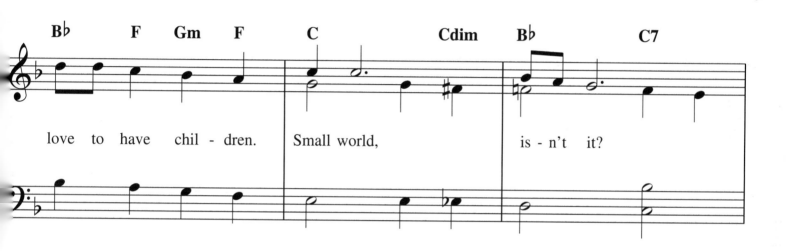

love to have chil - dren. Small world, is - n't it?

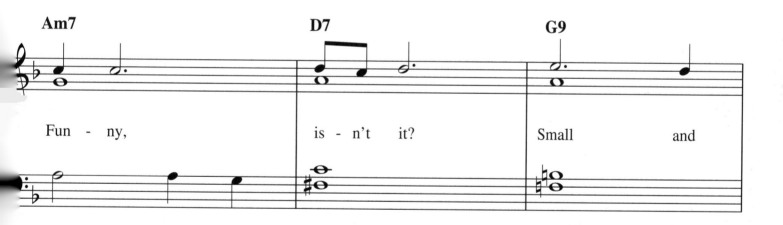

Fun - ny, is - n't it? Small and

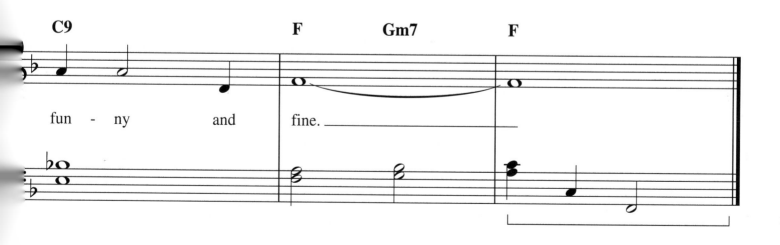

fun - ny and fine. _____

SOFTLY AS IN A MORNING SUNRISE

from THE NEW MOON

Lyrics by OSCAR HAMMERSTEIN II
Music by SIGMUND ROMBERG

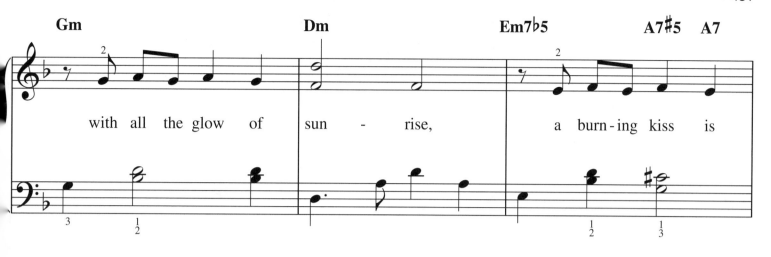

with all the glow of sun - rise, a burn-ing kiss is

seal - ing the vow that all be - tray.

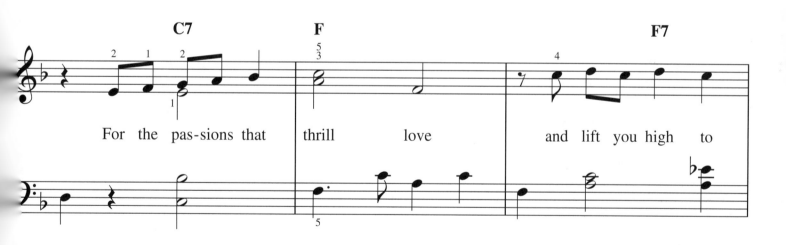

For the pas-sions that thrill love and lift you high to

heav - en are the pas-sions that kill love

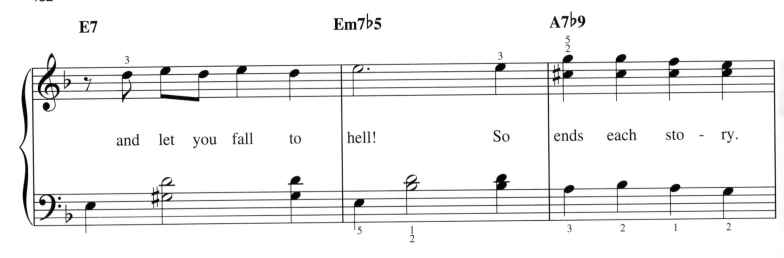

E7   **Em7♭5**   **A7♭9**

and let you fall to hell! So ends each sto - ry.

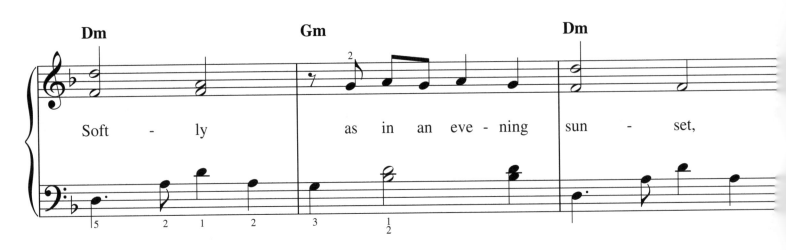

Dm   **Gm**   **Dm**

Soft - ly as in an eve - ning sun - set,

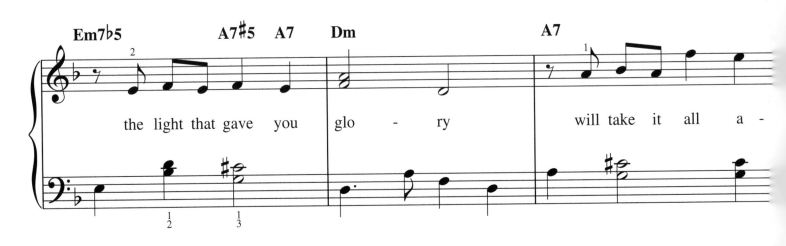

Em7♭5   **A7♯5** **A7** **Dm**   **A7**

the light that gave you glo - ry will take it all a -

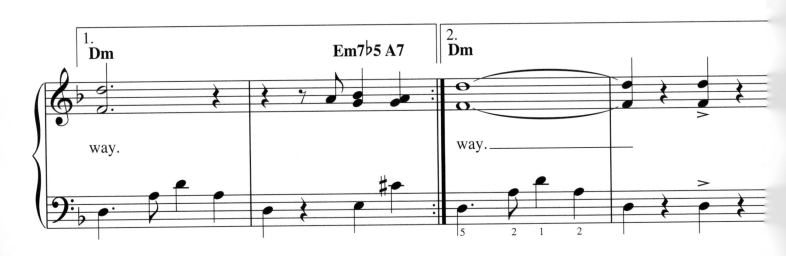

1.
Dm   **Em7♭5 A7**   **2.**
Dm

way.   way._____

SOMEONE NICE LIKE YOU

from the Musical Production STOP THE WORLD – I WANT TO GET OFF

Words and Music by LESLIE BRICUSSE
and ANTHONY NEWLEY

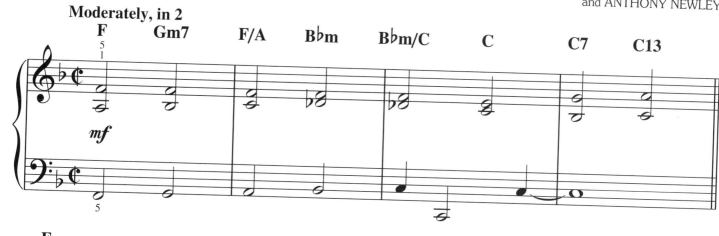

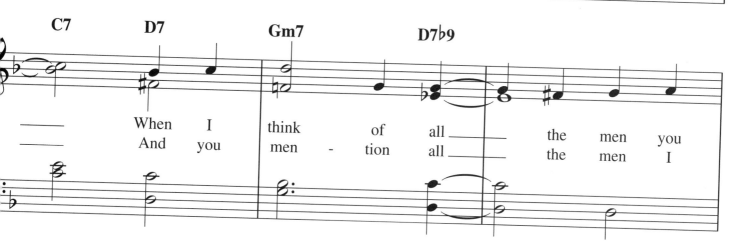

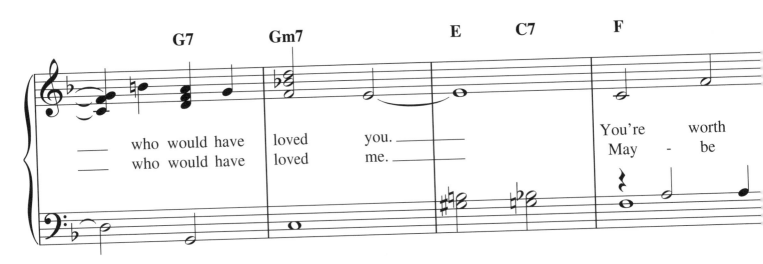

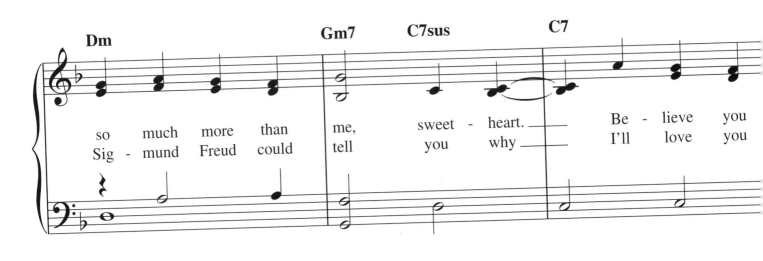

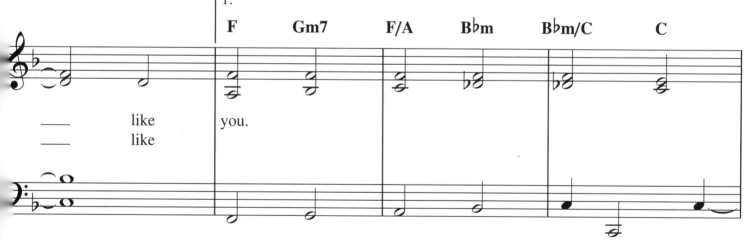

SOMEBODY LOVES YOU

Words by CHARLIE TOBIAS
Music by PETER DE ROSE

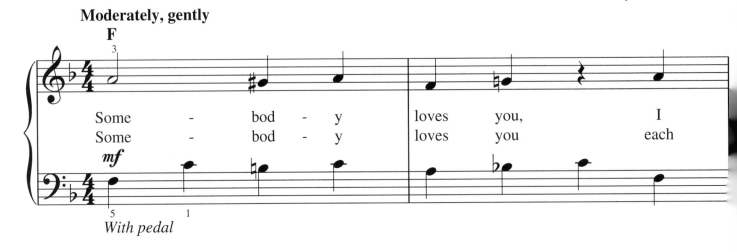

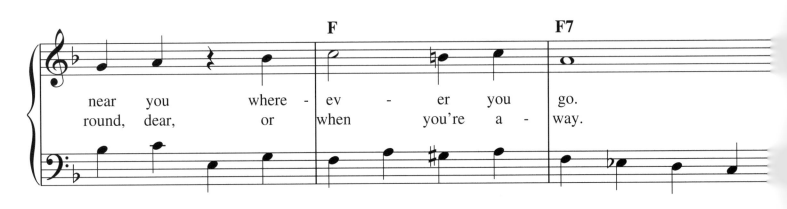

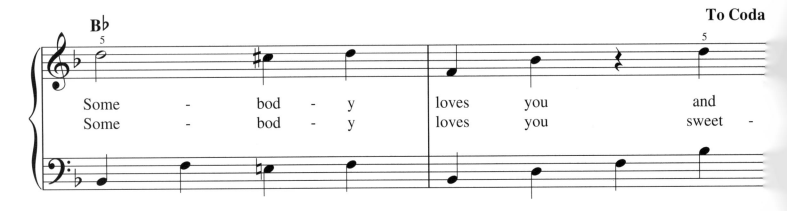

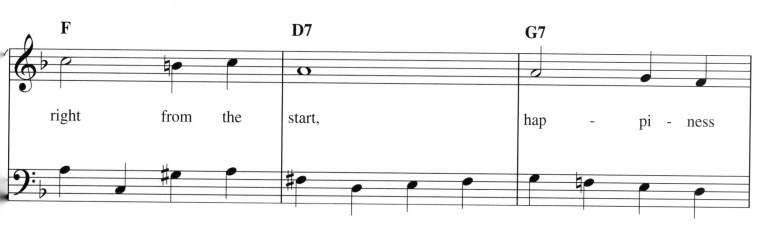

right from the start, hap - pi - ness

D.C. al Coda

flew in - to some - one's heart. ____

CODA

heart, can't you see? And that some -

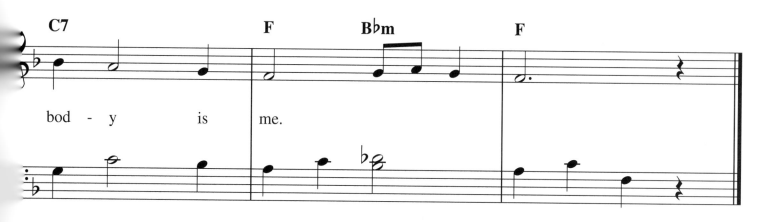

bod - y is me.

SOMETHING GOOD

from THE SOUND OF MUSIC

Lyrics and Music by
RICHARD RODGERS

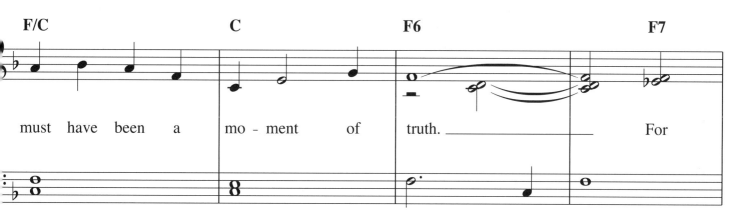

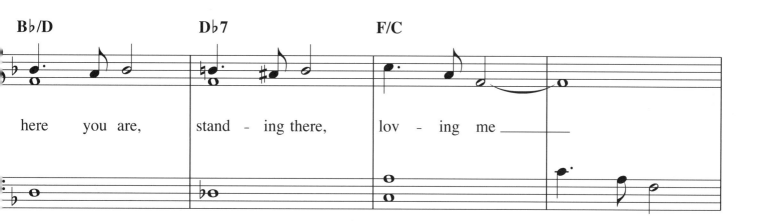

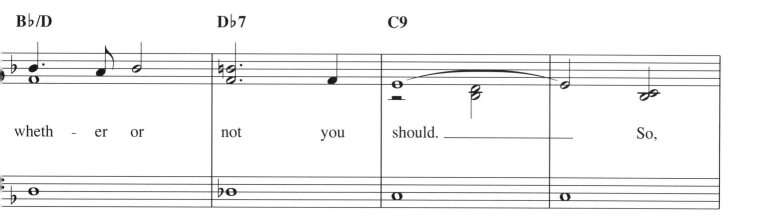

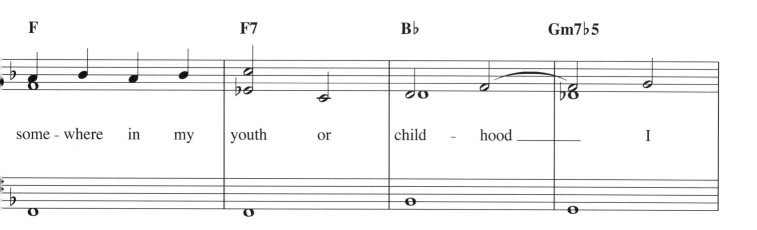

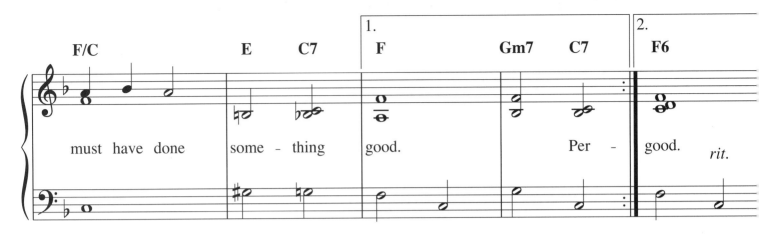

must have done some - thing good. Per - good. *rit.*

Slower

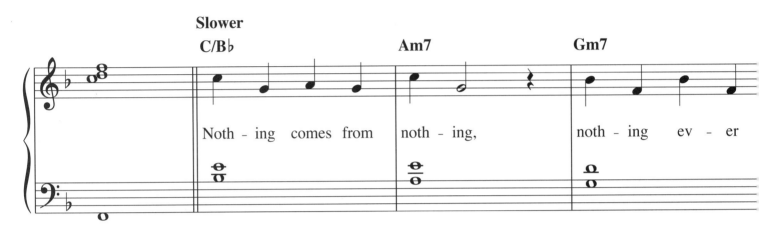

Noth - ing comes from noth - ing, noth - ing ev - er

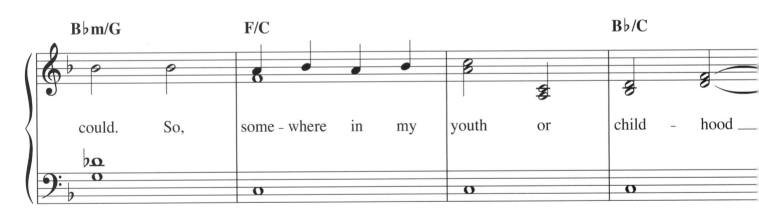

could. So, some - where in my youth or child - hood ___

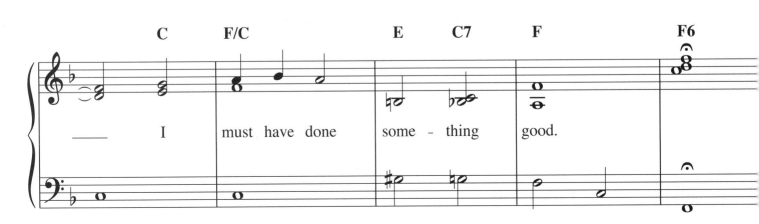

___ I must have done some - thing good.

SOPHISTICATED LADY

Words and Music by DUKE ELLINGTON,
IRVING MILLS and MITCHELL PARISH

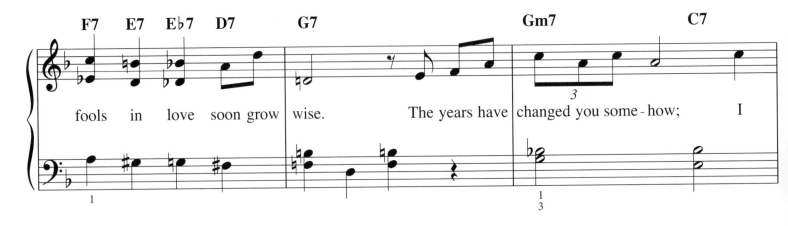

fools in love soon grow wise. The years have changed you some-how; I

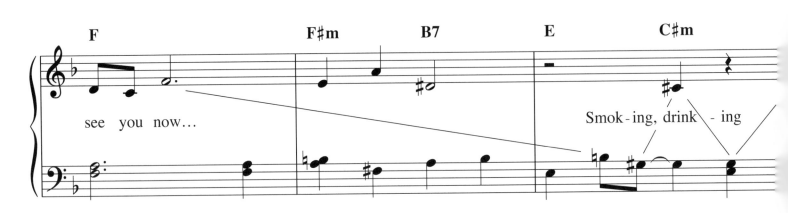

see you now... Smok-ing, drink - ing

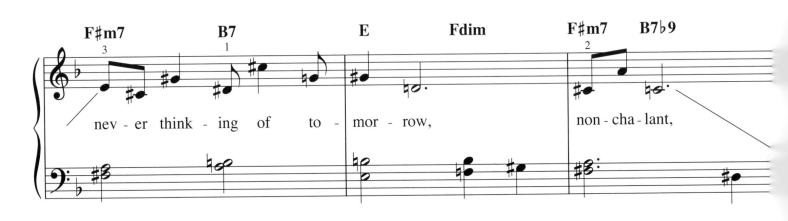

nev - er think - ing of to - mor - row, non - cha - lant,

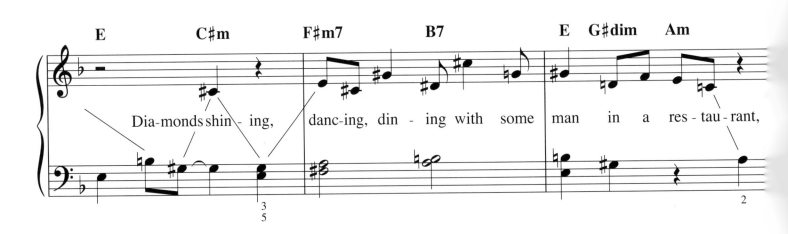

Dia-monds shin - ing, danc-ing, din - ing with some man in a res - tau - rant,

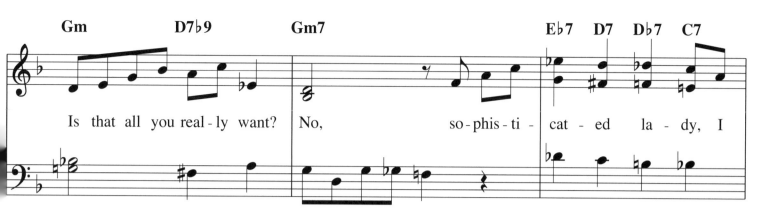

Is that all you real-ly want? No, so-phis-ti- cat- ed la- dy, I

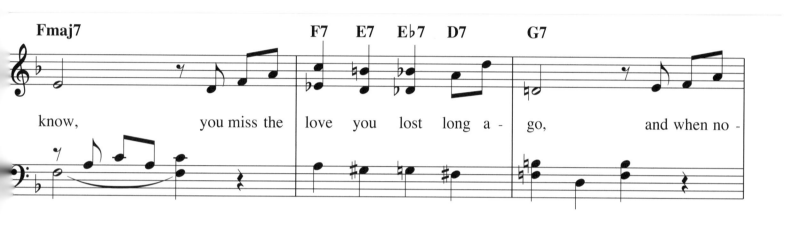

know, you miss the love you lost long a- go, and when no-

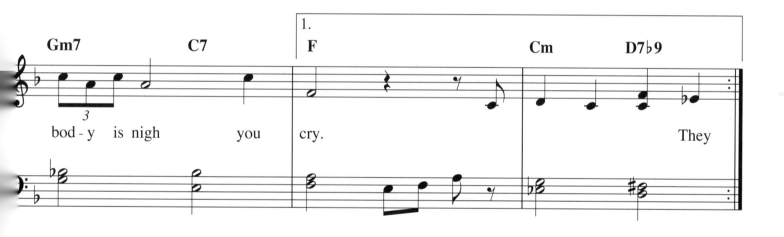

bod-y is nigh you cry. They

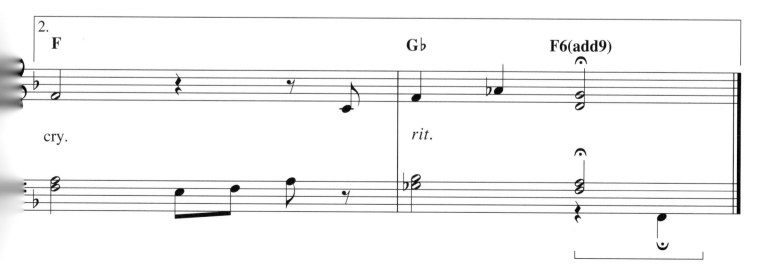

cry. *rit.*

SPANISH EYES

Words by CHARLES SINGLETON and EDDIE SNYDER
Music by BERT KAEMPFERT

445

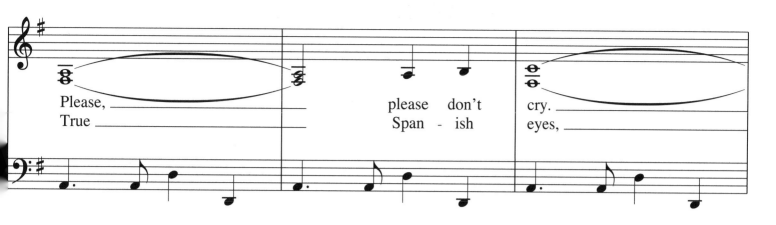

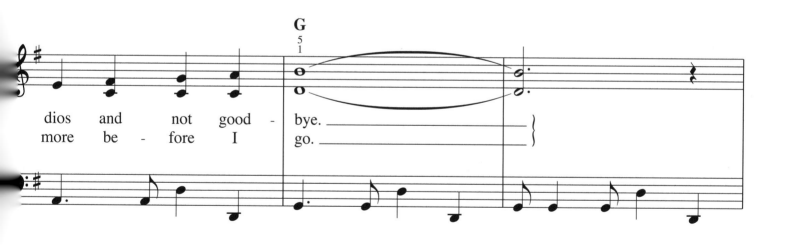

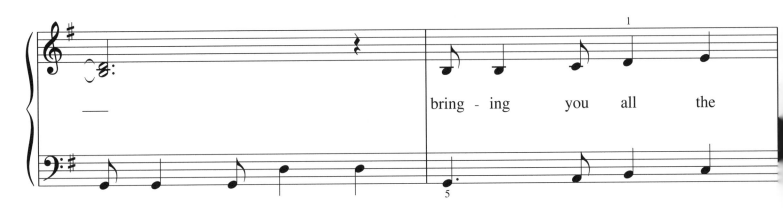

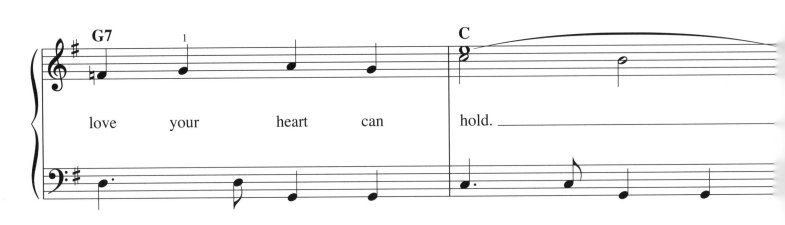

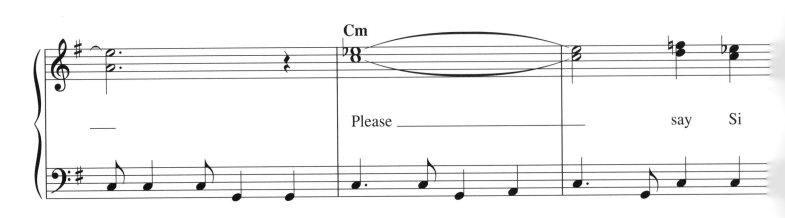

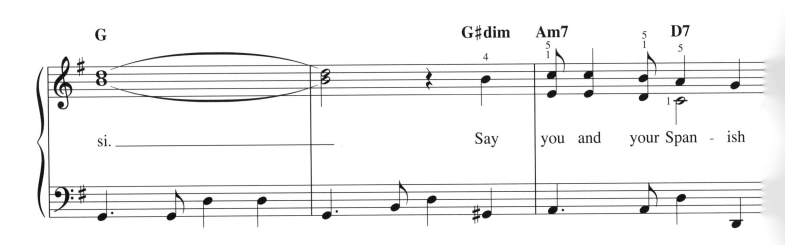

447

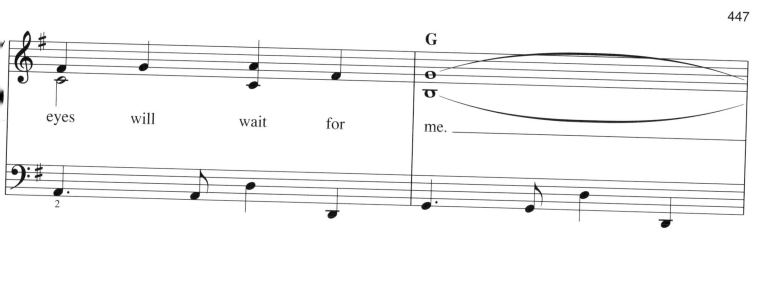

eyes will wait for me. _____

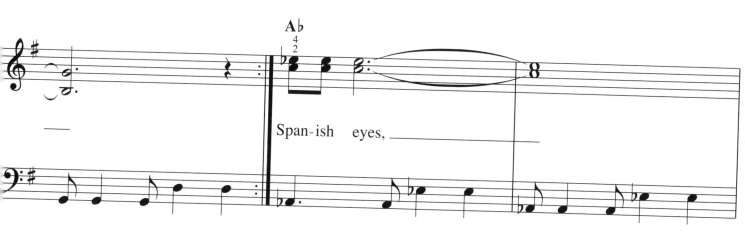

_____ Span-ish eyes, _____

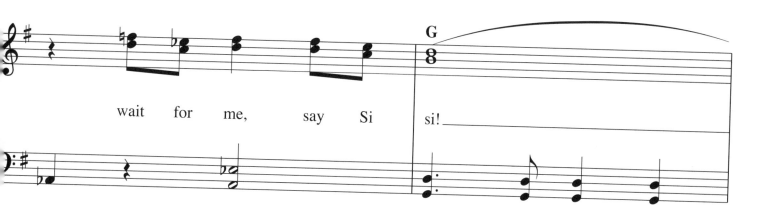

wait for me, say Si si! _____

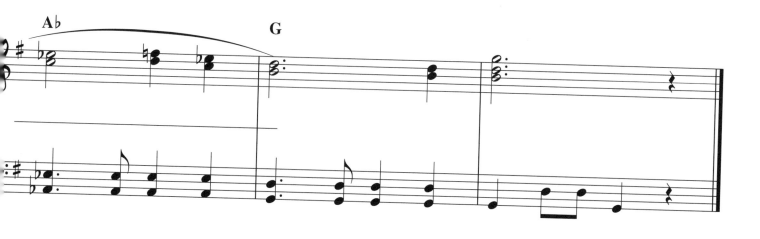

STEPPIN' OUT WITH MY BABY

from the Motion Picture Irving Berlin's EASTER PARADE

Words and Music by
IRVING BERLIN

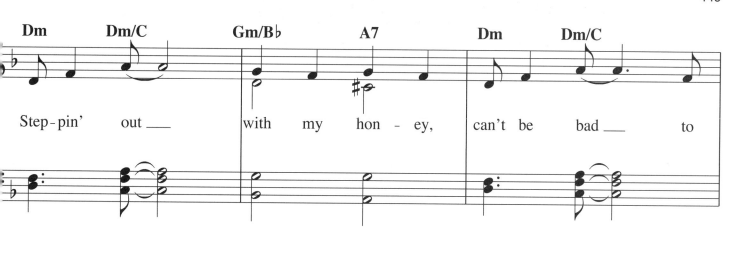

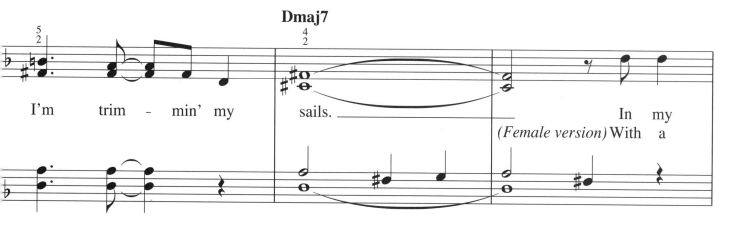

450

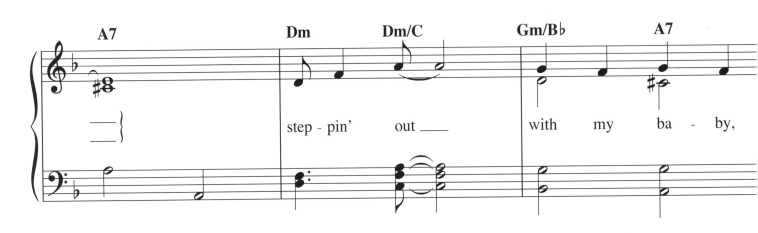

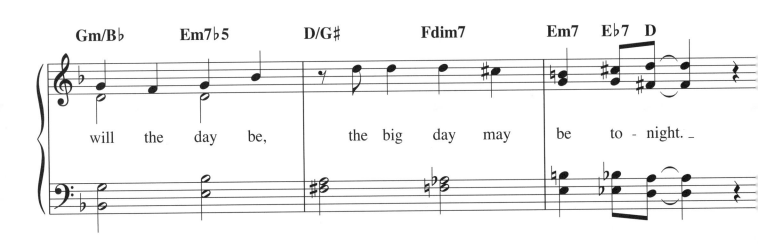

TANGERINE
from the Paramount Picture THE FLEET'S IN

Words by JOHNNY MERCER
Music by VICTOR SCHERTZINGER

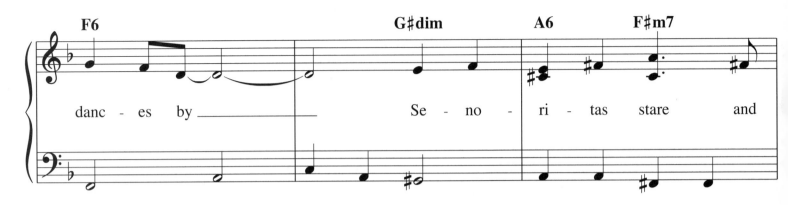

danc - es by _____ Se - no - ri - tas stare and

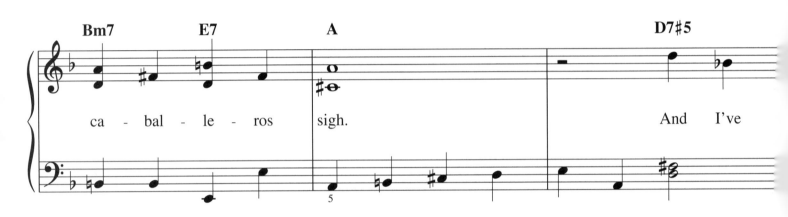

ca - bal - le - ros sigh. And I've

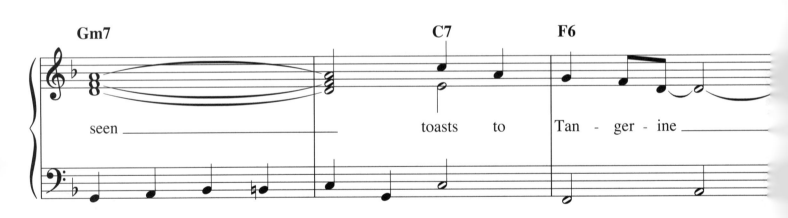

seen _____ toasts to Tan - ger - ine _____

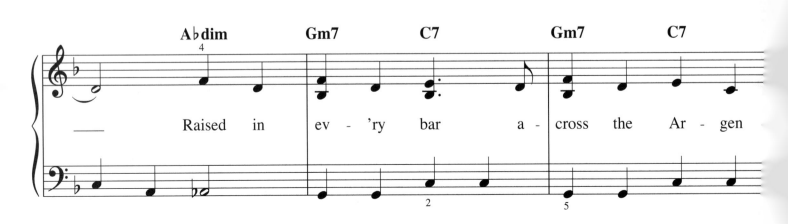

_____ Raised in ev - 'ry bar a - cross the Ar - gen

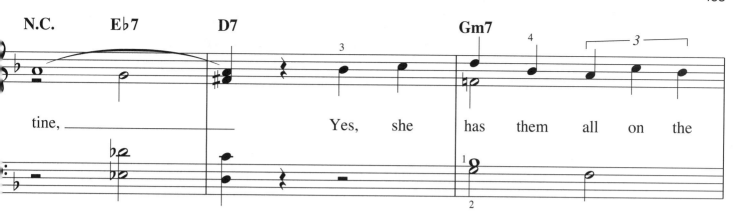

tine, _____ Yes, she has them all on the

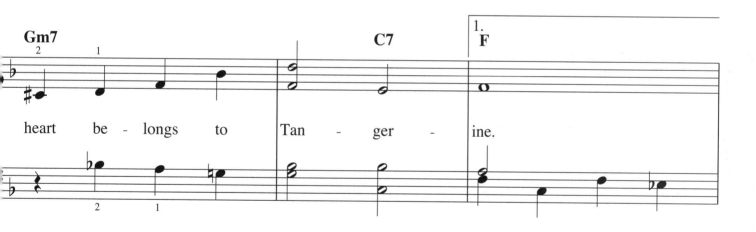

run, But her heart be - longs to just one. Her

heart be - longs to Tan - ger - ine.

Tan - ger - ine.

SUNRISE, SUNSET
from the Musical FIDDLER ON THE ROOF

Words by SHELDON HARNI[...]
Music by JERRY BO[...]

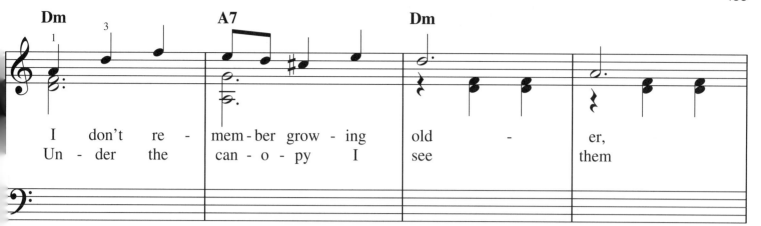

I don't re - mem - ber grow - ing old - er,
Un - der the can - o - py I see them

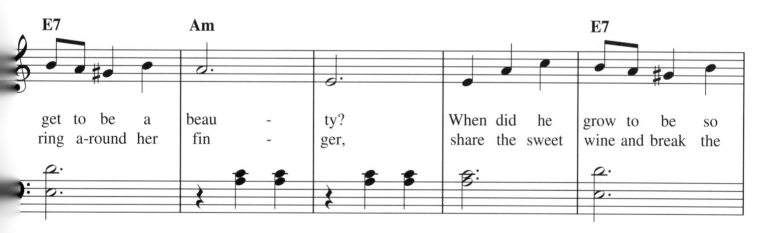

when did they? When did she
side by side. Place the gold

get to be a beau - ty? When did he grow to be so
ring a-round her fin - ger, share the sweet wine and break the

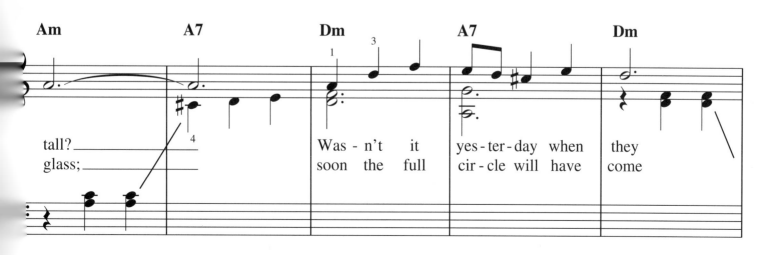

tall? Was - n't it yes - ter - day when they
glass; soon the full cir - cle will have come

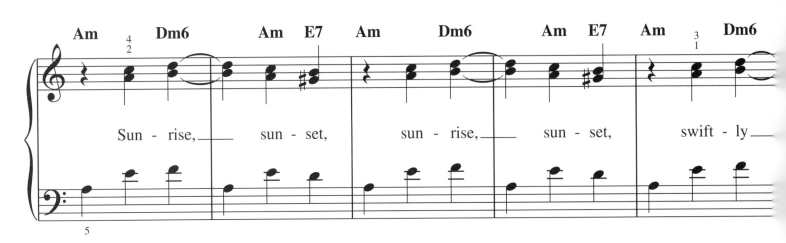

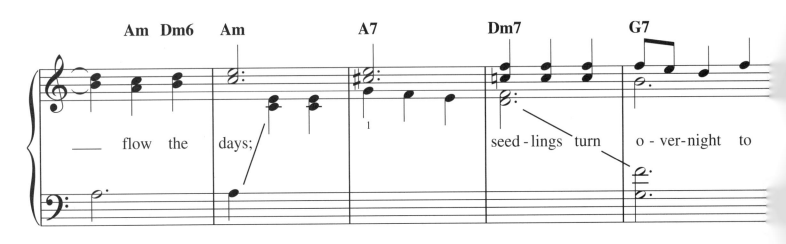

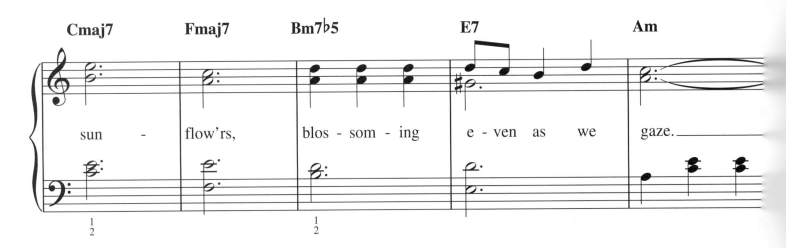

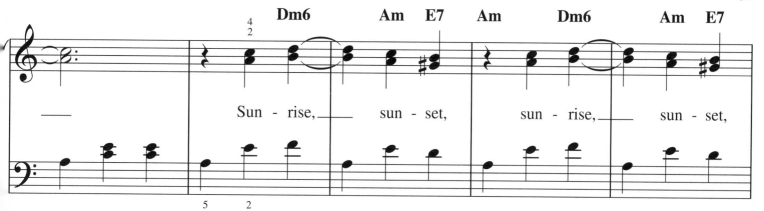

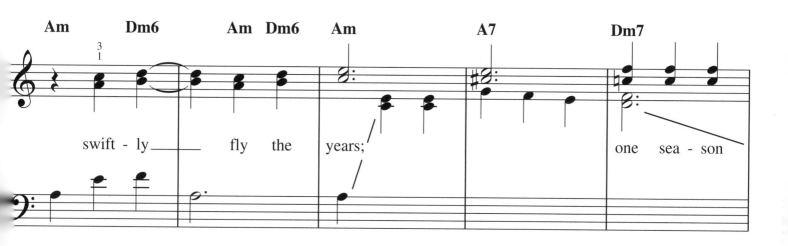

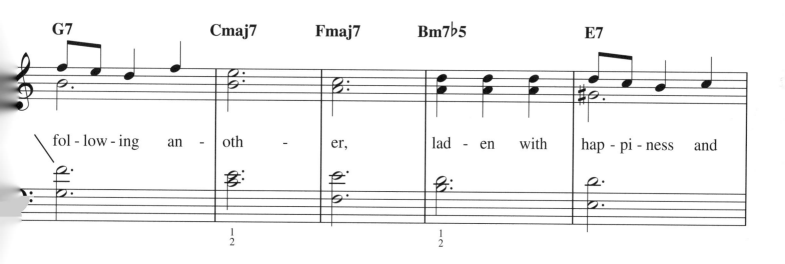

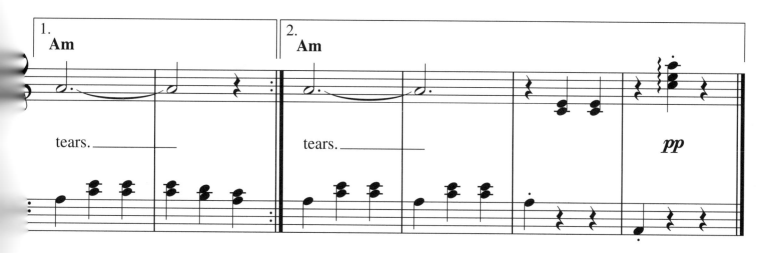

THERE WILL NEVER BE
ANOTHER YOU

from the Motion Picture ICELAND

Lyric by MACK GORDON
Music by HARRY WARREN

songs to sing, an-oth-er fall, an-oth-er spring, but

there will nev-er be an-oth-er you.

There will be oth-er lips that I may

kiss, but they won't thrill me

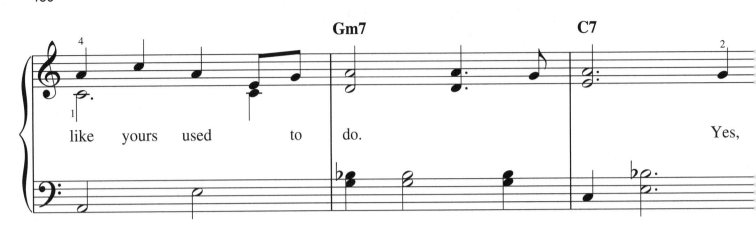

like yours used to do.   Yes,

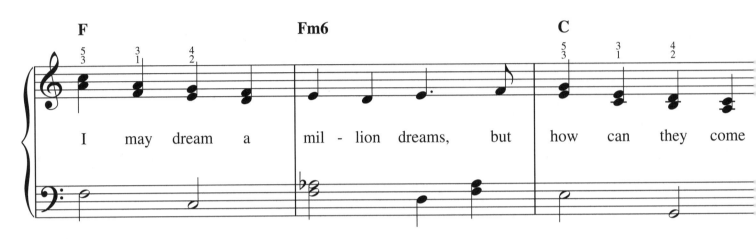

I may dream a   mil - lion dreams,   but   how   can   they   come

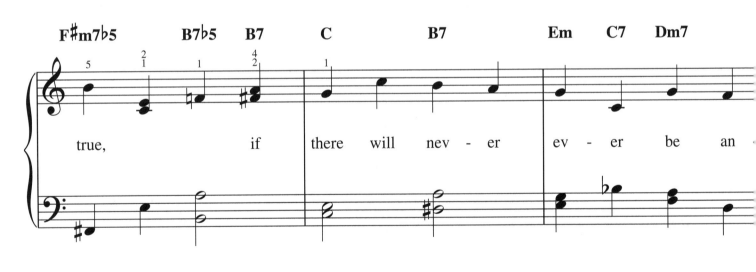

true,   if   there   will   nev - er   ev - er   be   an

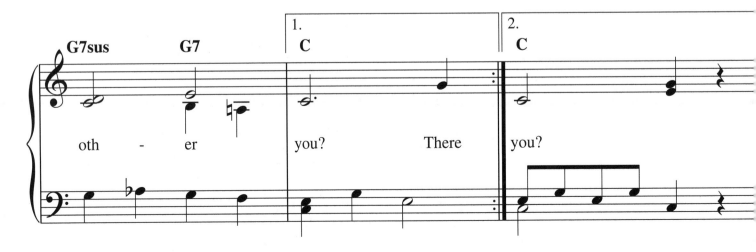

oth - er   you?   There   you?

THIS CAN'T BE LOVE

from THE BOYS FROM SYRACUSE

Words by LORENZ HART
Music by RICHARD RODGERS

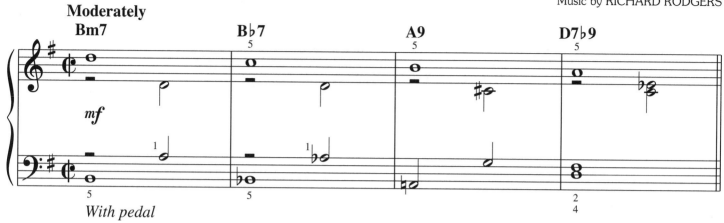

Moderately

With pedal

No pedal

This can't be love be-cause I feel so well, __

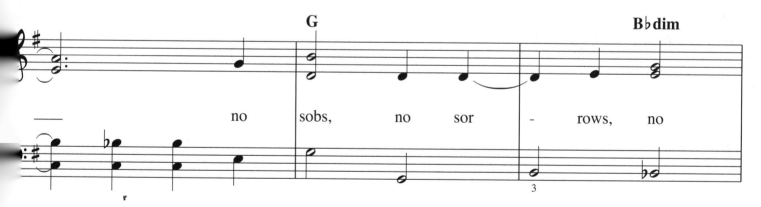

__ no sobs, no sor - rows, no

sighs. __ This can't be

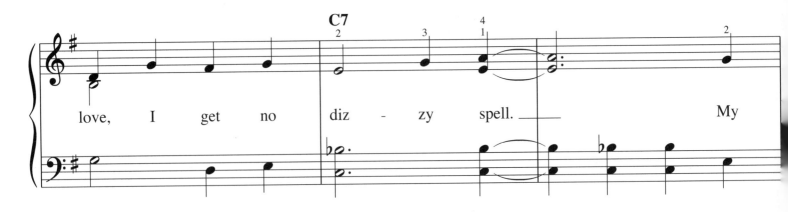

love, I get no diz - zy spell. ____ My

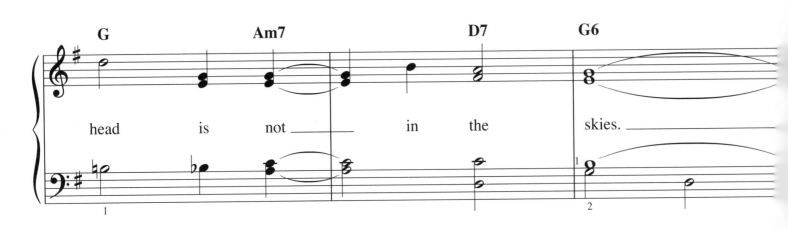

head is not ____ in the skies. ____

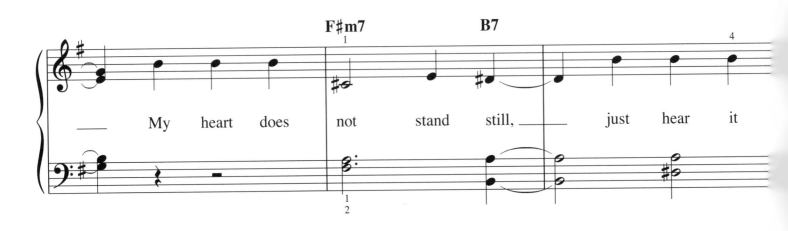

____ My heart does not stand still, ____ just hear it

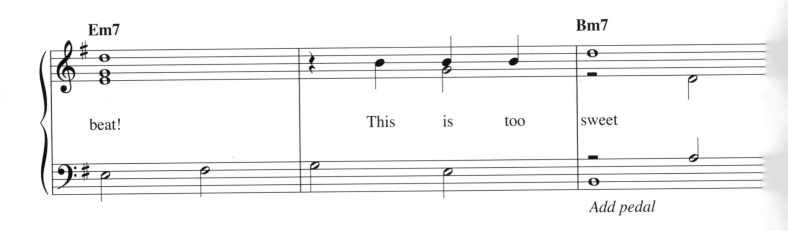

beat! This is too sweet

Add pedal

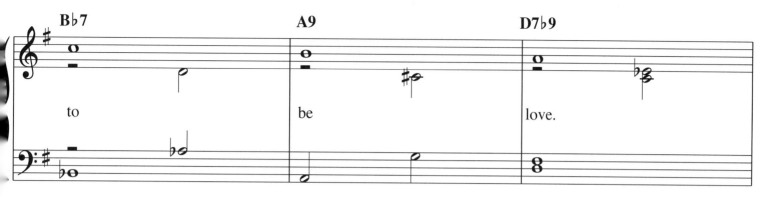

to be love.

This can't be love be - cause I feel so well. ___

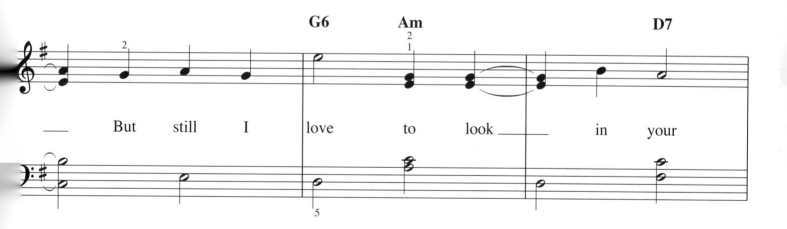

___ But still I love to look ___ in your

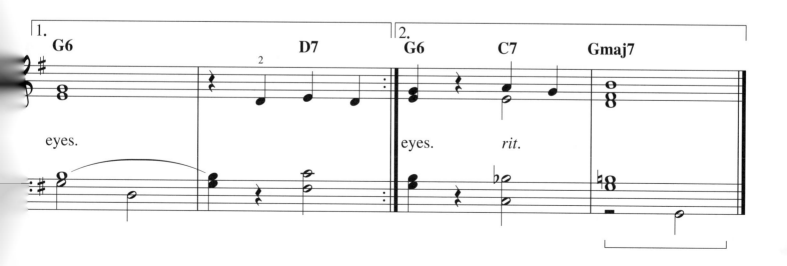

eyes. eyes. *rit.*

THERE'S A SMALL HOTEL

from ON YOUR TOES

Words by LORENZ HART
Music by RICHARD RODGERS

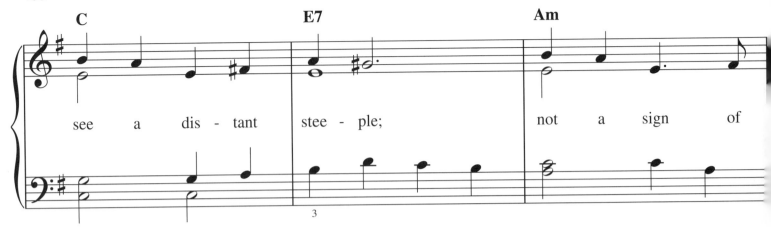

see a dis - tant stee - ple; not a sign of

peo - ple. Who wants peo - ple?

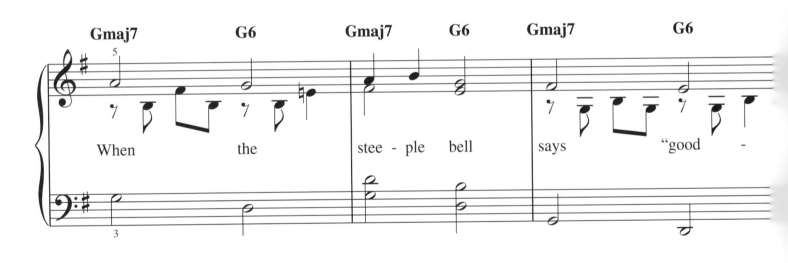

When the stee - ple bell says "good -

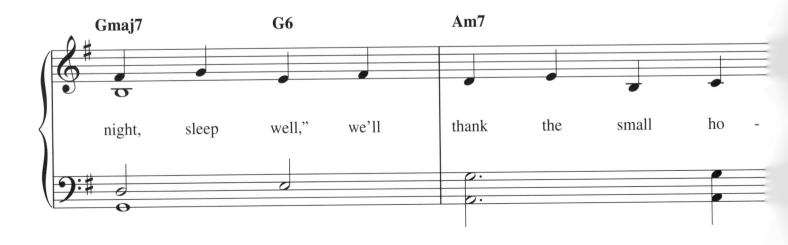

night, sleep well," we'll thank the small ho -

TO LOVE AGAIN
Theme from THE EDDY DUCHIN STORY

Based on Chopin's E Flat Nocturne
Words by NED WASHINGTON
Music by MORRIS STOLOFF and GEORGE SIDNEY

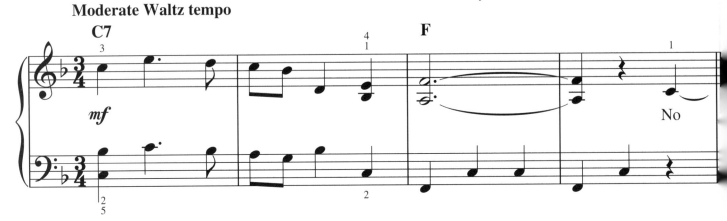

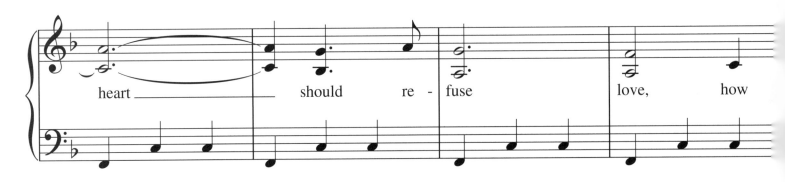

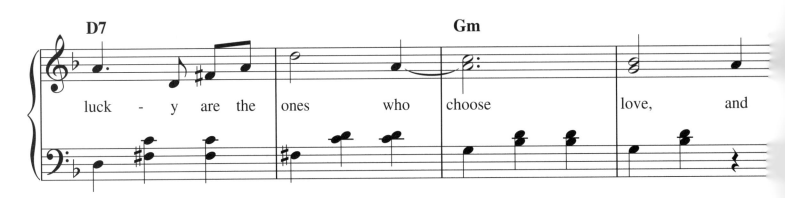

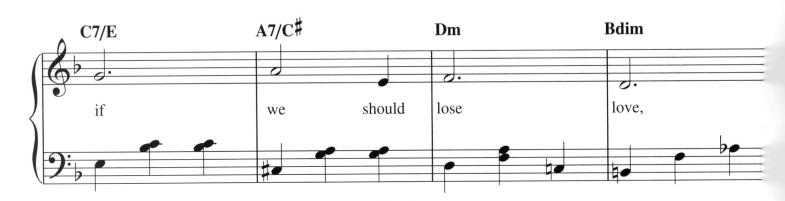

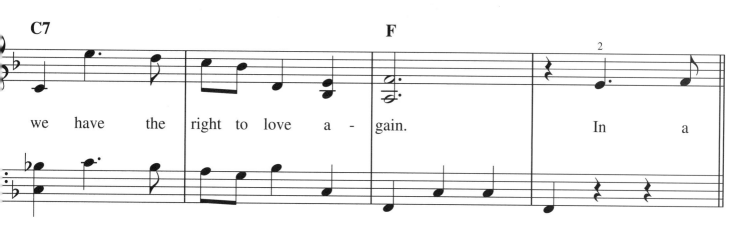

we have the right to love a - gain. In a

A little faster

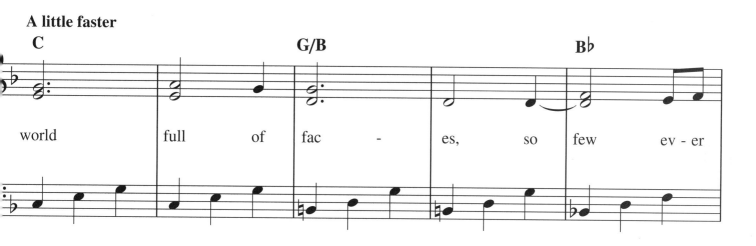

world full of fac - es, so few ev - er

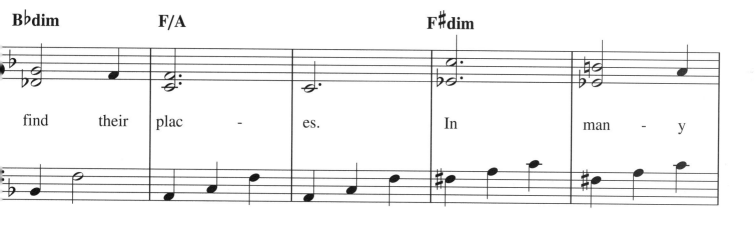

find their plac - es. In man - y

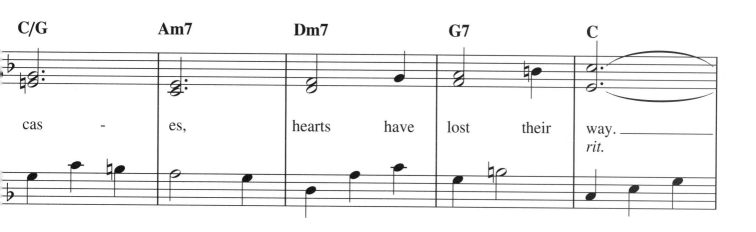

cas - es, hearts have lost their way. *rit.*

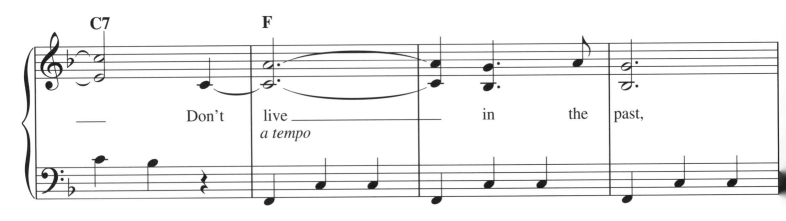

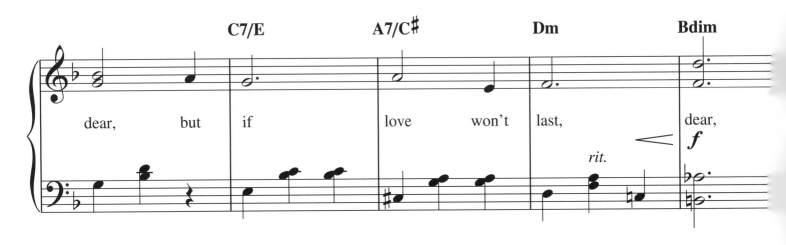

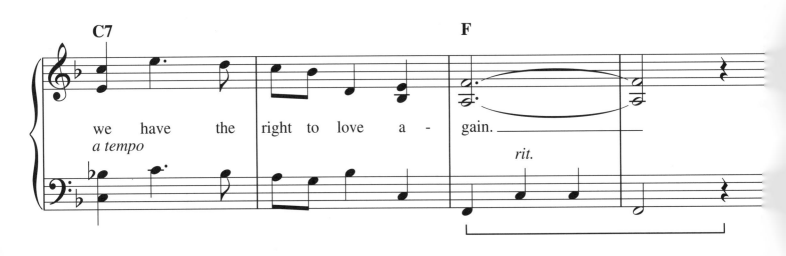

THE VERY THOUGHT OF YOU

Words and Music by
RAY NOBLE

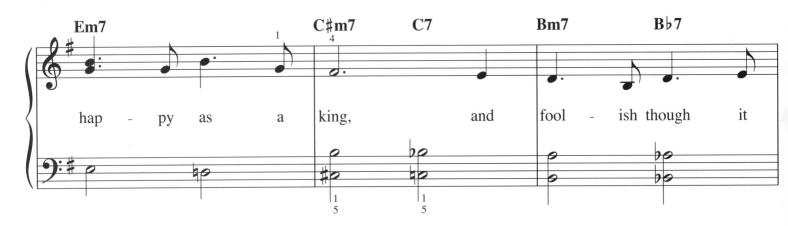

hap - py as a king, and fool - ish though it

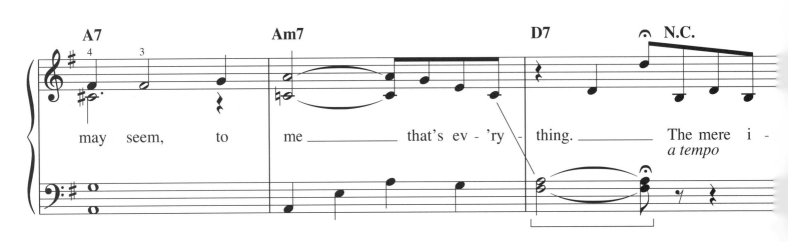

may seem, to me _____ that's ev - 'ry - thing. _____ The mere i -
a tempo

dea of you, the long-ing here for you,

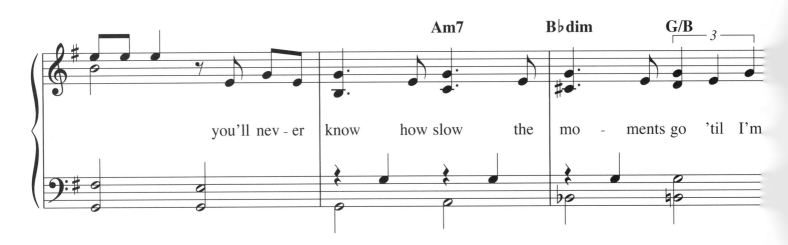

you'll nev - er know how slow the mo - ments go 'til I'm

WHAT A DIFF'RENCE A DAY MADE

English Words by STANLEY ADAMS
Music and Spanish Words by MARIA GREVER

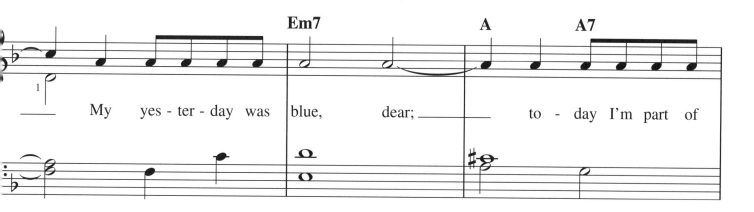

My yes-ter-day was blue, dear; to - day I'm part of

you, dear; my lone-ly nights are through, dear,

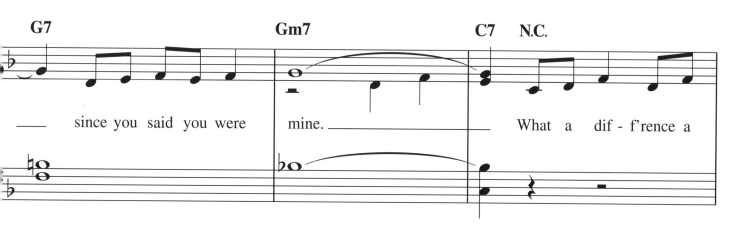

since you said you were mine. What a dif-f'rence a

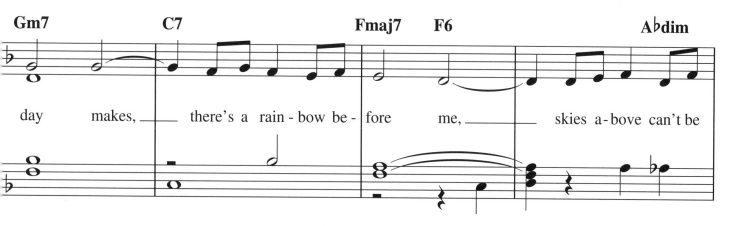

day makes, there's a rain-bow be-fore me, skies a-bove can't be

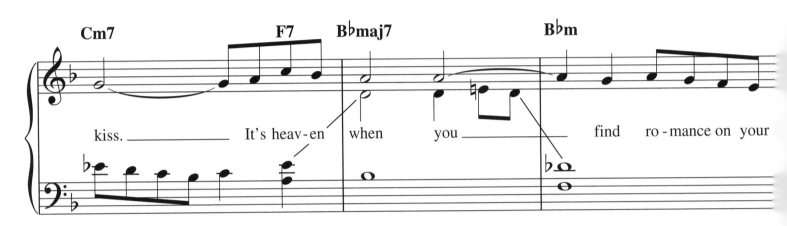

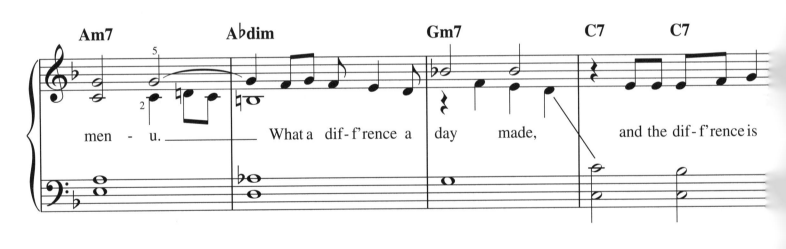

WHO CAN I TURN TO
(When Nobody Needs Me)
from THE ROAR OF THE GREASEPAINT – THE SMELL OF THE CROWD

Words and Music by LESLIE BRICUSSE
and ANTHONY NEWLEY

Slowly, with expression

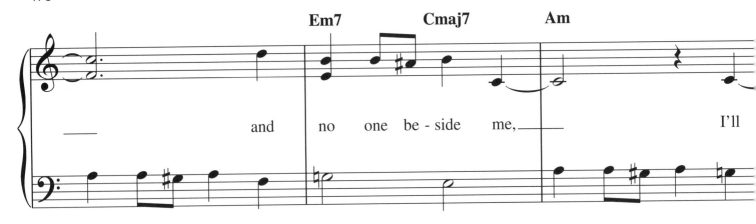

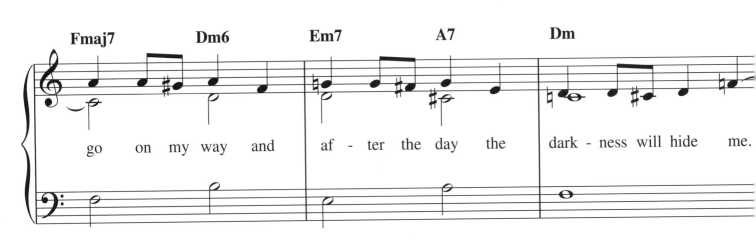

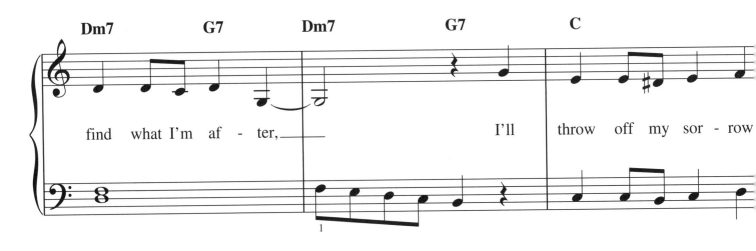

WHAT NOW MY LOVE
(Original French Title: "Et maintenant")

Original French Lyric by PIERRE DELANOE
Music by FRANCOIS BECAUD
English Adaptation by CARL SIGMAN

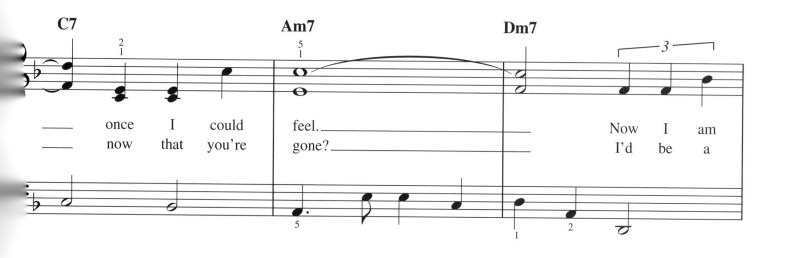

WILLOW WEEP FOR ME

Words and Music by
ANN RONELL

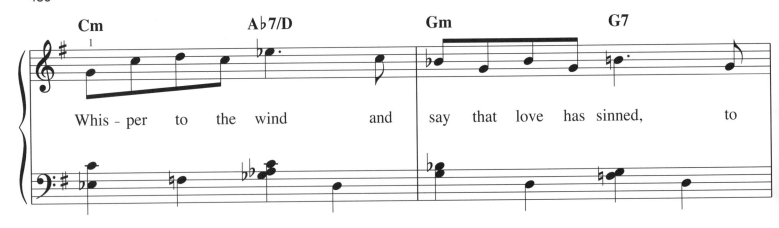

Whis - per to the wind and say that love has sinned, to

leave my heart a - break - ing and mak - ing a moan. _

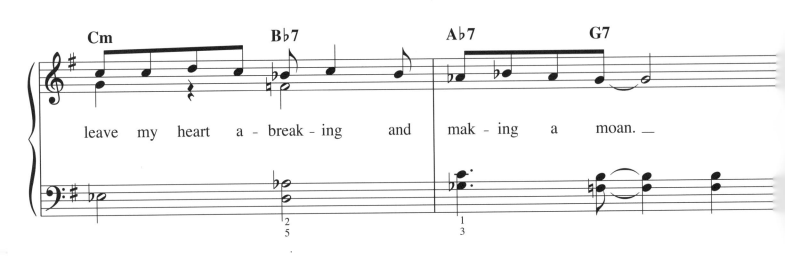

Mur - mur to the night to hide her star - ry light, so

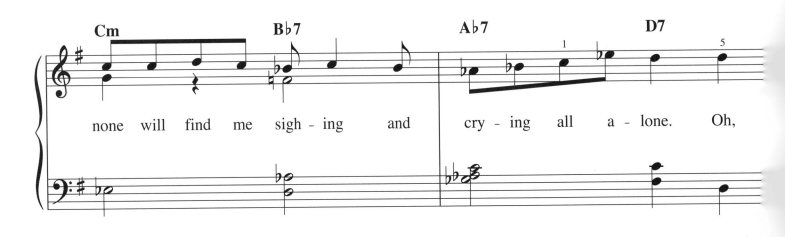

none will find me sigh - ing and cry - ing all a - lone. Oh,

weep - ing wil - low tree, weep in sym - pa - thy,

bend your branch - es down a - long the ground and cov - er me.

When the shad - ows fall, bend, oh wil - low, and weep for

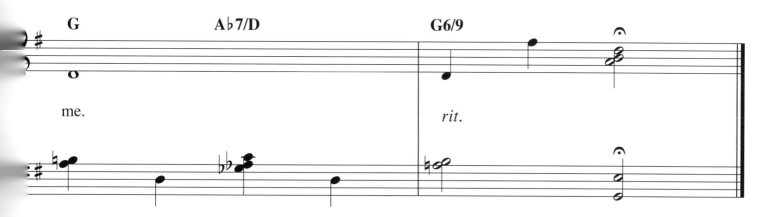

me. *rit.*

WON'T YOU BE MY NEIGHBOR?
(It's a Beautiful Day in the Neighborhood)
from MISTER ROGERS' NEIGHBORHOOD

Words and Music by
FRED ROGERS

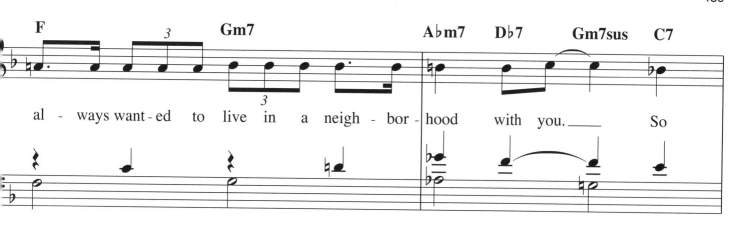

al - ways want - ed to live in a neigh - bor - hood with you.____ So

let's make the most of this beau - ti - ful day, since we're to - geth - er we might as well say,

Would you be mine? Could you be mine? Won't you be my neigh - bor?

Won't you please, Won't you please? Please won't you be my neigh - bor?

YESTERDAYS

from ROBERTA
from LOVELY TO LOOK AT

Words by OTTO HARBACH
Music by JEROME KERN

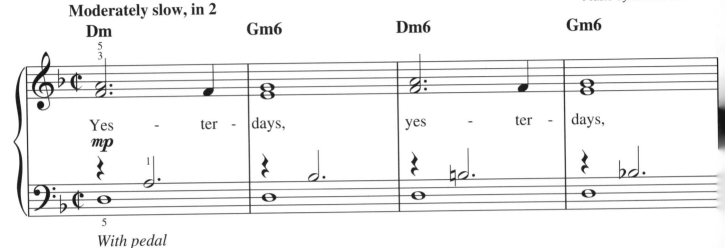

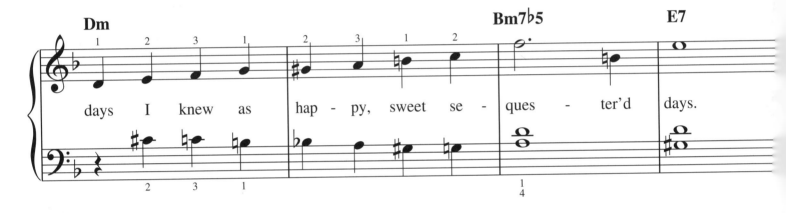

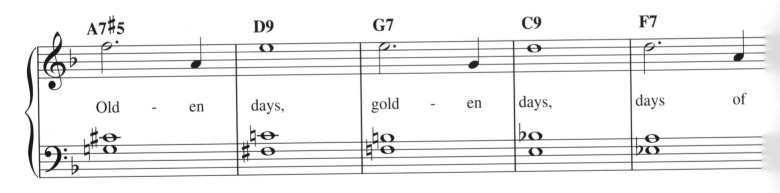

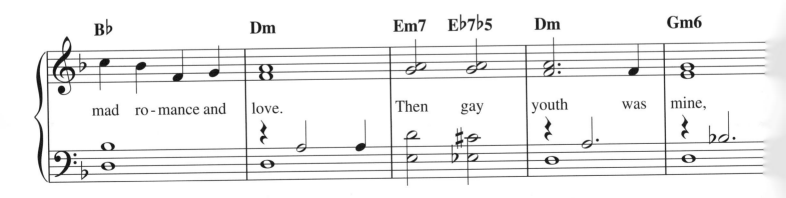

truth was mine, joy - ous free and flam - ing life, for -

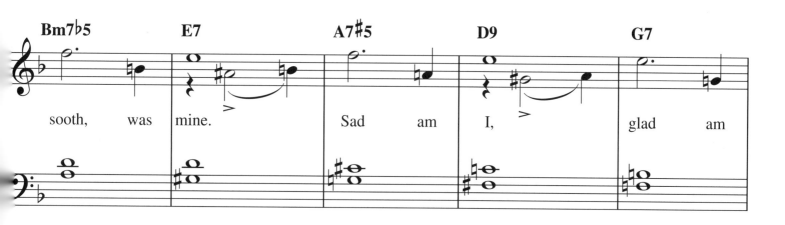

sooth, was mine. Sad am I, glad am

I, for to - day I'm dream-ing of yes - ter -

days.

rit. al fine

YOU ARE BEAUTIFUL
from FLOWER DRUM SONG

Lyrics by OSCAR HAMMERSTEIN II
Music by RICHARD RODGERS

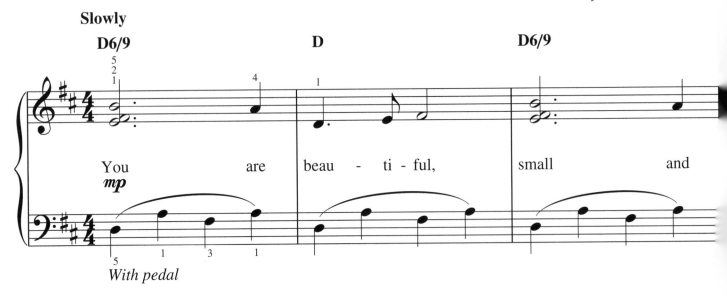

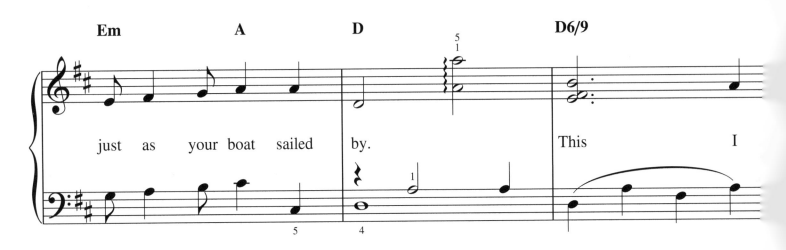

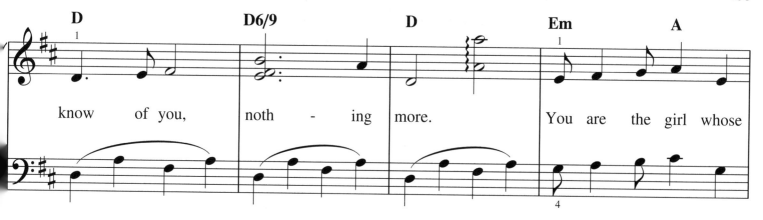

know of you, noth - ing more. You are the girl whose

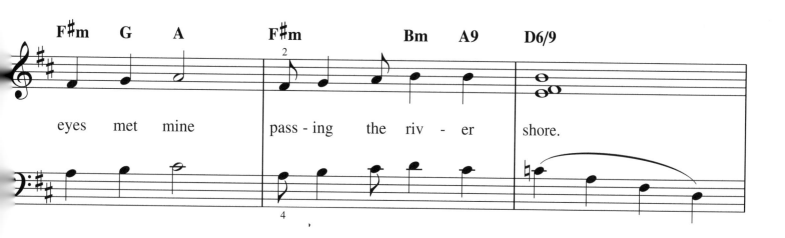

eyes met mine pass - ing the riv - er shore.

You are the girl whose laugh I heard, sil - ver and soft and

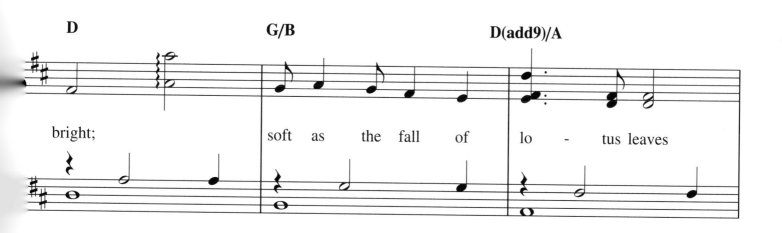

bright; soft as the fall of lo - tus leaves

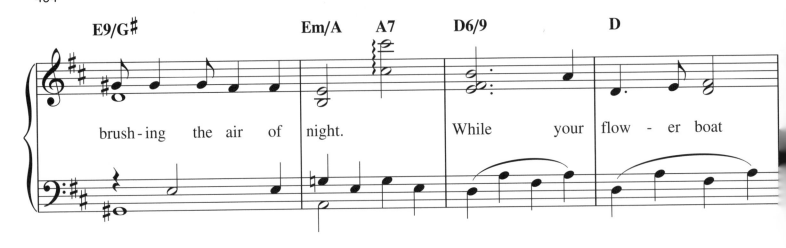

brush - ing   the   air   of   night.   While   your   flow - er   boat

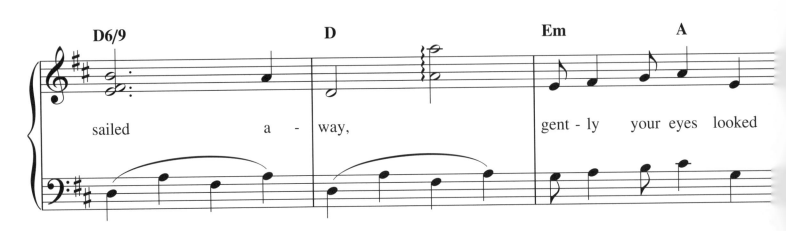

sailed   a   -   way,   gent - ly   your   eyes   looked

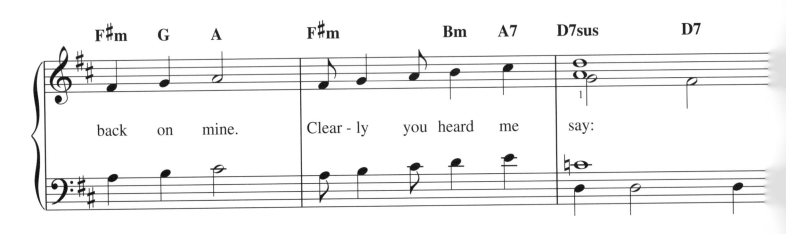

back   on   mine.   Clear - ly   you   heard   me   say:

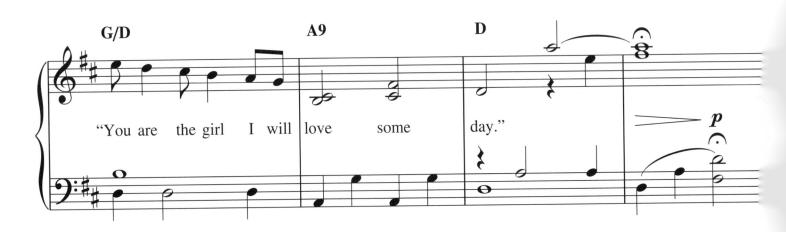

"You   are   the   girl   I   will   love   some   day."

YOU LIGHT UP MY LIFE

Words and Music by
JOSEPH BROOKS

Moderately slow

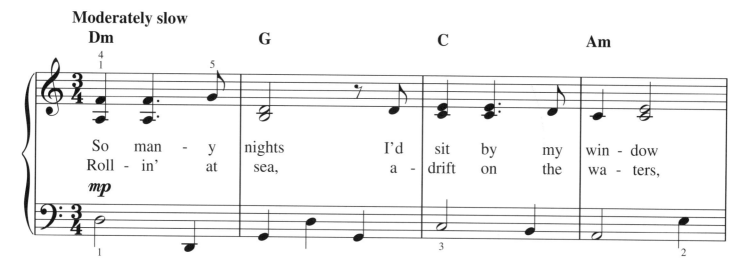

So man - y nights I'd sit by my win - dow
Roll - in' at sea, a - drift on the wa - ters,

wait - ing for some - one___ to sing me his song.
could it be fi - n'lly___ I'm turn - ing for home.

So man - y dreams I kept deep in - side me, a -
Fi - n'lly a chance to say, "Hey! I love you."

lone in the dark, but now you've come a - long.
Nev - er a - gain to be all a - lone.

And

you light up my life, you give me hope

to car - ry on. You light up my days and fill my

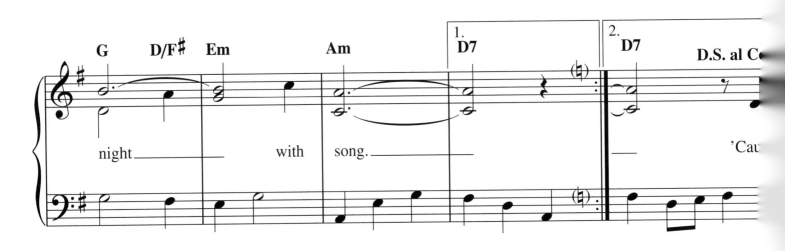

night_____ with song._____ 'Cau

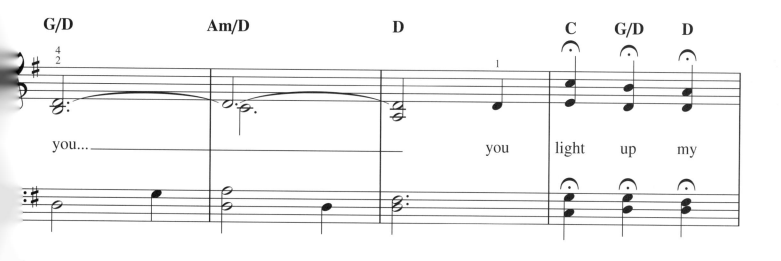

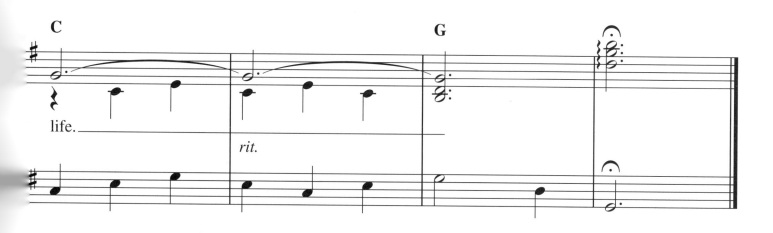

YOU'D BE SO NICE TO COME HOME TO

from SOMETHING TO SHOUT ABOUT

Words and Music by
COLE PORTER

Slowly and expressively

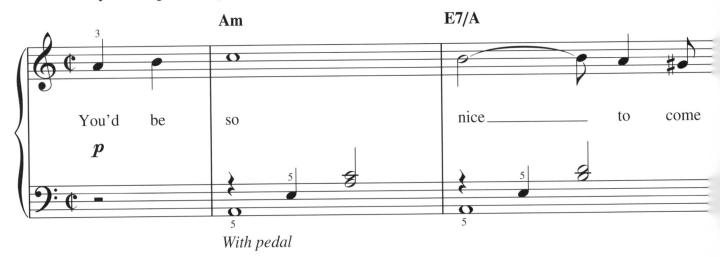

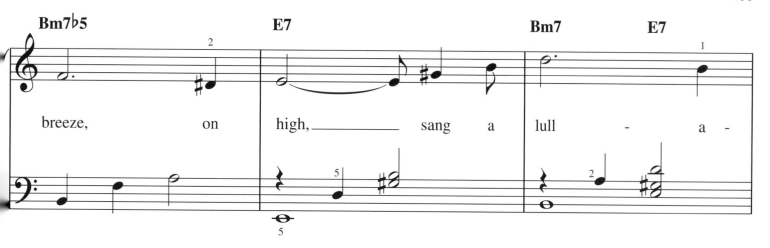

breeze,   on   high,_____ sang a   lull - a -

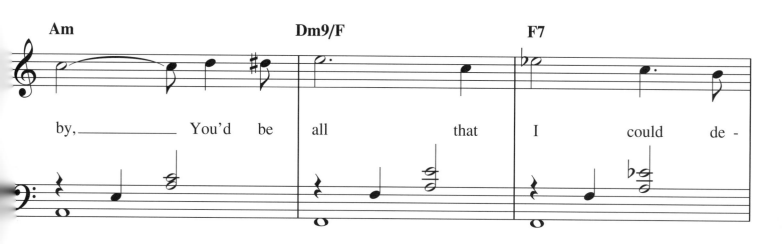

by,_____ You'd   be   all   that   I   could de -

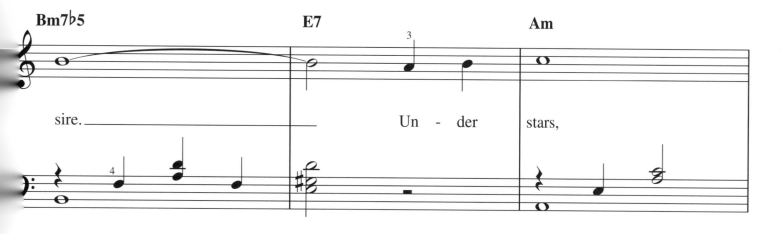

sire._____ Un - der   stars,

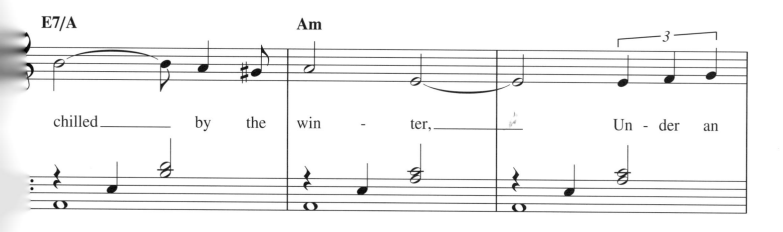

chilled_____ by   the   win - ter,_____   Un - der an

YOU'LL NEVER WALK ALONE

from CAROUSEL

Lyrics by OSCAR HAMMERSTEIN II
Music by RICHARD RODGERS

Moderately flowing

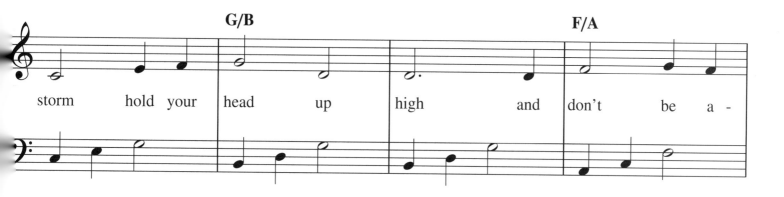

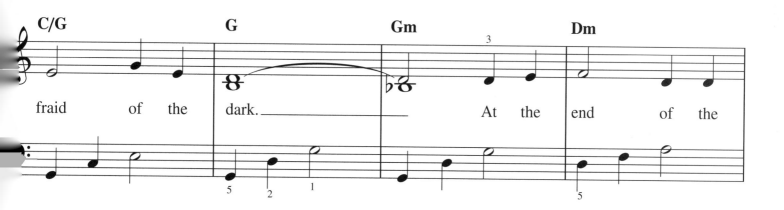

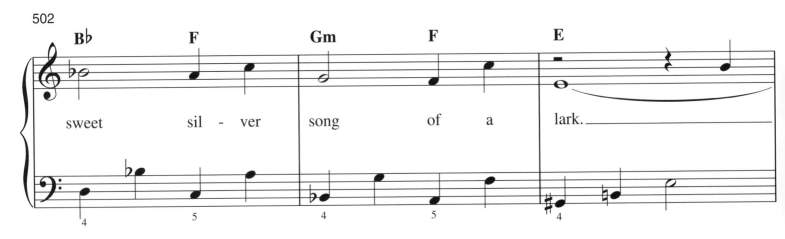

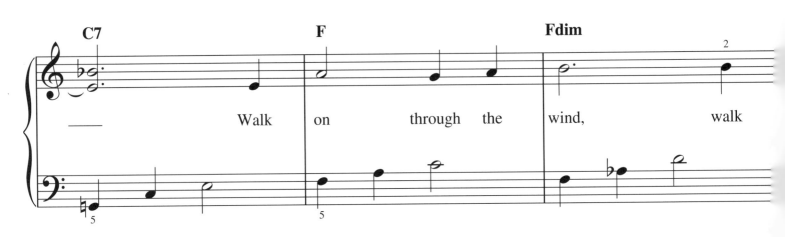

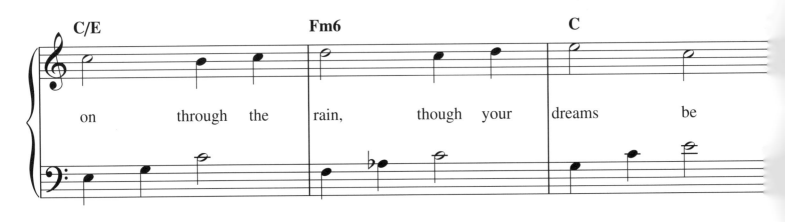

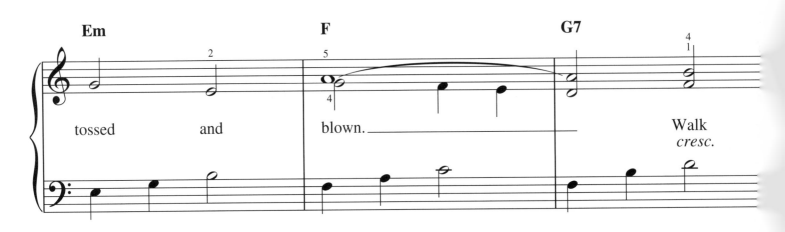

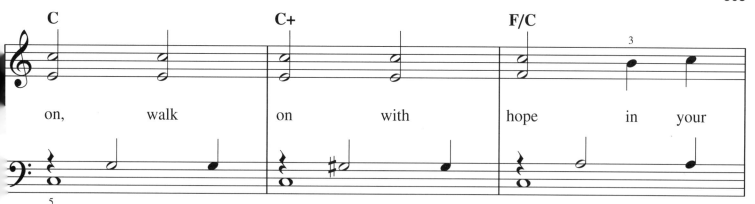

on, walk on with hope in your

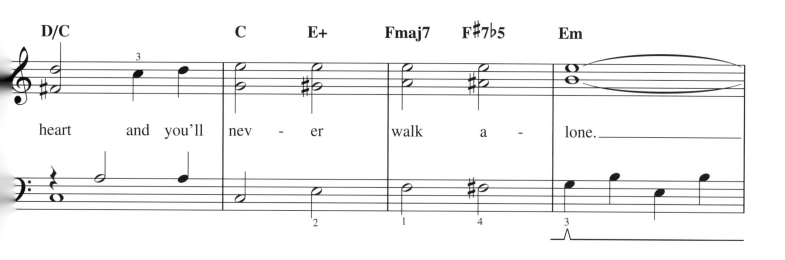

heart and you'll nev - er walk a - lone.____

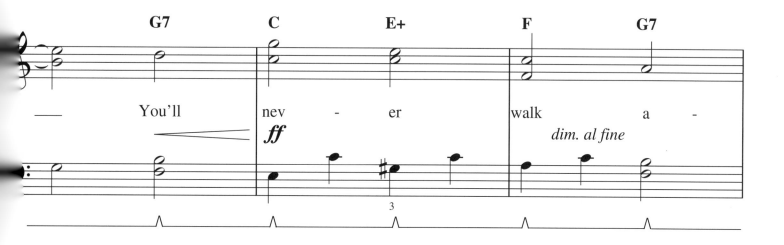

____ You'll nev - er walk a -

ff

dim. al fine

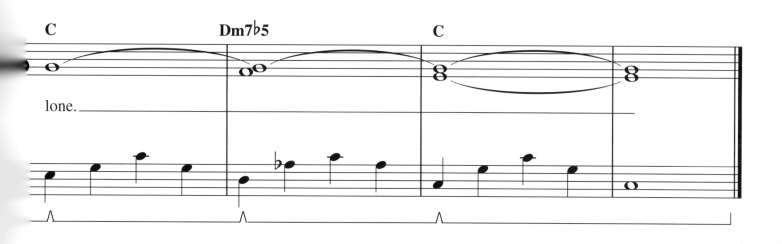

lone.____

YOU'RE NOBODY 'TIL SOMEBODY LOVES YOU

Words and Music by RUSS MORGAN,
LARRY STOCK and JAMES CAVANAUGH

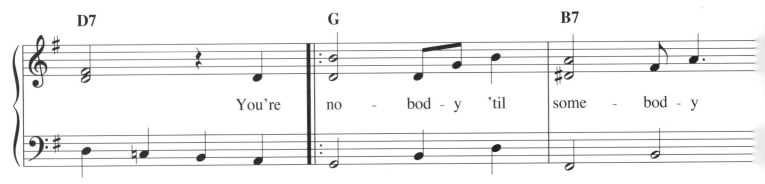

You're no-bod-y 'til some-bod-y

loves you. ___ You're no-bod-y 'til some-bod-y

cares. You may be king, ___ you

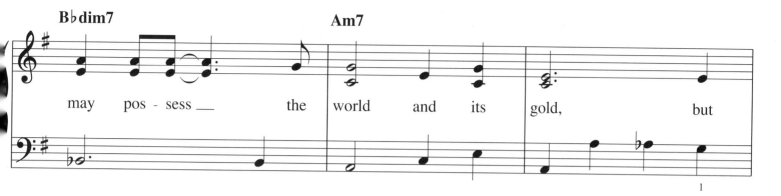

B♭dim7   **Am7**

may pos - sess __ the world and its gold, but

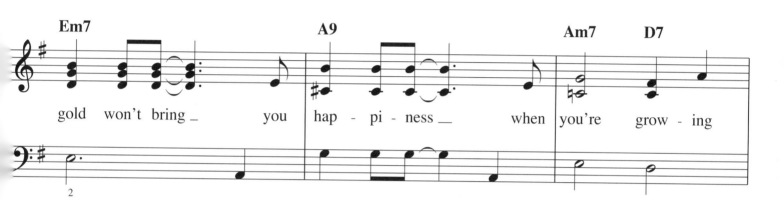

Em7   **A9**   **Am7**   **D7**

gold won't bring __ you hap - pi - ness __ when you're grow - ing

G   **B7**

old.   The world still is the same, you'll nev - er

E7   **Am**   **E7**

change it. _____ As sure as the stars shine a -

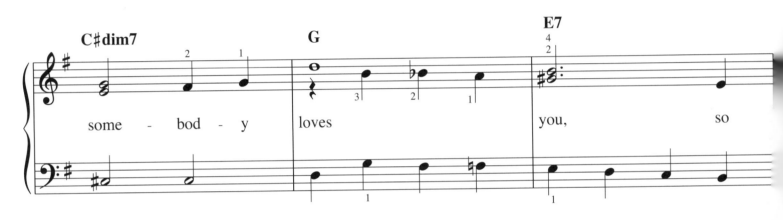

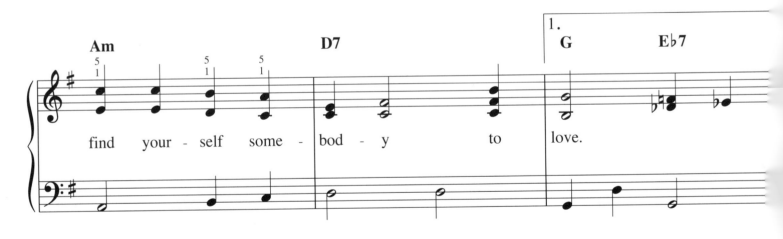

YOUNGER THAN SPRINGTIME

from SOUTH PACIFIC

Lyrics by OSCAR HAMMERSTEIN II
Music by RICHARD RODGERS

ZIP-A-DEE-DOO-DAH

from Walt Disney's SONG OF THE SOUTH

Words by RAY GILBERT
Music by ALLIE WRUBEL

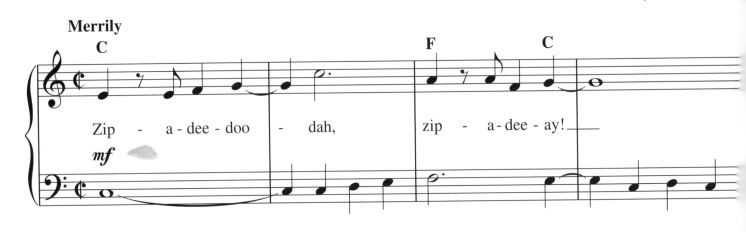

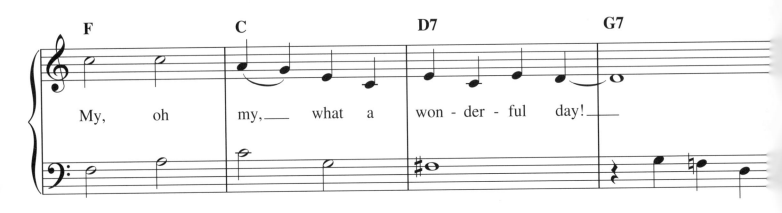

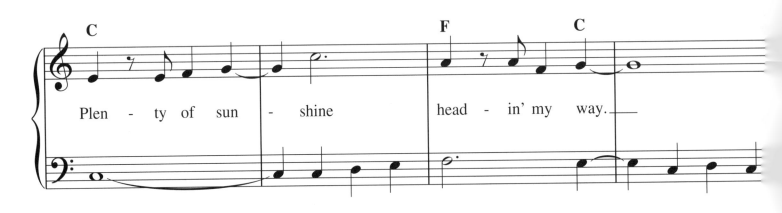

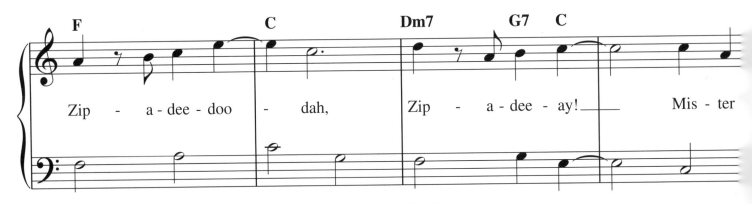

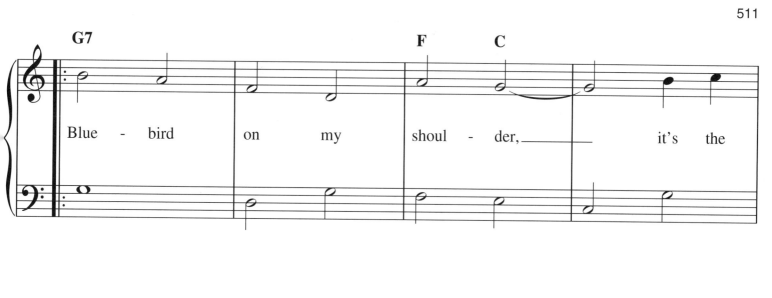

Blue - bird on my shoul - der, _____ it's the

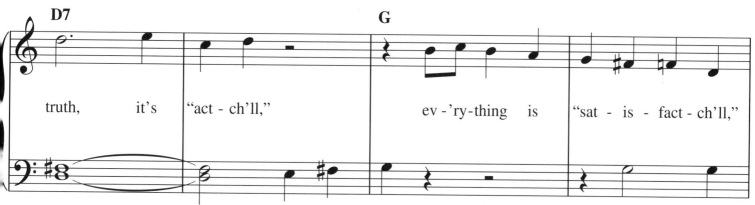

truth, it's "act - ch'll," ev -'ry-thing is "sat - is - fact - ch'll,"

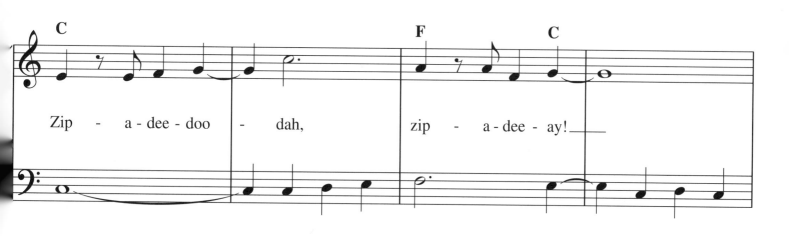

Zip - a - dee - doo - dah, zip - a - dee - ay! ___

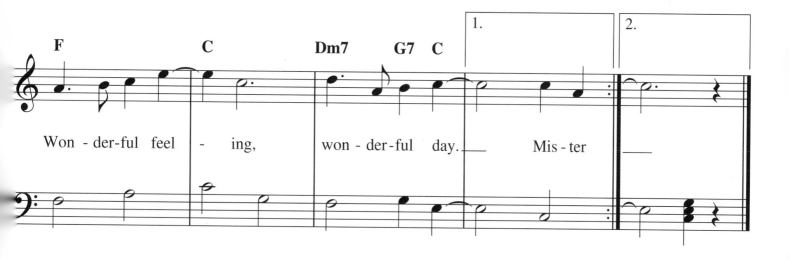

Won - der-ful feel - ing, won - der-ful day. ___ Mis - ter

EASY PIANO
CD PLAY-ALONGS
Orchestrated arrangements with you as the soloist!

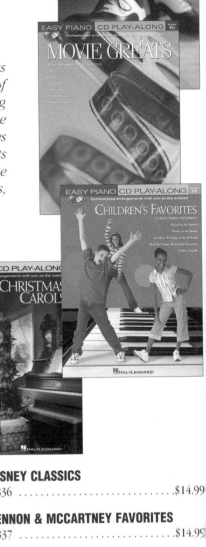

This series lets you play along with great accompaniments to songs you know and love! Each book comes with a CD of complete professional performances and includes matching custom arrangements in easy piano format. With these books you can: Listen to complete professional performances of each of the songs; Play the easy piano arrangements along with the performances; Sing along with the recordings; Play the easy piano arrangements as solos, without the CD.

1. GREAT JAZZ STANDARDS
00310916 . . . .$14.95

2. FAVORITE CLASSICAL THEMES
00310921 . . . .$14.95

3. BROADWAY FAVORITES
00310915 . . . .$14.95

4. ADULT CONTEMPORARY HITS
00310919 . . . .$14.95

5. HIT POP/ROCK BALLADS
00310917 . . . .$14.95

6. LOVE SONG FAVORITES
00310918 . . . .$14.95

7. O HOLY NIGHT
00310920 . . . .$14.95

8. A CHRISTIAN WEDDING
00311104 . . . .$14.95

9. COUNTRY BALLADS
00311105 . . . .$14.95

10. MOVIE GREATS
00311106 . . . .$14.95

11. DISNEY BLOCKBUSTERS
00311107 . . . .$14.95

12. CHRISTMAS FAVORITES
00311257 . . . .$14.95

13. CHILDREN'S SONGS
00311258 . . . .$14.95

14. CHILDREN'S FAVORITES
00311259 . . . .$14.95

15. DISNEY'S BEST
00311260 . . . .$14.95

16. LENNON & MCCARTNEY HITS
00311262 . . . .$14.95

17. HOLIDAY HITS
00311329 . . . .$14.95

18. HIGH SCHOOL MUSICAL
00311752 . . . .$16.99

19. HIGH SCHOOL MUSICAL 2
00311753 . . . .$17.99

20. ANDREW LLOYD WEBBER – FAVORITES
00311775 . . . .$14.99

21. GREAT CLASSICAL MELODIES
00311776 . . . .$14.99

22. ANDREW LLOYD WEBBER – HITS
00311785 . . . .$14.99

23. DISNEY CLASSICS
00311836 . . . .$14.99

24. LENNON & MCCARTNEY FAVORITES
00311837 . . . .$14.99

25. HIGH SCHOOL MUSICAL 3
00311838 . . . .$17.99

26. WICKED
00311882 . . . .$16.99

27. THE SOUND OF MUSIC
00311897 . . . .$14.99

28. CHRISTMAS CAROLS
00311912 . . . .$14.99

29. CHARLIE BROWN CHRISTMAS
00311913 . . . .$14.99

Disney characters and artwork © Disney Enterprises, Inc.

PEANUTS © United Feature Syndicate, Inc.

Prices, contents and availability subject to change without notice.

FOR MORE INFORMATION, SEE YOUR LOCAL MUSIC DEALER, OR WRITE TO:

HAL•LEONARD
CORPORATION
7777 W. BLUEMOUND RD. P.O. BOX 13819 MILWAUKEE, WI 53213

www.halleonard.com

08